Making Gender, Making War

Routledge Advances in Feminist Studies and Intersectionality

Core editorial group: Dr. KATHY DAVIS (Institute for History and Culture, Utrecht, The Netherlands), Professor JEFF HEARN (managing editor; Linköping University, Sweden; Hanken School of Economics, Finland; University of Huddersfield, UK), Professor ANNA G. JÓNASDÓTTIR (Örebro University, Sweden), Professor NINA LYKKE (managing editor; Linköping University, Sweden), Professor CHANDRA TALPADE MOHANTY (Syracuse University, USA), Professor ELŻBIETA H. OLEKSY (University of Łódź, Poland), Dr. ANDREA PETŐ (Central European University, Hungary), Professor ANN PHOENIX (Institute of Education, University of London, UK)

Routledge Advances in Feminist Studies and Intersectionality is committed to the development of new feminist and profeminist perspectives on changing gender relations, with special attention to:

- Intersections between gender and power differentials based on age, class, dis/abilities, ethnicity, nationality, racialisation, sexuality, violence, and other social divisions.
- Intersections of societal dimensions and processes of continuity and change: culture, economy, generativity, polity, sexuality, science and technology;
- Embodiment: Intersections of discourse and materiality, and of sex and gender.
- Transdisciplinarity: intersections of humanities, social sciences, medical, technical and natural sciences.
- Intersections of different branches of feminist theorizing, including: historical materialist feminisms, postcolonial and anti-racist feminisms, radical feminisms, sexual difference feminisms, queerfeminisms, cyberfeminisms, posthuman feminisms, critical studies on men and masculinities.
- A critical analysis of the travelling of ideas, theories and concepts.
- A politics of location, reflexivity and transnational contextualizing that reflects the basis of the Series framed within European diversity and transnational power relations.

1 **Feminist Studies**
A Guide to Intersectional Theory, Methodology and Writing
Nina Lykke

2 **Women, Civil Society and the Geopolitics of Democratization**
Denise M. Horn

3 **Sexuality, Gender and Power**
Intersectional and Transnational Perspectives
Edited by Anna G. Jónasdóttir, Valerie Bryson and Kathleen B. Jones

4 **The Limits of Gendered Citizenship**
Contexts and Complexities
Edited by Elżbieta H. Oleksy, Jeff Hearn and Dorota Golańska

5 **Theories and Methodologies in Postgraduate Feminist Research**
Researching Differently
Edited by Rosemarie Buikema, Gabriele Griffin and Nina Lykke

6 **Making Gender, Making War**
Violence, Military and Peacekeeping Practices
Edited by Annica Kronsell and Erika Svedberg

Making Gender, Making War
Violence, Military and Peacekeeping Practices

**Edited by Annica Kronsell
and Erika Svedberg**

NEW YORK LONDON

First published 2012
by Routledge
711 Third Avenue, New York, NY 10017

Simultaneously published in the UK
by Routledge
2 Park Square, Milton Park, Abingdon, Oxon OX14 4RN

*Routledge is an imprint of the Taylor & Francis Group,
an informa business*

© 2012 Taylor & Francis

Typeset in Sabon by IBT Global.

First issued in paperback 2013

The right of Annica Kronsell and Erika Svedberg to be identified as the authors of the editorial material, and of the authors for their individual chapters, has been asserted in accordance with sections 77 and 78 of the Copyright, Designs and Patents Act 1988.

All rights reserved. No part of this book may be reprinted or reproduced or utilised in any form or by any electronic, mechanical, or other means, now known or hereafter invented, including photocopying and recording, or in any information storage or retrieval system, without permission in writing from the publishers.

Trademark Notice: Product or corporate names may be trademarks or registered trademarks, and are used only for identification and explanation without intent to infringe.

Library of Congress Cataloging-in-Publication Data
Making gender, making war : violence, military and peacekeeping practices / edited by Annica Kronsell and Erika Svedberg. — 1st ed.
  p. cm. — (Routledge advances in feminist studies and intersectionality ; no. 6)
  Includes bibliographical references and index.
  1. Sex role. 2. Masculinity. 3. Women and the military.
 4. Women and peace. 5. Peace-building. I. Kronsell, Annica.
 II. Svedberg, Erika.
  HQ1075.M345 2012
  355.0082—dc22
                           2011012428

ISBN13: 978-0-415-84936-4 (pbk)
ISBN13: 978-0-415-89758-7 (hbk)
ISBN13: 978-0-203-80320-2 (ebk)

Contents

Preface: Those Difficult War Questions in Feminism   ix
CHRISTINE SYLVESTER

Acknowledgments   xiii

1   Introduction: Making Gender, Making War   1
ANNICA KRONSELL AND ERIKA SVEDBERG

THEME I
Conceptualizing Gender, Violence, Militarism

2   Gender Relations as Causal in Militarization
and War: A Feminist Standpoint   19
CYNTHIA COCKBURN

3   Men/Masculinities: War/Militarism—Searching (for)
the Obvious Connections?   35
JEFF HEARN

THEME II
Making Gender and (Re)Making the Nation

4   What Does a Bath Towel Have to Do with Security Policy?
Gender Trouble in the Swedish Armed Forces   51
MAUD EDUARDS

5   Friendly War-Fighters and Invisible Women: Perceptions
of Gender and Masculinities in the Norwegian Armed
Forces on Missions Abroad   63
TORUNN LAUGEN HAALAND

6   The 'Rotten Report' and the Reproduction of
    Masculinity, Nation and Security in Turkey   76
    ALP BIRICIK

7   Men Making Peace in the Name of Just War:
    The Case of Finland   90
    PIRJO JUKARAINEN

THEME III
Institutional Practices and Traveling Concepts

8   Analyzing UN and NATO Responses to Sexual
    Misconduct in Peacekeeping Operations   107
    LAURA HEBERT

9   A Gendered Protection for the 'Victims' of War:
    Mainstreaming Gender in Refugee Protection   121
    JANE FREEDMAN

10 Experiences, Reflections and Learning: Feminist
    Organizations, Security Discourse and SCR 1325   135
    LAURA McLEOD

THEME IV
Gender Subjectivity in the Organization of Violence

11 Nordic Women and International Crisis Management:
    A Politics of Hope?   153
    ELINA PENTTINEN

12 Women in Militant Movements: (Un)Comfortable
    Silences and Discursive Strategies   166
    SWATI PARASHAR

13 In the Business of (In)Security? Mavericks, Mercenaries
    and Masculinities in the Private Security Company   182
    PAUL HIGATE

14 Reenvisioning Masculinities in the Context of Conflict
   Transformation: The Gender Politics of Demilitarizing
   Northern Ireland Society   197
   FIDELMA ASHE

Conclusions

15 Is Feminism Being Co-Opted by Militarism?   209
   ANNICA KRONSELL AND ERIKA SVEDBERG

   Contributors   215
   Bibliography   219
   Index   247

Preface
Those Difficult War Questions in Feminism

Christine Sylvester

Erika Svedberg and Annica Kronsell describe themselves and a feminist contingent of PhD students at Lund University in the mid-1990s as 'homesteaders.' They graciously tip their hats to early ideas on feminist homesteading that I presented in Feminist Theory and International Relations in a Postmodern Era (1994); and then they shape the concept further for use in their particular circumstances. I recently heard Erika explain to a group of Women's Studies staff and students at Malmö University, where she teaches, that when the Lund group introduced feminist research themes to the department of Political Science, they did so with the intent of homesteading Swedish International Relations (IR). 'We made it clear to the department and to Swedish scholars of international relations,' she said, 'that feminist analysis is here to stay: It is not a passing trend but a permanent feature that scholars must accommodate.' Erika and Annica proved their point by raising funds to host a major feminist IR conference at Lund in 1996, the first in the Nordic countries, and carried on to produce the first generation of Swedish feminist IR PhD theses and scholarship. As a speaker at their first conference, I could see that this cohort of feminist scholars was indeed there to stay, and stay it has.

There are numerous topics that fall under the auspices of feminist IR. Early on, it was clear that Annica and Erika shared an interest in what Annica would later term 'institutions of hegemonic masculinity' (Kronsell 2005; 2006: 108) in the Nordic region, the military being a prime subject. They wrote together and separately about gender in the Swedish military and in its conscription practices (Kronsell and Svedberg 2001), drawing attention to the contradictions of a Swedish military intent on breaking the association of armed forces with violence to become a peacekeeper and development-oriented military, and yet carrying forward gendered understandings of bodies best suited to various tasks in a new military. The 'men' were the backbone of the peace army as of the previous defense army and there was no debate on the matter at large or within Swedish political circles. Women, citizenship and military institutions were a silence within a state that was otherwise seeking to homestead inherited military frameworks differently. By tackling this kind of war question in feminism—what are the gender norms built into the new Swedish military?—before the phrase 'war question in feminism' was introduced in feminist IR (Sylvester 2005), Annica and Erika became pioneers in the field.

In their latest collaboration, Erika and Annica raise the bar on gender and military issues and they homestead feminist IR by doing so. War and feminism is a topic of relevance to many around the world; yet until recently it has been assumed in feminism that war and feminism is an uncomfortable if not impossible combination. It is the wrong framing of the problematic of violence in a world that tends to find war a regrettable but acceptable social institution. Thus, many war questions in feminism remained unarticulated, subterranean or couched only in terms of women and the military or women as victims of war. Perhaps one would say that war questions were less systematically raised and examined than issues of peace and feminism—the more usual feminist point of entry to questions of armed conflict (Sylvester 2010b).

Once again, though, Annica and Erika launched their own transition in thinking from gender and the military to the larger topic of war and feminism by holding a conference on the War Question in Feminism at the Örebro University in 2008. I was there; and that conference was much more fiery than the first one. Participants argued about whether any shift in focus from peace to war was warranted or constituted a sellout of feminist values. The weight of opinion seemed to be that feminists should continue to refuse war talk and war analysis: There was no war question in feminism at all; there was only a continuing peace question to be both asserted and fleshed out. Whether the peace question in feminism was capacious enough to include women who asserted agency through armed conflict, women who made careers out of preparing for conflict and women who found they gained in other ways from armed conflict was not the issue for many. Feminism was outside war, above it and in a position of belligerence to it. By implication, women warriors must be captives of delusion or false consciousness. They could not actually choose violence as a politics, perhaps even a feminist politics.

In this volume from the War Question conference, the focus is on gender norms embedded in a variety of locations and practices of war. The editors might not put it this way, but there is a sense that the matter at hand is whether feminism is homesteading wars of our time or war is homesteading feminism by sending out old war appeals to women and men wrapped in gender-equality packaging. Even UN Security Council Resolution 1325 could be seen as a way of infusing old gender concerns into post-conflict situations. Warrior men usually make decisions, no matter who sits at the negotiating rounds, and women are encouraged to speak out and then go home to a status quo ante. That is to say, even progressive efforts to bring gender front and center in war-fighting and war-ending can assume that women's war experiences, war skills and war labors are inappropriate in peaceful societies. Those who narrate an ended war as history and memory can present progress as a reenactment of stable gender norms that the war disrupted. The degree to which that gendered outcome of many wars (Elshtain 1995), one I watched unfold in Zimbabwe in its postindependence years, should be queried today is a war question for feminism and for the institutions and groups that advance peace and reconciliation while also advancing state- and nation-building agendas. And, of course, one of the challenges of the day is to take into account local gender particularisms as they interact with powerful institutions that can protect human rights by waging war—humanitarian armed intervention—using a kill-to-be-kind logic.

The contributors to this book come at these and myriad other questions of war; masculinity; militarization; patriarchy; gender violence, norms, culture and agency; and feminist security in new ways. Their chapters are not comforting to read, but they do tackle war questions that feminists must square up to and debate with as much energy and determination as the major states and institutions of politics and political economy expend on refining and reiterating their war questions.

Acknowledgments

The idea for this book came in connection with the War Question in Feminism Conference that we arranged at Örebro University, Sweden, in September of 2008. Scholars showed their interest for the subject by the great response to our call for papers. The conference was organized around theme workshops. The chapters in this volume were presented in their first draft in one of five different workshops. There were many great papers, insightful and inspiring discussions in workshops and in various conference sessions and we want to thank all of the conference participants for being so enthusiastic and interested in the topic. You gave us support and the courage to take on the project of putting together a book on the subject. Although it was difficult to select among such a range of excellent papers, we see this book in a way as a continued conversation that is being carried on from the conference to everyone interested in questions relating to gender, war, violence and peacekeeping.

The smaller group of scholars contributing to this book has worked on this collectively; the authors have commented constructively on each others' texts and provided inputs to the discussions of the general themes. This has been extremely useful for the quality of the book. Without doubt, this book is the result of a successful interactive process and we, as editors, are very grateful to the authors for all input. We also extend our thanks to our sponsors; the Swedish Research Council, the Swedish Institute and the Bank of Sweden Tercentenary Foundation. Since the time when we were PhD students at Lund University, we have enjoyed the support of and benefited in so many ways from being part of the Feminist Theory and Gender Studies section of the International Studies Association. Now, this is our contribution to a community of researchers interested in feminist IR.

Annica and Erika, Lund, February 2011

1 Introduction
Making Gender, Making War
Annica Kronsell and Erika Svedberg

The making of war in the contemporary world is a highly diversified activity. War is ethnified, privatized and criminalized and pursued by states, private companies, warlords and guerrilla movements. This is not particularly new. What seems new, and rather paradoxical, is that the making of war is increasingly associated with peace. For example, state militaries and alliances take the 'responsibility to protect' and are engaged in peace-enforcement, peace building, conflict prevention and crises management all over the world. Means and resources used by militaries in the past to wage war are now brought into a conflict zone for a whole set of other purposes. Making war is increasingly done in the name of peace. This change is also associated with a reevaluation of the skills needed. 'Womanly' skills and competencies, previously thought to damage the military's fighting capabilities, are now cherished and regarded as necessary for peace building tasks. Skills like cooperation, caring and empathy are associated with women in peacekeeping (Olsson and Tryggestad 2001; Skjelsbaek and Smith 2001; Valenius 2007). Hence, war-making of today is closely connected with the making of gender and vice versa: The aim of this book is to discuss and problematize this.

After some 30 years of intense, curiosity-driven research and writings, leading feminist scholars maintain that we are only beginning to make sense of the complexity of gender in international relations (IR) (Hutchings et al. 2008). We have begun to unravel the seemingly simple question of what gender is, or means. Understanding gender as perhaps the most central social institution in the life of humans, a practice that constructs and reconstructs power relations throughout the centuries, remains central to feminist work in IR. Ontologically speaking, the authors of this volume come from a constructivist outlook on gender. We see gender being made and remade through the practices of individuals, organizations, militaries and states. The making of gender is always part and parcel of what has been called patriarchy, the gender-power system or gender order. Thus, the making of gender implies that gender is an organizing principle for social life. Laura Sjoberg argues, 'Feminists see gender subordination as constitutive of the global political world' (2009b: 205). Gender sensitivity is an outlook not necessarily shared by other constructivist or critical theoretical approaches.

IR feminist Ann Tickner explains that feminist analyses use 'gender as a socially constructed and variable category of analysis to investigate these power dynamics and gender hierarchies' (2006a: 24). In the making of gender we include subjectivities like men and women, masculinities and femininities as well as gender-power relations, norms and principles.

Today, a major challenge for feminist researchers is to include questions about war, but what *is* the war question for feminism? In our view, as inspired by IR scholars before us, like Christine Sylvester, Cynthia Enloe, Ann Tickner, Lene Hansen and many others, the war question represents a research program that wishes to challenge feminist researchers to take up theoretical as well as empirical work on questions related to war. Christine Sylvester has for decades insisted that feminist IR scholars take seriously and engage with the task of analyzing war. Lately, she has been looking at war as a sensational experience. War is also an experience of the body and she says that while all of us are touched by war in times of globalization, even when we stand 'outside' it, few security and war scholars are willing to recognize this fact (Sylvester 2010c: 34). Sylvester encourages a wide range of feminist research on war and we take her long-standing challenge to heart with this project.

Cynthia Cockburn seems to echo those same thoughts, although in a slightly different way. In her contribution she insists that the standpoint of women engaged in antiwar activities generates a profound and solid knowledge that war is intricately connected to the gender system via a continuum of violence. Women's experiences both from the outside and the inside of war are important for this research agenda as shown in, for example, Laura McLeod and Swati Parashar's chapters in this volume. At the same time, the analyses of the making and remaking of masculinities by Jeff Hearn, Alp Biricik, Paul Higate and Fidelma Ashe all pay close attention to another highly relevant but understudied gender aspect of contemporary war-making, the connection between the obvious (so obvious that it is deemed 'natural' and not questioned): masculinity—nation—efficiency—violence—war—peacekeeping. Our specific take on war and contribution to feminist research in this volume is to study how gender norms are embedded in practices of war and how they relate to gender subjectivities, be they notions about military men, masculinity's relation to violence or women's roles. With this book, we want to contribute to an emerging research program called Feminist Security Studies (cf. Sjoberg 2009a).

RESEARCH QUESTIONS

Processes of making gender and making war are intertwined and the objective of this book is to show this interconnectedness in relation to violence, military practices, peacekeeping and peace building. We do this around four themes. The first theme is conceptual and raises questions about the connection between gender, violence and military practices, and pays specific attention to the importance of the making of masculinity to military practice, violence and war. With the second theme we explore, in much detail, the important connection between military practices and nation building. This theme touches upon, on the one hand, the modernist practice of conscription, when the making of gender is in concurrence with the making of the nation, as in the case of masculinity constructions in Turkey discussed by Biricik. On the other hand, this theme also analyzes masculinity constructions in relation to so-called new war-making and military practice. It argues that what we see is also a remaking of the nation where processes of gender construction play a crucial role. The question addressed is: How is gender made when nations are remade in the context of new military practices? A third theme calls attention to United Nations (UN) Security Council Resolution 1325 on Women, Peace and Security from 2000 (SCR 1325), which has come out of the hard work of women's and other activist groups to bring a feminist security agenda to the Security Council of the UN. This agenda is a response to the gender consequences of war and military practice and a tool to reshape gendered practices, specifically in peacekeeping and peacemaking activities. In three chapters we look at how this resolution has traveled, been interpreted and found its way into organizations that deal with war and gender. The final theme of this volume considers the meaning of gender: How are femininities and masculinities made in the context of organized violence?

It is important to note that the ambition of this book is not only a matter of providing rigorous academic research on contemporary war issues. That we take as given. We also wish for the reader to see that amidst the complexity of war, presented by the many authors of this book, there is one common normative ambition in the visualization that feminism can be a method and a tool to accomplish positive transformation towards greater justice. Feminism claims that we can leave behind an unjust system that assumes male supremacy, built upon and maintained by violence (Tickner 2006; Cohn and Ruddick 2004; Jaggar 2008; Davis 2009). As (Ackerley et al. 2006) show in their book on feminist methodologies, there are many different ways to do feminist research. Feminism and critical masculinity studies as a tool for change will indeed look different, it will speak to people differently and it will be used differently in different contexts. The authors of this book look at war and military practices and how they relate to femininities and masculinities, institutional gender norms and to gendered power relations in many parts of the world.

This book aims to make a contribution by advancing an institutional take on war. Institutions matter, and by that we mean that rules and organizational features influence actors and have political outcomes. Constructivist perspectives see institutions and norms as an integral part in the construction of identities, interest and meaning in political life. Feminists are often sympathetic to such approaches (Locher and Prügl 2001: 114).

Generally speaking, the chapters study institutions, albeit of varied kinds, where practices of military, violence and security are confronting gender norms. They exemplify institutional practices of making war and making gender, like national militaries, private military companies, North Atlantic Treaty Organization (NATO), United Nations High Commissioner for Refugees (UNHCR) and feminist NGOs.

Institutions tend to have pattern-bound effects over time, which lock into place certain practices, creating norms and thereby contributing to path dependency. Norms of gender and war are embedded in institutions and have implications for practice. They are stable and slow to change. Nevertheless, institutions and the gendered military practices carried out by them also give rise to criticism and resistance. We think that the changes we sketched in the preceding are evidence of this. There is a common methodology of sorts shared by many chapters. In addressing these globalized norms of war and postwar, they look at how gender is carried out in 'everyday' practices within institutionalized contexts of war-making. This is a highly appropriate research methodology because gender norms tend to become invisible and taken for granted as they are put into everyday practice of the institution.

Militaries and international organizations have made certain subjectivities possible as individual men and women engaging in organizational activities tend to search for meaning and sense of purpose in what they do in their daily work. March and Olsen (1989) call this the creation of meaning. In going about their daily activities, individuals appeal to institutional norms and this way, they also do or perform gender practices, reproducing the male-as-norm and/or challenging it. So institutions matter because they are both enabling and constraining. Or, in the words of Locher and Prügl, institutions matter because they delimit our world in a systematic manner. They distribute privilege and create patterns of subordination (Locher 2007; Locher and Prügl 2001: 117) while simultaneously providing opportunities.

With a feminist constructivist approach and an institutional focus, how can we study change and transformation when it comes to war/peacemaking? Institutions are thick, inert and slow to change, and institutional norms are, too. The male-as-norm is persistent but, as we have argued, norms are constructed and enacted, performed when individuals engage with them on a daily bases within the institution, for example, while doing peacekeeping or military exercises. Since norms are constructed they can also be made to change and transform themselves, rethink policies and objectives, often as a reaction from pressures from social and political actors and movements. Transnational feminism and women's grassroots' activism are important change agents when it comes to gender in IR and institutions. The historical legacy of feminism as a social movement is that critique, resistance and activism can be crucial in triggering processes of political reform to bring about justice and fairness. The SCR 1325 is but one, albeit important, example of how feminist activism has influenced the global security agenda. Feminist theory as an ethical framework and as political activism has shown that changing long-standing constructions such as men's supremacy and domination over women does not come about automatically. Rather, during the last 150 years, women and a few men have relentlessly and bravely acted; they put up resistance to existing norm systems and demanded change.

In the following paragraphs we introduce the four themes of the book and briefly present the different chapters that address each theme.

THEME I: CONCEPTUALIZING GENDER, VIOLENCE, MILITARISM

The question we pose in this part is of a theoretical nature and asks how gender relates to war-making via a focus on violence and militarism. By militarism we mean the underlying value system that permeates military organizations and war activities. Militarization, on the other hand, is the process of preparing and engaging in the actual war-related practices. According to radical feminist thinkers, violence is at the core of maintaining the gender order of male supremacy and female subordination. Betty Reardon (1985/1996) argues that militarism and the gender order are interdependent. According to this thinking, militarism and the gender order are so closely related to social violence that, metaphorically speaking, they are two sides of the same coin. If violence in one form or other is constitutive to the construction and reconstruction of masculinity, or, in other words, if male supremacy over women is at the core of what it is to be masculine, then the gender order too is based on, or even presupposes, men's violence against women. Kimberly Hutchings (2008: 389) explores the connection between war and masculinity and contends that there is a functional relationship between masculinity and militarism because qualities like aggression and physical courage are defined as essential components of both masculinity and war. Based in part on Galtung's (1969) notion of structural violence, Cynthia Cockburn urges us to think of violence as a continuum:

> The power imbalance of gender relations in most (if not all) societies generates cultures of masculinity prone to violence. These gender relations are like a linking thread, a kind of fuse, along which violence runs. The thread of violence runs through every field (home, city, nation-state, international relations) and every moment (protest, law enforcement, militarization), adding to the explosive charge of violence in them. (2004: 44)

Cockburn explores this theme further in Chapter 2 in this volume and looks at gender as a driving force in militarization and war. She argues that patriarchy is what 'predispose[s] our societies to war' and thus, that patriarchal relations 'are among the causes of war' (119). What happens in war is that sexual divisions become even deeper through war-making and so do class and ethnic divisions. That gender violence is linked to war as a continuum, says Cockburn, does not mean that it is a direct cause for war, like the fight for territory or resources can be, it is a thread from militarism as a mind-set expressed in the media and by politicians, the mobilization for war or defense in the economy, to the aftermath of war, the peace talks, the unsteady developments and sporadic violence and the return of soldiers to civilian lives. Cockburn articulates these insights from a feminist standpoint based on antiwar activism, a standpoint that conceives of gender power as a system of intersections. Her argument is that war-making has neither a beginning nor an end, but waxes and wanes. War making has a cyclic life over time, and gender relations are 'pushing the wheel around' (29). The implications are extensive; theories of war are flawed if they lack a gender dimension and every strategy to end war for peace must include a change of gender relations.

In Chapter 3 Jeff Hearn explores this further by unraveling patriarchy's relation to war, militarism and violence from the perspective of critical studies on men and masculinities. He shows how men, although in massive presence and domination in wars and militaries are naturalized, normalized in relation to war-making and thereby also un-gendered. He states: 'men and militarism are so obviously coupled, that it is hard to know where to start' (36) in analyzing masculinities' relation to war, violence and militarism. Hearn approaches the topic by focusing on various connections between war and masculinity, from the material to the interrelation between different masculinities at different levels, from IR to practices of military training and different types of war and military actors. Thereby, Hearn gives a rich account of the variation in masculinities and enriches Cockburn's notion of the continuum of violence in war.

'Gendering militarism and war,' Hearn insists, involves attending to both gender and sexuality. It is not only the relation of women to militarism and war that should be in focus. It is necessary to explicitly ask 'how men, masculinities and men's practices relate to militarism and war' (38). An important clarification that he conveys is that power works also in the construction of diverse masculinities; the power dimension of gender is not in relation to femininity and women alone, but far more complex and intersectional. Hearn speaks of 'a wide web of masculine activities within the militarism-war-violence complex(es)' (36). Masculinity, too, is stratified along ethnic, sexual, class and other dimensions, and through this power relations are created and maintained; contributing and reinforcing the gender dimension of war. The importance of looking at the relation between men, or rather masculinities, is stressed, as Hearn argues that 'the collective, historical power of men may be maintained by the *dispensability* of some men' (39), as with the general acceptance of loss of soldiers in war.

He goes on to assert that the 'sacrifice' of single men may indeed strengthen collective structural power.

In sum, what we learn from these chapters is that in an effort to conceptualize violence, militarism and war it is essential and useful to think of the gender order as a web, a continuum of relations that are implicated in the subjectivities of the various actors active in the field.

THEME II: MAKING GENDER AND (RE)MAKING THE NATION

We argue, as many have done before us, that the military is a key institution for feminists interested in the war question. Institutions that have historically been governed by men are constituted on norms associated with masculinity and heterosexuality (Kronsell 2005) and the war-military-machinery is among these. About state military institutions we can say that militarism supports the state's threat of, and use of, coercive force. Thus, the state is implicated in the support of violence with the acknowledgment of and investments in a military organization. This is a view that departs from classical IR theory. In realism, war is seen as the outcome of rational decisions based on states' interests. In Clausewitzian terms, war is simply politics by other means. Our perspective is that military institutions are at the core of the formation of states, to defend against the 'enemy' is an important nation-building activity. Collective identity associated with nation building is gendered, based on the different ways men and women have been situated within discourses of nationalism and militarism (Kronsell and Svedberg 2001: 154).

Thus, military practice and national identity formation are linked and materialized in the state, which gives the armed forces a kind of influence and privilege seldom matched by other societal institutions (Enloe 2000: 46; Tilly 1990). Militarism names the normative conceptual construction involved in militaries, defense politics and war-making whereby the effective use of violence by trained staff is a key element. Militarism does not necessarily imply an excessive use of military violence (Carlton 2001) but supports the idea that a potential for violence and aggression is needed for the state and the nation's defense and well-being. This is observed in countries that have not recently been engaged in explicit war practices, like the Nordic countries referred to in this book.

All the chapters included in this theme study, with much interesting detail, how embedded gendered norms relate both to military practices, like increasing emphasis on peacekeeping, and to nation-making—i.e., how the collective 'we' in the War on Terror world is rearticulated as the demands on the military institutions are changing. The chapters study closely how gendered norms are reflected in security practices, in terms of different tensions around femininity and masculinity constructions but also how the construction of the national is both challenged and reaffirmed through the situation of 'making of war in the name of peace' that we are studying here. These studies are important because they provide insight into the relationship between militarism and gender and how such norms are played out in military institutions, but also because they provide empirical evidence from a context of midsize powers, with a certain status or position to be upheld in the global security context, known as 'peacekeepers.' For example, the Nordic countries are heavily engaged in international peacekeeping and crises management and provide good examples of militaries doing peace-related activities. Also, some of the countries presented in this theme are often in the forefront of gender equality efforts; thereby, the empirical material brings evidence from militaries in countries where gender and equality issues have become salient on the national political agenda and efforts have been made to try to implement the norms in many societal sectors.

This is certainly the case in Maud Eduards's chapter with its focus on recent changes that have taken place in the Swedish Armed Forces (SAF), both regarding its internal organizational practices around who the contemporary soldier is and the image that the SAF are projecting in the world as they engage in rapid deployment forces abroad. Eduards shows how various strategies, like equality plans to combat gender discrimination and plans to implement SCR 1325, have, in the hands of the military organization, simultaneously become a form of marketization of the Swedish military at home and abroad; i.e., it is an effort to present the Swedish nation to the world. For example, the focus on SCR 1325 in the rapid deployment forces is promoting the SAF as both gender aware and gender equal. In view of this, Eduards calls attention to the great expectations that are put on Swedish women as soldiers and officers in missions abroad as they should help create a better world and let the name of Sweden gain honor around the globe. Hence, she writes, gender equality policy is expected to combine Sweden's national and global interests. In her analysis of daily practices within the SAF, Eduards notes the many discrepancies between ambitious statements and the daily experiences of women soldiers and officers. Eduards's overall conclusion is that gender is made trivial in the organization, paradoxically as it may seem, because equality activities are based on the notion that inequality can be nullified through gender neutrality, and men's actions and culture has no space in this.

Torunn Laugen Haaland takes on the idea that Nordic countries are in the forefront in the way they deal with gender issues and analyzes whether the internal perception of gender and masculinity of the Norwegian Armed Forces (NAF) matches these views. Haaland's research is based on material produced internally in the military, like memory books and contingency reports. She analyzes how the norms on masculinity and militarism impact how the NAF operate abroad in peacekeeping operations and argues that the military remains deeply conservative regarding gender relations, evident in how they perceive women in their own ranks and local women where they are deployed. Women are invisible and approached as if they are 'one of the boys.' While women's visibility appears constant it varies according to type of mission and type of unit (for instance, field hospital versus combat maneuver units). Haaland compares her studies of gender in the NAF with Sandra Whitworth's (2004) findings on masculinity in the Canadian military in peacekeeping operations. Whitworth's study pointed to a serious contradiction between what soldiers were trained for—combat like tasks—and what they actually did when peacekeeping. Also the NAF who went abroad were trained for war and combat and they too had some problems adjusting to the demands in the real peacekeeping or peace-enforcement situation, which seldom resembled that of a combat situation. More common tasks were social patrols, watch duty and the challenge to endure boredom. Yet, Haaland suggests that in the NAF, a different masculinity than the Canadian one emerges. In this masculinity, 'aggressiveness was not a commonly praised quality,' but rather 'the need for restraint and control' was emphasized' (71). In other words, the masculinity projected by the NAF is in terms of a 'friendly war-fighter.'

Alp Biricik analyzes how security, nation-state building and male bodies are closely intertwined in reproducing norms of masculinity for the continuous reconstruction of ideal manhood in Turkey. The focus is on young men resisting becoming conscripted soldiers in the Turkish military. Homosexuality (or homosexual behavior, rather) may be a reason for exemption from military service in Turkey. Inspired by Foucauldian thinking, Biricik shows how medical doctors at the military hospitals through the practices of medical screening of the draftees are performing a safeguarding of 'normal' heterosexual Turkishness. This results oftentimes in contradictory, even absurd, practices. In his empirically based analysis, Biricik shows how a dichotomous relationality of heterosexual/homosexual masculinity is reproduced through institutionalized military practices. Young men in Biricik's study wishing to be exempt from military training engage in active information seeking, sharing, rehearsing and finally reenactment of just the right way to perform homosexuality under the scrutinizing gaze of the state officials of the medical profession. Who will succeed and be diagnosed as a true gay man?

This tight connection between nation-making and the military organization is verified in Pirjo Jukarainen's research on the Finnish Armed Forces (FAF). Although the FAF are engaged in international missions, which is also part of their image as a peacekeeping superpower, Jukarainen shows how this activity is more about confirming a Finnish national identity than caring about distant others in the name of human rights. The masculine heroism associated with the peacekeeping role is intimately connected to the traditional gendered notions in the FAF based on decades of all-male conscription practice. This masculine heroism is carried over, rather than challenged, with the new tasks of peace building abroad. The concern seems to be more about playing out heroism and bravery toward the Finnish home nation, and less for people in faraway places. Women peacekeepers seem to be a contradiction in terms in the Finnish context where the staff of the operations is derived from the conscripted all-male military.

Evidence from Norwegian, Finnish, Turkish as well as Swedish militaries in the various studies of this book show that in addressing the war question, assumptions regarding masculinity and militaries also need to become more nuanced. Militaries in the Nordic countries, to some extent, hang on to notions of combat, militarism and conservative masculinity, but as Haaland shows there is evidence that other 'softer' qualities also are valued. Does this mean that militaries are diversifying in the way that masculinity is understood and articulated?

THEME III: INSTITUTIONAL PRACTICES AND TRAVELING CONCEPTS

During the period between the end of the Cold War and the War on Terror, the concept of security became less associated with the military capacity of states and more sensitive to the well-being of individuals (Joachim 2003: 260), which more closely reflected a feminist interpretation of security (such as Tickner 2001: 36–64). A global emphasis on human security made women's issues more relevant to the work in international organizations while providing an opportunity to reframe the agenda of the Security Council. The adoption of SCR 1325 in 2000 is the most prominent example of this (True-Frost 2007: 156). While the 'opening' of the UN structure was imperative to setting a new agenda sensitive to women's and feminist concerns, it would never have been possible without the lobbying activities of various women and feminist NGOs at local, national, transnational and international levels (Cockburn 2007). To women's NGOs and transnational feminist activists, the UN has been an important arena for putting women's issues on the international agenda of global concerns (Kronsell 2010). At the same time this has provided an impetus for the transnationalization of feminism and the feminist movement (Rai 2004; West 1999; Winslow 1995).

In the preparation for UN conferences, NGOs and other civil society actors from different regions and ideological perspectives were able to join forces and create transnational alliances of NGOs concerned with, for example, violence against women (Keck and Sikkink 1998: 165–198; Cockburn 2007). Friedman et al. claim that the success of this form of activism is due to the nature of the UN as 'both an intergovernmental organization of nation-states and an adaptive transnational organization that reflects emerging non-state-based values and interests' (2005: 24). Barnett and Finnemore (2004: 164) argue similarly that international institutions have autonomous influence and the constitutive power to define interests, deploy human and financial resources, and persuade others to accept new preferences and new policy goals. The UN is expected to respond to global problems and has become increasingly open to participation, direct and indirect, by nonstate actors. The end of the Cold War 'freed up agenda space' (Joachim 1999: 151), and the UN and other international organizations emerged as moral actors in global affairs, bringing a new kind of thinking on IR (Barnett and Finnemore 2004: 165).

Institutions and institutional norms, albeit being resilient and persistent, can indeed change. In the case of SCR 1325, it was transnational feminism and the women's movement that in the end pushed it onto the Security Council's agenda. With the aim to strengthen and develop means for the implementation of SCR 1325, three more resolutions have been taken, SCR 1820 (2008), SCR 1888 and SCR 1889 (2009). Calling for a gender perspective in peacekeeping operations, SCR 1325 has provided a guideline for how gender can be understood in the context of peacekeeping particularly, but also more generally, at least for European militaries. The concept of gender and gender mainstreaming has thus traveled from transnational feminist thinking and activism to the UN Security Council's agenda of international norms building and then further on into the military organizations and the crisis management authorities of some member states.

We propose that the term *traveling concepts* can be adopted to analyze change from an institutional perspective. *Traveling concepts* is a term used to connote processes whereby feminist thinking from one place goes through transitions and adjustments on its way to make sense and become valuable tools for feminist analyses in new sites and settings. In feminist scholarship it has been used as an analytical tool to trace the changing meaning of specific concepts as they meet and rub against institutional practices (see also Griffin and Braidotti 2002). Like looking at pieces of glass mirrored in a kaleidoscope, a slight shift makes a completely new pattern—the original ideas are changed in the process. How does the UN's or NATO's utilization of the concept *gender* differ from other uses, such as the women's movement, or more strategically by certain actors, such as a post-Yugoslavian local women's group?

The authors who discuss the second theme of the book, present studies that—broadly speaking—trace how feminist theory and concepts travel into institutional settings where feminism and feminist thinking has not traditionally been housed; in national military settings, the UNHCR, NATO, Women in Black (WiB) in Serbia. The aforementioned resolutions on women, peace and security constitute in practical terms a venue for the traveling of feminist thinking and women's organizing into places and institutions as far removed from feminism as can be imagined. In this process, the traveling has already begun to transform the concepts.

In her chapter on mainstreaming gender in refugee protection, Jane Freedman's research reveals a UN apparatus where gender mainstreaming no longer means the same thing as feminist thinkers and the women's movement intended. Within UNHCR there was appallingly little actual change in the thinking going on; *gender* meant women and *gender mainstreaming* in practicality meant to bring more women into the operation. Valenius's (2007) research on Finnish peacekeeping operations shows a striking similarity to Freedman's work on how gender and gender mainstreaming is conceptualized by those involved. Freedman concludes that one of the major problems is the failure of transmission of the goals of gender sensitivity through such a large bureaucracy as the UNHCR. Most feminist analyses of SCR 1325 and its implementation have pointed to the same basic concern that gender has come to simply mean women and that gender mainstreaming in practice means increasing the number of female peacekeepers. However, this situation might not be merely the unintended result of a slow-moving, large-scale bureaucratic institution. Laura Hebert's study in this volume on UN and NATO responses to sexual misconduct in peacekeeping operations points to something like an intentional inertia on the part of officials, rather than accidental oversight. Building on a feminist constructivist perspective, Hebert argues that 'as long as the fundamental association between security threats, military capacity, and the masculine soldier ideal persists, we can expect that efforts aimed at gender mainstreaming will continue to take the form of integrating women into already-defined masculine structures. Efforts to address peacekeeper sexual misconduct will remain palliative rather than preventive' (119).

The term *traveling concepts* is closely intertwined with ideas of contemporary transnational feminism, as it was originally coined by scholars in European Women's/Gender Studies. In their attempt to forge a field of gender studies in an 'EU-European' university setting, which was marked by serious divisions, they found *traveling concepts* to be a useful term in that it made those involved focus on understanding that the other had another, unfamiliar and perhaps uncomfortable way of thinking about 'regular' feminist concepts. The way the concept was developed and conscientiously utilized was action oriented and all this makes it closely linked to transnational feminism both within and outside of academia. *Traveling concepts* as a term conveys a process that, in itself, constitutes an important part of transnational feminism. The term *transnational* puts the focus on the politics of the global–local and center–periphery spectrum of gendered power relations today. Transnational links penetrate all spheres and levels of social existence.

In her study on WiB in Serbia, Laura McLeod points out that for a concept like 'gender security' to really travel, it needs to have direct relevance to the local context where it will be adopted and transformed in the process. She focuses on the way that perceptions and attitudes towards war and nationalism in ex-Yugoslavia is both a product and productive of actions relating to SCR 1325. McLeod's study uncovers how, to WiB in postwar Serbia, the concept of security and SCR 1325 are closely linked with their hopes for a postwar revival of a secure society. Interestingly, McLeod's study highlights how a feminist understanding and awakening takes place via the war, as a direct outcome of post-conflict policies pertaining to SCR 1325. Clearly, concepts do not travel by themselves, they have to be somehow carried by people or groups, but what is interesting for us is how they are interpreted and put into practice within a specific context.

THEME IV: GENDER SUBJECTIVITY IN THE ORGANIZATION OF VIOLENCE

Making gender is about the construction of feminine and masculine subjectivities, which we argue are intimately connected to the making of war in contemporary international politics. To reach a deeper understanding of this relationship in all its complexity it is necessary to explore and unravel the way such subjectivities are constructed in specific war-related contexts. In this section, four related chapters do just this. With rich empirical data and theoretical sharpness they survey feminine and masculine subjectivities in relation to crises management practices, militant groups, private security companies (PSCs), peace building and organizing.

Many scholars have pointed to the essentializing tendencies related to gender subjectivity. This has been particularly the case when skills like cooperation, caring and empathy have been connected to women in peacekeeping (Olsson and Tryggestad 2001; Skjelsbaek and Smith 2001; Valenius 2007). Elina Penttinen's chapter takes issue with this. She studies gender subjectivity and asks whether the view that women have special skills, such as being emphatic and caring, is relevant to the Finnish organization of international crises management. She is highly critical to what she views as the almost taken-for-granted notion that women 'add something' to peacekeeping. What is it exactly that they add, she asks. Through an in-depth case study of policewomen carrying out their work in Kosovo, Penttinen shows how the institutions who think they benefit and take advantage of 'traditional' feminine skills to advance crises management and security concerns are actually looking for skills that are not essentially feminine but have to do with personal knowledge, interests and values. She calls this a politics of hope.

This critique of the essentializing tendency in feminist scholarship is followed up in Swati Parashar's chapter. She argues that in feminist IR scholarship the association of women with peace and antiwar strategies has silenced important aspects of the discourse on women, gender and the war question and limited the understanding of women's subjectivity and agency in war and violent contexts. When women are included in military institutions, its peacekeeping and policing activities, it also becomes possible to empirically examine the much taken-for-granted connection between woman, care and empathy. The challenges that it poses run on many levels simultaneously in institutions such as the military, where the male-as-norm has been practiced over a long historical time span. On the other hand, women also have the capability to be violent and femininity can also be connected to violence. Sjoberg and Gentry (2007) have collected war experiences describing women capable of brutality and misconduct in war situations. Parashar, too, shows how women are part of violent political projects not simply as victims. She studies women's role in the armed movements in Kashmir and Sri Lanka and what implication this has for how fear and violence is perceived. Parashar pays close attention to the paradoxes and ambiguities that are associated with the subjectivities of militant women and the way that these subjectivities clash and counter with the gender norms of society.

Paul Higate's chapter deals with PSCs through a focus on the institutional-identity dimensions of their gendered terrain. Drawing on a range of secondary data he illuminates diversity of social practice within the industry, ranging on the one hand from the use of violence against civilians—noted as a key moment of (re)masculinization—through, on the other, to the unreported, myriad acts of restraint exercised by private security contractors in their everyday work. In making sense of these complexities he examines the military-masculine characteristics of the sphere, within the context of its majority proportion of former armed services' personnel recruited from around the globe. In conclusion, Higate argues that feminists might wish to politicize the veteran figure more explicitly, thereby opening the way for a more concerted and critical concern with their impact on security. In sum, he raises pressing questions around the relationship between militarism and masculinity in different contexts, including those that are privatized, in contemporary warfare.

In the final chapter, Fidelma Ashe develops a feminist reading of post-conflict Northern Ireland. Over the years, this conflict has received much scholarly attention. Ashe found that for the most part, studies on the political transition in Northern Ireland have elided gender aspects. Moreover, by placing issues of gender and sexuality at the forefront of the analysis of 'peace processes' the chapter examines the effects of conflict transformational processes and narratives on gender and power relationships in Northern Ireland. In particular, she explores the effects of processes of demilitarization in the region and highlights the gender-power effects of those processes.

As set out at the beginning of this chapter, we want to encourage feminists to engage with issues pertaining to war. A reason why this has not been done adequately in the past is that feminists (and women) have, explicitly or implicitly, associated themselves with antiwar sentiments and pacifism. In the preface to this book, Christine Sylvester poignantly sketches what seems to be an irreconcilable conflict within feminism: 'Feminism was outside war, above it and in a position of belligerence to it.' There is a dimension of exclusionary politics at work here. In our view the war question for feminism deals with these conflicting ideas about the relationship between gender, violence and war. We are concerned about the implications of this.

One implication is that feminists can no longer position themselves above questions of war and conflict. In our view there has to be space for feminism and feminists to ask the question whether there are times when violence might actually be necessary. Looking at violence as a possible option, not a desirable one, for example, in the protection of gross violations of human rights, genocide, mass rape, etc., does not mean a glorification of violence or an acceptance of militarism. In practicality, women would be barred from the opportunity to provide alternative security and defense policies in IR and diplomacy.

Furthermore, the war question for feminism underlines gender as a relational term. Associating women with pacifism is based on a simplified dichotomy (woman-peace, man-war) (cf. Elshtain 1995), which also has the effect of excluding nonviolent men and, hence, it does not allow us to conceptualize nonviolent masculinities.

Theme I
Conceptualizing Gender, Violence, Militarism

2 Gender Relations as Causal in Militarization and War
A Feminist Standpoint[1]
Cynthia Cockburn

In many countries and regions around the world, women are organizing in women-only groups and networks to oppose militarism and militarization, to prevent wars or bring wars to an end, to achieve justice and sustainable peace. From early in 2005 I carried out two years' fulltime empirical research investigating the constitution and objectives, the analyses and strategies of such organizations.[2] The research involved 80,000 miles of travel to twelve countries on four continents, and resulted in case studies of ten country-based groups, fourteen branches of Women in Black in five countries, and three other transnational networks—the Women's International League for Peace and Freedom, Code Pink and the Women's Network against Militarism. Yet this was only a slender sample of the movement of movements that is women's engaged opposition to militarization and war in the contemporary world.

In this article I summarize or encapsulate the unique feminist analysis of war that women seemed to me to be evolving from their location close to armed conflict combined with their positionality as women, and the activism to which they had been provoked. I draw out here only the boldest of its themes, the 'strong case' on gender and war. It is that patriarchal gender relations predispose our societies to war. They are a driving force perpetuating war. They are among the *causes* of war. This is not, of course, to say that gender is the only dimension of power implicated in war. It is not to diminish the commonly understood importance of economic factors (particularly an ever-expansive capitalism) and antagonisms between ethnic communities, states and blocs (particularly the institution of the nation-state) as causes of war. Women antiwar activists bring gender relations into the picture not as an alternative but as an intrinsic, interwoven, inescapable part of the very same story.

A FEMINIST STANDPOINT ON WAR?

Approaching this field of study, I read back into feminist standpoint theory by which many of us had been guided some decades ago, a Marxian way of thinking that had been eclipsed in the conservative era of the 1990s. In the late 1970s, Nancy Hartsock, inspired by Marx, Luka s and Gramsci, began rethinking their concept of working class consciousness and the emergence of a 'proletarian standpoint'. Material life, they had suggested, structures but sets limits to the way we understand society and its relations. The ruling class and the working class, situated at either end of a power relation, may be expected to have radically different understandings of the world. The vision of the rulers is liable to be both partial and perverse, while that available to the oppressed group, born of struggle, may be able to 'expose the real relations among human beings as inhuman' and so have a potentially liberatory role (Hartsock 1983:232; See also Hartsock 1998). To summarize its features, then, a standpoint is an account of the world constituted by (and constitutive of) a collective subject, a group. It is derived from life activities and achieved in struggle. It is subversive of the hegemonic account. It is potentially the foundation of oppositional and revolutionary movement. Locating and accounting for the emergence of a feminist movement, Hartsock applied a Marxian historical materialist approach to *women's* life activity and the phallocratic institutions that structure it, supposing that here too was the ground for a distinctive consciousness, another and different oppositional standpoint. Analysing the sexual division of labour she showed how women's distinctive activity, their experience of domestic, servicing, reproductive and caring work, characteristically unpaid or underpaid, can indeed generate a feminist standpoint that contradicts the hegemonic understanding of political economy.

A number of feminist theorists in those productive years were questioning the basis of knowledge claims (Rose 1983, Jaggar 1983, Harding 1986, Smith 1987). Donna Haraway, addressing the multiplicity and diversity of feminist subjects and life experiences, developed the plural concept of 'situated knowledges'. One cannot expect, she affirmed, to generate an understanding useful to subjugated groups from the universalizing standpoint of the master. After all, he is 'the Man, the One God, whose Eye produces, appropriates, and orders all difference' (Haraway 1988:193). Diverse views from below, clearly rooted in life experiences, were a better bet for more reliable accounts of the world. But 'reliable' seemed to claim 'objectivity'. On what basis could such partial knowledge be considered objective? Haraway, and a little later Sandra Harding, reclaimed objectivity for situated knowledges. Reframing feminist standpoint theory for the postmodern and poststructuralist context of that moment, Harding clarifed that giving up 'the goal of telling one true story about reality' need not mean that 'one must also give up trying to tell less false stories' (Harding 1991:187). On the contrary. Science had never been value-free, as scientists liked to claim. A stronger version of objectivity could be achieved by combining the view from below with enquiry that was *reflexive*, by researchers who named and clearly situated themselves, coming clean about power, interests and values, as informative about the subject and source of knowledge as about the studied objects. I aimed in my empirical research therefore, as indeed I have always done, to be maximally reflexive. I named myself as a long-time feminist antiwar activist in a war-sourcing country, and as a researcher in a white, Western academic world. I set out a research strategy that gave the greatest possible influence over resulting texts to the women whose activity I would research, using a website and weblog as a tool for discussion, negotiation and review of interim and final writings (see 'Introduction' in Cockburn 2007).

However—could I legitimately understand women's face to face involvement with *militarization and war* as a situation capable of giving rise to a feminist standpoint? As other socialist-feminists have tended to do (e.g. Hartmann 1991, Weeks 1998), Hartsock had stayed close to Marx in focusing on *labour* as the quintessential human activity. She had brought to view and built a feminist standpoint on the hidden, marginalized (though necessary) activity allocated to women in the sexual division of labour. But a disadvantaged place in the labour force was not the only characteristic of women's life experience. Could not a situation at the receiving end of gendered physical violence in militarization and war (and indeed in so called peace), subjected to the will of those who possess the means of coercion, likewise be expected to generate a certain feminist consciousness, a feminist oppositional standpoint? My belief that it could was strengthened by finding that other theorists had dealt with a variety of aspects of women's experience and activity as the source of a knowledge claim. Chapters of a reader edited by Sandra Harding (2004a) showed Sara Ruddick arguing for the experience of mothering, Dorothy Smith for women's bodily engagement in the 'everyday world', and Maria Mies and Vandana Shiva for women's survival and subsistence in the third world, as all generative of feminist standpoints. I feel a certain confidence, then, in describing as a standpoint the outcome of my engagement with the understandings of feminist antiwar / antimilitarist activists and the feminist researchers and writers (many of them also activists) who have documented and analysed their experiences. In fact I titled the book that reported the research *'From Where We Stand'*, signalling 'standpoint' while problematizing the 'we' and the 'where' to leave open the possibility of different positionalities in relation to power and differing locations in relation to violence generating subtly varied perspectives.

Framing war, however, calls for a generously holistic conception of power. It must account for women's experience not only of labour, subsistence, mothering *etcetera*, but also of physical violence. War-makers and their apologists are capitalists, but not only capitalists. They are phallocratic, but not only patriarchs. They are white supremacists, but also located advantageously in other power systems (cultural, religious). In 1998 Kathi Weeks (striving to heal the antagonism between modernism and postmodernism) had reformulated feminist standpoint theory, invoking what she calls 'totality', that is to say dimensions of power seen not as one, nor even as several, isolated forces, but rather as 'systems that traverse the entire social horizon and intersect at multiple points' (1998: 5). Weeks, like Hartsock, had located her standpoint in women's labour. Nonetheless her notion of the 'social totality', 'the whole of society seen as a process', seemed to me helpfully to promise a perspective inclusive of more than mode of production and labour processes. It approximated rather well, I thought, to the view from a refugee camp, a military brothel or the picket at the gates of a military airfield.

THINKING FEMINIST, PERCEIVING PATRIARCHY

I found women antiwar activists, with few exceptions, unhesitating in naming themselves feminist. Take, for example, *La Ruta Pacifica de las Mujeres* (Women's Peaceful Road), a state-wide network in Colombia organizing for an end to half a century of internal war. They identify feminism and pacifism as their two 'political bastions' (baluartes politicas). They write of their organization, 'These theoretical foundations have led to its recognition as a novel movement, because there have been prejudices against both of these concepts in the traditional social movements' (*La Ruta Pacifica* 2003:63).[3]

This identification with feminism may seem surprising in view of a widely reported hesitation among contemporary women in Western and 'developed' contexts to adopt the perspective, due among other things to the counter-offensive that has defamed the movement (Faludi 1992, Scharff 2008). There is however plentiful evidence in a global context of a feminist response to circumstances, such as third world indebtedness, neo-liberal economic 'reforms', environmental exploitation or threatened incursions by corporate capital into poor communities, that heighten the contradictions women experience (e.g. Basu 1995).

We should perhaps not be surprised, then, to find that a feminist consciousness is readily generated by close encounters with militarization and war. In the context of war-resistance, I found some women, reaching for an understanding of gender power relations, had had access to transnational feminist theoretical work. The Women in Black group in Belgrade, for instance, travelled widely to other countries during the years of the Yugoslav wars. They exchanged ideas with the feminist antimilitarist women in Spain and Italy who hosted their speaking tours. Their written analyses of their situation cite a transnational body of feminist work including that of Cynthia Enloe, Judith Butler, Adrienne Rich and Nira Yuval-Davis (WinB 2005a). At the same time, they were themselves influential thinkers and writers. Many of them had been active in the feminist movement that blossomed in Yugoslav cities in the 1980s. When rival nationalisms started to tear the state apart they found that, along with all else, they were losing the gains they had made as women. They recognized this as a resurgence not just of militarism and nationalism but also of patriarchy. Their boldly stated disloyalty to nation, state and church inspired women antiwar activists in other countries (Cockburn 2007, ch.3).

Other women's antiwar organizations I met had been stimulated to work out their own ideas by reference to newspapers and TV, while yet others had learned from each other and gathered ideas circulating through the Internet within the transnational movement. In some cases networking and funding organizations such as the Swedish *Kvinna till Kvinna* had been instrumental in transmitting feminist ideas between war zones. It was regional women's networks, including *Femmes Africa Solidarité*, that helped bring into existence the Mano River Women's Peace Network (MARWOPNET), that intervened to stop war in Sierra Leone (Cockburn 2007: 24–33).

So what kind of feminism is this? Extraordinarily holistic it seems to me. By definition it is *transnational*. Secondly, it is necessarily *social constructionist*. An essentialist view of sex differences as 'given' cannot coexist with a goal of transformative change in gender relations. Knowing male pacifists and women who celebrate violence rules out any view of men and women being deterministically shaped by biology. For instance, the women of the Indian groups Forum against the Oppression of Women and Awaaz-e-Niswan, who organized the International Initiative for Justice in Gujarat (see Cockburn 2007:13–22), could hardly hold an essentialist view of women as 'naturally peace-prone'. In the profoundly patriarchal culture of India's Hindu extremist organizations, women may be cast as the selfless wife and mother. Yet during the massacre of Muslims in Gujerat in 2002 the women's wings of the Sangh Parivar and other institutions of the Hindutva movement were out on the streets chiding the men for 'wearing bangles'—urging them to be prove their manhood by killing and raping Muslim women.

Third, looking through the prism of war has made us acutely conscious of the way women are oppressed and exploited through our *bodies*, our sexuality and reproductive capacities. War deepens already deep sexual divisions, emphasizing the male as perpetrator of violence, women as victim. In particular, it legitimates male sexual violence, enabling mass rape of women. It magnifies the distance between femininity and masculinity and enhances men's authority in a quantum leap. So this feminism sees women's subordination as more than the by-product of political inequality or an exploitative economic system. However, antiwar feminism inevitably has a wider range of concerns than this. It cannot fail to have a *critique of capitalism*, and new forms of imperialism and colonization, class exploitation and the global thrust for markets, since these are visibly implicated among the causes of militarization and war. Many wars besides involve intra-state and inter-state nationalisms, so this feminism is necessarily conscious of and *opposed to exclusions* on grounds of race, religion or other aspects of ethnicity. Abuses in war give rise to energetic movements for human rights, including *women's rights*, and the struggle to obtain UN Security Council resolution 1325 (Cockburn 2007, chapter 5) involved a demand for *representation*, suggesting that antiwar feminism also has these so-called liberal demands on its complex agenda. Many organizations and networks are concerned to create horizontal structures and prefigurative forms of activism (Cockburn 2007:178–80), presupposing a feminism that has a critique of the meanings and operation of *power*.

There is thus no way the thinking of women antiwar activists can be reduced to those limited categories we so often, unhelpfully, brand as 'radical', 'socialist' and 'liberal' feminism. It is better encompassed by what Chela Sandoval terms a 'differential' mode of oppositional consciousness. It has not been unique to feminism, she says, but common to all the great liberation movements of the late 20th century, to have several tendencies. She names them: equal rights (we're similar and want equality); revolutionary (we're different and want radical change); supremacist (we're different and better); and separatist (we'll build a better world alone). They are not mutually exclusive. Sandoval's 'differential' is a metaphor suggestive of a gear box and thus of a feminism that intelligently and tactically slips from one to another analysis of women's condition as circumstances demand (Sandoval 2004).

As I found women antiwar activists on the whole comfortable with the word 'feminism' I also found them, both in the global south and global north, routinely and without hesitation using the term 'patriarchy' in everyday speech. They know patriarchy well—they live in it. The Women's Network against Militarism has member groups in a scatter of countries from the Caribbean to the Pacific rim, all of them plagued with US military bases and personnel, weapons technology and related environmental destruction. These well-informed women activists are clear about the part played by patriarchy and masculinism in the region. "The basis of militarism is the strengthening of the patriarchal system," Aida Santos, of the Philippines told me, referring to the effect the US presence was having on her own country's gender relations. They recognize the significance of masculinism in sustaining patriarchal structures. In one of their pamphlets the Network write 'We need a redefinition of masculinity, strength, power and adventure; an end to war toys and the glorification of war and warriors' (Cockburn 2007:63–67).

An easy reference to patriarchy in some ways marks a difference between feminist activists and feminist academics, who today often hesitate before invoking patriarchy. Thirty or forty years ago it was possible to feel confident of using the term. We had evolved the notion of a *sex/gender system* (Rubin 1975) or *gender order* (Connell 1987) as one of the significant dimensions of power in human societies. While in theory, almost any set of sex/gender arrangements could be found in our world, all societies we knew of and those of which we had reliable knowledge from the past, had been, with institutional variations, patriarchies, characterized by male domination, female subordination.

But feminist thinking in the 1980s noted that we needed to take account of historic phases of male dominance, which varies in form with changing modes of production and the rise and fall of empires. With the passage of time, as we became alert to the ways in which rule by the 'fathers' in the sex/gender system of European society was giving way to rule by men in general (Pateman 1988), and familial authority was giving way to more public expressions of male power (Walby 1990), the word 'patriarchy' began to sound a little archaic. On the other hand nobody came up with a satisfactory alternative. 'Fratriarchy' and 'andrarchy' might be more accurate designations of the gender order in Western Europe today, but they have failed to find favour. We are left with a very powerful reality that academics are uncertain how to name.

Popularly, however, the term lives on. This does not mean feminist anti-war activists are blind to its complexities and contradictions, in fact these are widely discussed. For instance, women are certain that there *is* in fact a sexual division of war, just as there's a sexual division of labour, a strong gender skew that makes for gender-specific experiences. Yet they can hardly fail to be alert to anomalies. Most rape victims are women, but some are men. While most soldiers are men, a growing percentage are women. At the same time, we see that the exceptions to the norm, like those that fulfil the norm, experience their anomalous fate in profoundly gendered ways. The implication of rape are very different for women and men. Women, unlike men, can become pregnant as a result of rape. Males experience rape as 'feminizing', a trauma specific to masculine identity (Zarkov 2007). As to soldiering, one need look no further than US female soldier Kayla Williams' startling account of her service in Iraq. Aspiring to equality through military service alongside men, she emerged from the experience reduced in her own eyes to 'a slut'—which is how her male comrades had perceived and treated her. It is not the same thing to be a woman soldier as a man soldier, nor is it seen as one (Williams 2004).

So, observing the sexual division of war and especially observing its vagaries, it becomes clear that the case for gender as a power relation implicated in the perpetuation of war cannot rest on what individual men and women do. It is not written in stone that the cultures we live in will capture and 'normalize' the gender performance of each and every one of us. Some of us escape, some of us do not match up, some of us fail to live our gender 'properly', some individuals resist gender norms. There are no certainties, only probabilities. The case rests more firmly on the patriarchal gender relation itself, which is a phallocratic relation between a supreme masculine principle and a secondary feminine one, where masculinity is associated with transcendence (rising above the mundane) and femininity with immanence (immersion in the daily round), where the masculine is a source of authority (de Beauvoir 1953) . It is the *gender order itself*, predicated on coercion and violence, that comes to view as bearing on militarization and war in interesting and significant ways.

A WAY OF SEEING WAR: AS CULTURAL; AS SYSTEM; AS CONTINUUM

What I have learned in listening to feminist antiwar activists is that a particular perception of war comes from a combination of a certain location and a certain positionality. Being located close to war, in the flesh or in the imagination, combines with the experience of being a woman in patriarchy to foster an understanding of the significance of gender. Women's reflections on war are closer to those of the culturally-attuned sociologist or anthropologist than those of the international relations discipline which, despite the recent intervention of feminists (Grant and Newland 1991, V .Spike Peterson 1992, J. Ann Tickner 1992), tends to speak for and from the abstract masculinity of statesmen, diplomats and military. The conventional view of war in this maintream discourse stresses its political, institutional, calculated and organized nature. It tends to downplay the messy *cultural* detail of armed conflict. For example, Colin Creighton and Martin Shaw in the introduction to their classic collection of articles *The Sociology of War and Peace* (1987:3) sum up this understanding in the words 'Aggression isn't force, force isn't violence, violence isn't killing, killing isn't war'.

They are right, of course. War is not fisticuffs. Yet—looking at war as a woman inside the war zone, or paying attention as a feminist to women's experience of war, it is not quite so easy to set aside 'ordinary' aggression, force or violence as 'not war'. Women are saying clearly that they experience coercion by men in disturbingly similar forms in war and so-called peace. Thus the women of the women's organization *Vimochana*, in Bangalore, whose antiwar activism is pitted both against the militarism of the Indian state and the bloody inter-communal conflict that besets India, told me, 'We didn't start as women against war, but as women against violence against women. Through that we came to take a stand against violence in the wider society.' While the frequent sexualization of violence in war is not the whole story, it is indicative. Feminists tend to delve beneath the cool 'international relations' representation of war, to break the academic taboo on looking at 'aggressiveness', and then, down at the level of cultures, when we see the violence clearly, to ask questions about social relations: what kinds of violence? who does them to whom? and what may they have to do with gender identities, gender antagonisms and gender power? War as institution, seen from a woman's location inside it, reveals itself as made up of, refreshed by and adaptively reproduced by violence as banal practice.

Secondly, war-fighting between two armies is only the tip of the iceberg, as it were, of an underlying, less immediate, set of institutions and relationships that can be understood as *systemic*. The author most often credited for the term 'war system' is Betty Reardon. In her text *Sexism and the War System* she employs the term to refer to society in its entirety, 'our competitive social order, which is based on authoritarian principles, assumes unequal value among and between human beings, and is held in place by coercive force' (Reardon 1996:10) While this accurately describes many modern societies, the women's organizations I have studied, in so far as I have come to understand their analysis, do not in the main share Betty Reardon's reduction of this social order to nothing other than a gender order. Few, I believe, would follow her in a belief that 'patriarchy ... invented and maintains war to hold in place the social order it spawned' (Reardon 1996:12). Looking at war from close quarters these women activists see all too clearly that other forces are at work in addition to gender. All the same, it is helpful to visualize 'war' using the idea of system as a conceptual model, imagining it as a set of interacting or interdependent entities, functionally related, with inputs and outputs, and information flows within and across its open borders. (For sociological applications of systems theory see for instance Bailey 1994, Checkland 1997). Seen this way it comprises linked organizations (Ministries of Defence, the arms manufacturing firms, training academies and military suppliers, the Chiefs of Staff and their commands), materiel (bombs, battleships, bullets), and governing ideologies (expressed in values, attitudes and cultures). War seen systemically reflects the perception of women transnational antiwar activists, located at varying sites they recognize as interconnected, engaged in distinct but related oppositional practices (opposing the international arms trade from London, demonstrating outside the Ministry of Defence in Serbia, or contesting military influence in children's education in the USA or Turkey). Such a systemic view of war readily opens up to a gender analysis. Its institutions, let us say the 'military industrial complex', can be seen as loci of several dimensions of power, economic, national—and patriarchal. We can see overlaps and information flows between the war system and other social systems in which a gender dimension is particularly significant, such as the educational system, recreation and media.

So, war as relational, war as systemic—and a third qualifier is important: the idea that wars are only phases in a sequence of conditions linked together as a continuum. It is from women I have met during my research that I have learned to see the continuum effect more clearly (Cockburn 2004). *La Ruta Pacifica* for instance write, '... we Colombian women are tired of so many kinds of violence: sexual violence, intrafamilial, social, economic, political violence—and armed violence as its maximal expression' (*La Ruta Pacifica* 2003:75).[4] As with 'war system', 'war as continuum' is a perception that arises from being linked in an international movement, yet variously located in relation to war fighting as it waxes and wanes. For example, some, like the Women's Network against Militarism whose focus is the US military bases in the Pacific and Caribbean, are particularly well informed on militarization, the state of preparedness for war. *La Ruta* is in mid-war. *Actoras de Cambio* in Guatemala are in a post-war moment, dealing with the terrible residues of massive armed sexual violence. In Sierra Leone, the women of MARWOPNET are organizing women along borders to monitor movements of men, guns and drugs to prevent a renewal of war (Cockburn 2007: ch.1,2). So, organizations and networks like this, spanning the globe and linked by electronic communications, tend to see 'war' not just as spasms of war-fighting, but as part of a continuum leading from militarism (as a persisting mindset, expressed in philosophy, newspaper editorials, political think tanks), through militarization (processes in economy and society that signify preparation for war), to episodes of 'hot' war, and thence to cease fire and stand-off, followed perhaps by an unsteady peace with sustained military investment, beset by sporadic violence that prefigures a further round in the spiral.

In fact, authors in mainstream war studies too are increasingly noting a continuum effect. Steve Schofield has shown how the UK's war-readiness was not relaxed at the end of the Cold War—rather militarization measured by military expenditure was maintained into the 1990s (Schofield 1994). Rupert Smith suggests that with the end of industrial warfare and the advent of the new paradigm of 'war among the people' the continuum effect has increased. War 'is no longer a single massive event of military decision that delivers a conclusive political result'—rather 'our conflicts tend to be timeless, since we are seeking a condition, which then must be maintained until an agreement on a definitive outcome, which may take years or decades' (Smith 2006:17). Berdal and Malone have collected a volume of essays that suggest that in contemporary civil wars, defeating the enemy in battle is no longer necessarily the aim. Rather, some participants have a 'vested interest in continued conflict' and in the long-term institutionalization of violence (Berdal and Malone 2000:2).

CAUSES OF WAR AND WHERE TO LOOK FOR THEM

Many women antiwar activists, then, see gender relations as causal in war. The mainstream analysis is blind to such causality. How can this incompatibility be resolved? Are they perhaps looking at different phenomena? The verb 'to cause', after all, has more than one inflection. Brian Fogarty writes that the reason for multiple theories of war is that even a particular war may have multiple causes. 'At the very least, every war probably has immediate causes, antecedent causes, and something like 'root causes' or 'favorable conditions' underlying them' (Fogarty 2000:77). The economic motivators of war are often, in Fogarty's sense, immediate. Usually they are rather clear to see, written into the news headlines. What are the aggressors demanding? What are the defenders defending? In early wars, five thousand years ago, we might see theft of grain surpluses; a little later maybe a demand for levies, taxes, tributes; water sources; control of trade routes. In internal revolutionary wars—let's say that of Russia in 1917—the aim may be to seize control of the means of production. In African wars today it is possible to see valuable minerals as a factor. The extraction of coltan and tantalite for computers and mobile phones features in the current profoundly destructive war in the Democratic Republic of Congo. Business interests can often be seen at work beneath the 'security' discourse of states (Blum 2003).

Ethno-nationalist issues, foreign-ness, the expression of the perceived security interests of an ethnic or national self in relation to its others, is a second major cause of war (Horowitz 1985, Gurr and Harff 1994, Hutchinson 2005). It is often an antecedent cause, in Fogarty's terms, if not an immediate one. Raids against the ones outside the walls of the first city states, the barbarians on the borders of the early empires. Later, the Infidel. Some contemporary wars are fought by an insurgent ethnic group trying to get recognition inside a larger polity, looking for more autonomy or it's own state: as Chechen separatists seek to escape from the Russian Federation while the Russian military mobilize to stop them. How can this kind of racializing cause in war be detected? By listening to what the ideologues are saying, the religious leaders. What is the propaganda, who is putting it out? What names are claimed, what names are being imposed on others?

By contrast, patriarchal gender relations as a cause of war, I would suggest, most often fall in the 'root cause' or 'favourable conditions' category, and here we have to pay attention to culture. With the exception of the abduction of the mythical Helen of Troy (and the spurious attempt of the George W. and Laura Bush to portray the invasion of Afghanistan in 2001 as a war to save Afghan women from repression by the Taliban) wars are not fought 'for' gender issues in the way they are sometimes fought 'for' oil resources, or 'for' national autonomy. Instead, they foster militarism and militarization. They make war thinkable. They make peace difficult to sustain. As noted above, women close to militarization and war are observant of cultures, cultures as they manifest themselves in societies before, in and after armed conflicts. If we think of the war system as having a cyclical or spiralling life, as a continuum over time, proceeding from the discourse of militarist ideology, through material investment in militarization, aggressive policy-making, outbreaks of war, short firefights, prolonged stalemates, ceasefires, demobilization, periods of provisional peace, anxieties about security, rearmament etc., and if we look closely at the social relations in which individuals and groups enact these various steps, that is where it is possible to see gender relations at work, pushing the wheel around.

The above account of a feminist standpoint, generating an understanding of war that contradicts the hegemonic view, is derived first and foremost from my empirical research among women's antiwar organizations and networks. But, closely involved with that movement, there is a world of feminist scholars (men as well as women) who have striven over the past three decades to articulate in a growing library of written work the understandings arising among women war survivors and activists. Many collected editions bring together research and reporting from a range of different countries and periods (for instance, Cooke and Woollacott 1993, Lorentzen and Turpin 1998, Moser and Clark 2001, Giles and Hyndman 2004). Research-based monographs show the influence of gender relations at points along the continuum of militarization and war. Robert Dean, for instance, in his study of the Kennedy administration taking the US to war in Vietnam, shows masculinism at work in preparation for war (Dean 2001). Susan Jeffords in *The Remasculinization of America* (1989), shows, through an analysis of films and novels, national efforts to salvage masculine pride after such a defeat. Many firsthand accounts show in painful detail how, in military training, patriarchal masculinity lends itself to exploitation for war fighting, and how violence is eroticized in masculine fantasy (Theweleit 1987). Together such studies articulate the feminist perception that patriarchal gender relations are among the 'root causes' of militarism and war.

THE VIOLENCE INHERENT IN LINKED SYSTEMS OF POWER

There are many dimensions along which power is distributed in the 'totality' of society (Weeks 1998). One is age. Others are skin color; physical strength and ability; or, say, the urban—rural dimension of advantage. As far as militarization and war are concerned however it is safe to say that three dimensions of power are the most significant and influential. The first is economic power. The second is ethnic or national power embodied in community, religious and state structures. This is often, but not uniquely, white supremacy. The third is gender power. Feminist studies have developed a way of addressing this multiplicity of sources of power from the perspective of the individual, using the concepts of 'positionality' and 'intersectionality'. They are ugly and tedious words, sometimes deployed to the point of fetishization, but they are genuinely useful because they enable us to take account of the way a person's sense-of-self and ascribed identity are partly defined by her or his positioning in relation to not one but several dimensions of power (Anthias 1998). What has too often been overlooked, I believe, in a 'post-structuralist' climate, is that intersectionality *also and always works at the macro level*. The power structures of economic class based on ownership of the means of production, the racializing power of ethno-nationalism expressed in community authorities and states, and the sex/gender hierarchy *together* shape human social structures, institutions and relational processes. Together they establish positions of relative power, thereby laying down the possibilities and probabilities for individuals and groups that variously inhabit them. No single one of them produces its effects in the absence of the other two.

Intersectionality means that it makes little sense to seek to isolate the institutions, the structures, of patriarchal gender power. The family may appear to be the 'real' one, the only one. It is not. Few if any institutions do a specialized gender job—or for that matter a specialized economic or other 'power mobilizing' job. A corporation or a bank may appear to be 'just' an economic institution, a church or a mosque may look as if it is simply an ethnic institution, a family may seem to be merely a sex/gender institution. But look inside them and you find each and all sets of relations functioning at one and the same time: they are all economic, ethnic and gender institutions, though differently weighted. In corporations, almost all senior people are men; churches often mobilize considerable wealth and all the monotheistic clerical institutions are bastions of male power; blood-and-earth nationalists have keen interests in the fecundity of the patriarchal family, and so on. It is not possible logically to disconnect them, neither the dimensions of power themselves nor the processes that are their vectors. They are distinct, they can be studied and named, but they are intersectional.

What, then, has the view of power as intersected sets of institutions and relations got to do with war? Here I think we need to depart from empirical material and undertake an exegesis, something like this. A class system built on economic surpluses, a racializing hierarchy of cities, then states and empires, and institutionalized patriarchy, emerged together within a definable historical period (at a different moment in different parts of the world). They were predicated on violence. They all involved constituting a self in relation to an inferiorized, exploited other—the rich man's landless labourer; the citizen's hated foreigner; the woman as men's property, commodified in bride price, sale or exchange price, in prostitution and the value of her children. All three processs were necessarily violent. Labourers will not build canal systems unless driven by hunger. Foreigners will not bow to another's hegemony if it is not backed by coercion. Women will not be subdued without force. It is not surprising therefore that institutionalized warfare, the augmentation and mobilization of what Charles Tilly terms the means of coercion (Tilly 1992), was born along with increasing accumulation of wealth, the early state and the establishment of patriarchies—innovations that signified the condition known as 'civilization'. Gerda Lerner's intensively researched book *The Creation of Patriarchy* shows this happening towards the end of the Neolithic in the emerging societies of the eastern Mediterranean (Lerner 1986). It has also been noted, several millennia later, in the American hemisphere. William Eckhardt, in a comprehensive study that reviews many other historians on war, evolves a 'dialectical evolutionary theory', as he calls it, suggesting that the more 'civilized' people became the more warlike they became. Civilization and war: it is a correlation he finds persisting in all regions and phases of history (Eckhardt 1992:4).

The suggestion here then is that militarization and war are caused, shaped, achieved and reproduced across millennia through all three dimensions of power. If one is at work, the others will be too. The gender drama is never absent: the male as subject, the female as alien, the alien as effeminate (both the one a man perceives out there, and the one he fears inside himself). This is why a theory of war and its causation is flawed if it lacks a gender dimension. Most theories of war, however, in sociology and in international relations, do indeed lack this necessary element. To those who evolve and deploy them, they seem perfectly complete and satisfying without it. When women, feminists, come along and introduce our insights into discussions of war, when we talk about women and gender, we are often told we are being trivial, we are forgetting 'the big picture'. Cynthia Enloe speaks from a feminist standpoint when she boldy interjects 'but suppose this IS the big picture?' (Enloe 2005:280)

CONCLUSION: GENDER TRANSFORMATION AS PART OF THE STRUGGLE FOR PEACE

To summarize the argument made above—looking closely at war with a sociologist's or anthropologist's eye reveals cultures, the detail of what is done and said. You see job advertisements for the military, you see training, you see discipline and indiscipline, killing, rape and torture. If, as well, you have a feminist's engaged standpoint, derived from women's lives and deaths in this maelstrom, you see the gender in it. And you turn again to evaluate so-called peacetime. You see that the disposition in societies such as those we live in, characterized by a patriarchal gender regime, is towards an association of masculinity with authority, coercion and violence. It is a masculinity (and a complementary femininity) that not only serves militarism very well indeed, but *seeks and needs militarization and war for its fulfilment.* Of course, the violence of war is in turn productive. It produces re-burnished ethnic identities, sharpened by memories of wrong and a desire for revenge. It produces particular gender identities–armed masculinities, demoralized and angry men, victimized femininities, types of momentarily-empowered women. But these war-honed gender relations, 'after war' (which may always equally be 'before war'), again tend to feed back perennially into the spiralling continuum of armed conflict, for ever predisposing a society to violence, forever disturbing the peace.

Why is it important to pay attention to the perceptions of a feminist standpoint on war, to address the possibility that gender-as-we-know-it plays a part in perpetuating armed conflict? Because there are practical implications in this for our worldwide, mixed-sex movements for demilitarization, disarmament and peace. After all, we are ready to recognize that a sustainably peaceful society must differ from today's war-torn societies. At the very least, its economic relations must be more just and equal. Additionally, its national and ethnic relations must become more respectful and inclusive. Women committed to organizing as women against war add a dimension to this transformative change. They ask the antiwar movement to recognize that, to be sustainably peaceful, a society will also have to be one in which we live gender very differently from the way it is lived today.

R.W.Connell has persistently analysed what cultural studies tell us about masculinity. In 2002 he wrote ' . . . men predominate across the spectrum of violence. A strategy for demilitarization and peace must concern itself with this fact, with the reasons for it, and with its implications for work to reduce violence' (Connell 2002:34). And he went on to say, 'Gender dynamics are by no means the whole story. Yet given the concentration of weapons and the practices of violence among men, gender patterns appear to be strategic. Masculinities are the forms in which many dynamics of violence take shape . . . *Evidently, then, a strategy for demilitarization and peace must include a strategy of change in masculinities*' (emphasis added, ibid:38). Connell has also been important for showing us the multiplicity and variation in masculinity, pointing to its subversive as well as hegemonic forms (Connell 1995). In countries such as Serbia and Turkey where military service for men is still obligatory, some homosexual men have been among the most politicised and challenging 'conscientious objectors', because of they way they have simultaneously refused militarism and conformity to patriarchal norms of manhood (Cinar and Usterci 2009).

So the message coming from feminist antiwar, antimilitarist and peace organizations of the kind I studied is that our many internationally-linked coalitions against militarism and war as a whole need to challenge patriarchy as well as capitalism and nationalism. 'We can't do this alone', women say. Sandra Harding has pointed out that 'everything that feminist thought must know must also inform the thought of every other liberatory movement, and vice versa. It is not just the women in those other movements who must know the world from the perspective of women's lives. Everyone must do so if the movements are to succeed at their own goals' (Harding 2004b:135). But the message emanating from a feminist standpoint on war has not so far been welcomed onto the mainstream agenda. The major antiwar coalitions, mainly led by left tendencies, contain many women activists. An unknown number, individually, may share in a feminist analysis of war, but their presence has not yet been allowed to shape the movements' activism. If antimilitarist and antiwar organizing is to be strong, effective and to the point, women must oppose war not only as people but *as women*. And men too must oppose it in their own gender identity—*as men*—explicitly resisting the exploitation of masculinity for war.

NOTES

1. I am grateful to the publishers of the *International Feminist Journal of Politics* for permission to reproduce this article which appeared in Vol.12, No.2, May 2010. The content derives from papers presented as the Bertrand Russell Lectures, in March 2008, in Hamilton, Ontario. It was also the theme I presented as the first annual *Feminist Review* public lecture in London in July 2008. I am grateful to the Centre for Peace Studies at McMaster University, the Keith Leppmann Memorial Fund, and the editorial board of *Feminist Review* for these opportunities.
2. The project was action-research in which I engaged both from my academic base in the Department of Sociology at City University London and my

involvement as an activist in the international network Women in Black. It resulted in a book, *From Where We Stand: War, Women's Activism and Feminist Analysis*, Zed Books, 2007, and the supporting materials are available on my website www.cynthiacockburn.org. The research was generously supported by grants from the Joseph Rowntree Charitable Trust, the foundation Un Monde par Tous, the Network for Social Change, the Ian Mactaggart Trust, the Lipman-Miliband Trust and the Maypole Fund.

3. My translation. 'Ambas bases teóricas han hecho que se le reconozca como un movimiento novedoso pues con uno y otro concepto han existido prejuicios en los movimientos sociales tradicionales' (*La Ruta Pacifica de las Mujeres* 2003:63).

4. My translation. '... [L]as mujeres colombianas estamos cansadas de tantas violencias: la sexual, la intrafamiliar, la social, la económica, la política y la armada como su maxima expresión' (*La Ruta Pacifica de las Mujeres* 2003:75).

3 Men/Masculinities
War/Militarism—Searching (for) the Obvious Connections?

Jeff Hearn

> There's something about all that male contact [in the army] that was almost beautiful to me.
> (British tank commander, interview broadcast in *Tanks*, part of *Soldiers* series, BBC1 TV, 30 October 1985)

INTRODUCTION

The military is one of the clearest and most obvious arenas of men's social power, violence, killing and potential violence and killing, in their many guises. It is an understatement to say that men, militarism and the military are historically, profoundly and blatantly interconnected. Many armies and other fighting forces of the world have been and still are armies composed exclusively of men, young men and boys. The world of the military and militarism is massive, and men are present throughout. Military matters are urgent and powerful; how militaries, armies and those in them are organized and act are literally matters of life and death. They are specifically geared to the ability, actual and potential, to inflict violence and other forms of harm. This applies in 'imperialist wars,' 'wars of resistance,' 'Just Wars,' 'unjust wars,' 'preemptive wars,' 'preventative wars,' 'preclusive interventions,' even 'peacekeeping.'

In recent years critical studies on men and masculinities have highlighted how men have been and often continue to be seen as ungendered or naturalized (Hearn 1998a; Kimmel et al. 2005). Studies range from masculine psychology and psychodynamics to societal, structural analyses of men, from detailed ethnographies of particular men's activities, to investigations into constructions of specific masculinities in discourses, and interrelations of unities and differences between men. While not wishing to play down debates between different traditions, some of the main themes within recent critical studies on men and masculinities can be summarized as:

- a specific, rather than implicit or incidental, focus on men and masculinities

36 *Jeff Hearn*

- taking account of feminist, gay and other critical gender scholarship
- recognizing men and masculinities as explicitly gendered rather than nongendered
- understanding men and masculinities as socially constructed, produced and reproduced
- seeing men and masculinities as variable and changing across time (history) and space (culture), within societies, and through life courses and biographies
- emphasizing men's relations, albeit differentially, to gendered power
- spanning both the material and the discursive
- interrogating the intersecting of the gender with other social divisions

All these points are relevant in considering men and militarism. Indeed, men and militarism are so obviously coupled that it is hard to know where to start; it might seem gratuitous to labor the point. The very obviousness of this coupling, at different levels of analysis, from the individual to the global, can easily naturalize or normalize it, so that its interrogation escapes serious critical scrutiny. However, the extent of connections is more extensive than often presumed. I begin by addressing what might be called some 'very obvious' connections, in which the 'facts' of the scale of militarism appear to speak for themselves. Then, there are so-called 'obvious' connections, that is, clear, undeniable connections around the gender structuring of militaries and militarism. Third are the less widely recognized, yet 'fairly obvious,' and indeed equally important, connections that may be less familiar, yet hard to refute. For example, in this last category, warring and war-related times and places provide contexts for men's many other actually or potentially violent and violating gendered practices in and by: corporations, privatized security forces, organized crime, foreign policy, diplomacy, arms trading, sex trade, financial exploitation and corruption. These are all dominated by men, with their own particular social structures and forms of organizing, with practices ranging from direct violence to trading, managing and working for a living.

Looking at differing degrees of 'obviousness' brings attention to a wide web of activities within militarism-war-violence complex(es). Crisis, whether individual, societal or global, is often a time when the embedded nature of power is made more visible. In the case of militaries and militarism, crisis may indeed be endemic, at least for those on the actual or potential receiving end of their actions. Thus, through explorations of various forms of 'obviousness,' this chapter seeks to make the familiar unfamiliar.

MEN/MASCULINITIES, VIOLENCE/WAR/MILITARISM: VERY OBVIOUS CONNECTIONS

I will begin with some very obvious and large-scale connections. The size and power of military spending worldwide is huge beyond belief. Military spending worldwide was about US$1,000 billion in 2002: 20 times development aid to relieve poverty. In 2002 the increase in US military spending was about the total poverty aid from rich to poor countries (Stockholm International Peace Research Institute [SIPRI] 2002, 2003; de Vylder 2004). In 2007 SIPRI estimated worldwide expenditure was over US$1,200 billion, having overtaken the figures from the late 1980s and the 'post–Cold War' dip in the 1990s. Stiglitz and Bilmes (2008) estimate the Iraq and Afghanistan Wars are costing over 3 trillion dollars.

In the twentieth century, estimates of about 188–262 deaths or more million caused by humans (about 5 percent of the total) have been made by experts in this field (Brzezinski 1993; Hobsbawm 1994; Rummel 1994; White 2001; Leitenberg 2006). The scale of very largely manmade death is difficult to appreciate. In many, perhaps most, wars and conflicts civilians bear the gravest consequences. In the Vietnam War, three million civilians died (Allukian and Atwood 2000). WHO estimated that in 2000 while 520,000 were killed through homicide, 310,000 were killed from war-related acts (WHO 2002). The ongoing conflict in the Democratic Republic of the Congo has led to 3.8 million deaths (Coghlan et al. 2006). Estimates of deaths from the First Gulf War alone are about 150,000 Iraqi troops killed (as against 400 Coalition troops), 3,000 Iraqi directly caused civilian deaths and between 100,000 and 240,000 civilian deaths caused indirectly (Messerschmidt 2010). In October 2006, a peer-reviewed survey estimated 186,000 civilians had been directly killed by the Coalition, following the 2003 invasion, out of an estimated total of about 655,000 excess Iraqi deaths above the number expected in a nonconflict situation, and about 601,000 excess deaths due to violence (Burnham et al. 2006).

Most of both of the spending and the killing is directed by and done by men. Men remain the specialists in violence, armed conflict and killing, whether by organized militaries, terrorism or indeed domestic violence. Men have dominated these individual and collective actions. In war and through militarism individual men, like women and children, may suffer, even be killed, but men's collective structural power may be undiminished, even reinforced.

Yet, on the other hand, there are easy ways to avoid this—perhaps it is so obvious that commentators seem embarrassed in mentioning, let alone analyzing, these connections. The excellent SIPRI *Yearbook* reviews the current state of 'Armaments, Disarmament and International Security' (2008). The summary covers 25 pages packed with information on these questions. As regards gender, there is a one-page section entitled 'Integrating Gender into Post-Conflict Security Sector Reform' written by Megan Bastick, noting:

> Participation of women in post-conflict security services is crucial to creating structures that representative, trusted and legitimate, and are able to meet the security needs of both men and women. . . . Gender mainstreaming—assessing the impact of SSR [security sector reform]

policies and activities on women, men, boys and girls at every stage of the process—is a key strategy. (9)

Thus there can be descriptions of gender-neutral military, militarism and armament, and then their gendered effects on women. Indeed whether we are talking about academic research, media commentaries or everyday practices of international politics, international relations (IR) and militarism are still not usually presented from a gender perspective. However, even when analyses of IR are gendered, this gendering often, even perhaps usually, does not extend to the gendering of men, an issue I return to later in this chapter.

MEN/MASCULINITIES, VIOLENCE/WAR/MILITARISM: OBVIOUS CONNECTIONS

Yet strangely, even very strangely, these two areas—of war and conflict, and men and masculinities—have generally not been put together. It has often either been simply accepted as taken for granted or gone unnoticed that military persons are largely men. Dominant forms and processes of militarism, in theory and practice, have long been seen as either 'gender neutral' or implicitly and simply men's/male, whether they represent widely adopted or more specialist forms of masculinity. Gendering militarism and war involves attending to both gender and sexuality, and not only the relation of women to militarism and war, but also explicitly gendering how men, masculinities and men's practices relate to militarism and war (for example, Hearn 1987; Enloe 1998; Goldstein 2001; Moser and Clark 2001; Higate 2002; Ferguson et al. 2004; Whitworth 2004; Hopton and Higate 2005). Militaries are part of the state and organized in association with political, economic and administrative power in the highest reaches of the state, including policing, security services, foreign policy and economic interests. They are concerned with both national and international offense and defense.

My own country of origin, the UK, has a long history of militarism and military ideology that continues to suffuse much national life (Dawson 1994). This is even with the UK's loss of empire (Tolson 1977) and abolition of conscription, as seen in the enactment of imperial masculinity in the Falklands War (Metcalf 1985). The UK, along with France, has fought most international wars since 1946, followed by the US and Soviet Union/Russia (Human Security Centre 2005). It has been a strong ally to the US, which has been involved in many further wars in the period. According to CIA and SIPRI (2008) estimates, the UK has the second largest military expenditure in the world, after the US, just above China and France. The UK is probably the second largest spender on military science, engineering and technology. In 2007 it became the largest arms exporter, according to government figures, overtaking the US, which normally leads in this respect (Fidler 2008).

Militarism and militaries are among the most clearly gendered of all governmental and related activities. Within the military men are the vast majority of active members, trained to inflict violence and other forms of harm on others, and overwhelmingly dominate the higher ranks of military management of such violence and harm (Higate 2002). The military provides resources for many kinds of military masculinities; it is an established way for boys and young men to become and be 'men.' The links between men, masculinity and the military are various and plural, so there are military masculinities, not just military masculinity, including homosocial, strongly masculinized and homophobic masculinities (Cammermeyer 1995; E. Hall 1995; Tatchell 1995). Moreover, many states specifically disallow gay/homosexual men from serving in the military, and in some countries men in the military who are defined in this way can be prosecuted. Intense contradictions can also occur between hypermasculinity and misogyny on one hand, and 'softer,' more tender masculinities on the other, not least in the throes of military survival (D. Morgan 1994). Similarly, making military gendered violence is a practical, continuous accomplishment, with military masculinities taking variable forms at the level of identity. The complex relations of militarism and masculinities can become identity projects and experiential worlds ripe for fantasy and psychodynamic processes (Theweleit 1987). More generally, international events and scenarios, such as US defeat in Vietnam, Russian defeat in Afghanistan and reassertions of imperial masculinity in wars and arms races have all been very largely in men's hands and have had clear implications for national and local constructions of masculinity.

The impact of the military, and military men and masculinities, upon those outside the military—women, men and children—is huge. This is so in terms of direct and indirect violence on other combatants and civilians in combatant areas, but also on the lives of men in the military and their family and friends. Violence may be done mainly to other men, mainly to women and children, or more randomly to people, regardless of gender. In some cases men are specifically targeted by men, including using boys and younger men to harm older men of their own ethnic or other category, as in gendercide (Jones 2004), itself more or less random or more systematic. Indeed, the collective, historical power of men may be maintained by the dispensability of some men, as with soldiers in war, even with violence to women and children, usually as noncombatants.

In most cases men dominate the military, both numerically and organizationally; there are, however, major complications in this gendered picture. First, not all armies consist of men. Historical relations of men and militarism should not obscure women's military activity at particular times and places (Hearn 2003b). In the mid-nineteenth century it is estimated that of the King of Dahomey's 12,000 strong army, 5,000 were women. In the 1941 Yugoslav Liberation War about 100,000 women carried arms as active fighters (Oakley 1972: 145). Over 10,000 women took part in the Algerian Liberation War armed struggle, of which a fifth suffered imprisonment or death. Women's involvement in nation formation, as in struggles against imperialist powers, has been formidable, if often later undermined with moves to 'peace' (Knauss 1987; Pankhurst 2007a). Women also perform key servicing or administrative positions within militaries; in some countries this specialization may be reinforced with moves to privatization of military functions (Tallberg 2009).

The detailed gendered effects of military service on individual men and women are clearly very important. Direct effects include injury and mental health problems, especially after active service. For example, about 10 percent of UK troops airlifted out of the Iraq war zone between January and October 2003 suffered primarily from psychological problems (Iverson et al. 2005). A reluctance to engage in help-seeking behavior is one pattern among some young veterans (van Staden et al. 2007). Other effects concern difficulties in adjusting to civilian life (Higate 2001). An issue taken up in some countries is the link between military service and domestic violence (Mercier and Mercier 2000), leading to some planned interventions in this arena. The UK Probation staff union NAPO said its figures suggested about 1 in 11 prisoners used to be in the armed forces ('Jails Hold 8,500 Ex-Servicemen' 2008). Up to 8,500 former members of the armed forces are serving sentences in UK prisons, it has been claimed. In addition, soldiers under 20 are 1.7 times more likely to kill themselves than civilians of the same age, according to figures from a 2004 Ministry of Defence Report (S. Hall 2004).

MEN/MASCULINITIES, VIOLENCE/WAR/MILITARISM: FAIRLY OBVIOUS CONNECTIONS

However, the extent of the connections is broader and more complex. The connections extend to gendered global histories, states and para-states, IR and differential analyses and explanations of military violence.

Some Global Histories

While the concept of Western men as 'world leaders' has become established over the last century or more, men have long been 'world leaders' in exploration, adventuring, conquest and warfare. The official histories of empires, nation building and militarism can be seen as largely histories of men, or certain kinds of men. These gendered processes have expanded through exertions of huge amounts of colonialist and imperialist violence, enacted largely by men. In developing global geopolitical analysis of men and masculinities, Connell (1998, 2005) outlined three forms of 'globalizing masculinities.' First, masculinities of conquest and settlement are those practices by men at frontiers of incipient empires. The men were often drawn from more segregated, even rootless sectors of metropole society, combining 'an unusual level of violence and egocentric individualism' (1998: 12) in their frontier activities. They were often, though not always, relatively autonomous from state control, especially in early phases of conquest and settlement. They sometimes enacted obliteration of local populations, as well as ideological change of local gender orders. Second, masculinities of empire refer to practices of men within more established empires. This involved, and continues to involve, gender ranking of different men and masculinities: some more highly valued, more 'masculine' (often imperialists, colonizers and certain resistant colonized); some more 'effeminized' (certain other, perhaps less resistant colonized). Empires create opportunities for imperial administrative masculinities, economic individualism at imperial margins, and new distinctions by 'expertise,' rather than direct violence, at the metropole. Third, decolonization processes challenge imperial gender orders, producing masculinities of postcolonialism and neoliberalism. Associations of resistance, masculinity and violence sometimes disrupt local gender orders, often involving violence, institutionally and interpersonally. With the breakdown of old empires, new postcolonial men and masculinities have developed in both metropoles and former colonies, in part through the operation of global capitalism and neoliberalism. In each of these historical phases, different globalizing masculinities operate in part through violence and militarism, as in adventuring, state consolidation and expansionism, and global–local armed conflicts respectively.

While the notion of 'globalizing masculinities' is applied more readily to Western histories, it is also useful in other contexts (Connell 2007). For example, refocusing globalizing masculinities on the transitional, post-Soviet nations of Central and Eastern Europe and Western and Central Asia suggests rather different masculinities to those stressed from Western perspectives. For example, important historical features here include: impacts of Czarist and Russian empires; the conquest and settlement of Siberia; development of Soviet Union seen as an empire; Stalinist 'ethnic cleansings' and mass political purges; processes of Russification; and the particular complex empires and national/ethnic formations and conflicts in the former Yugoslavia, including the Serbian empire. All of these have involved intersections of masculinity, violence and militarism. Such various globalizing histories highlight crosscutting complexities in the intersections of masculinities with gender, nationality, ethnicity, religion and other social divisions, with the complications of empires having multiple centers (Hearn 2003a).

States, Para-States and International Relations

The 'man question,' the problematic place of men in the gender order, is almost always present implicitly when talking of the state. The state has been seen as the dominant legitimate controller of violence—'a human community that (successfully) claims the monopoly of the legitimate use of physical force within a given territory' (Weber 1948: 78)—in military, police, custodial and repressive forces. This has brought huge collective violence that is linked to constructions of men and masculinities. The state has a dual meaning, as state actions and decisions, and their consequences, first, for its citizens within the state, and, second, for those outside the state in question. The state has traditionally sought to protect its citizens from outside threat, and from each other through sovereign power invested therein. This usually includes a dominant authority, controlling territory and representing its people in foreign policy and IR. State sovereignty provides grounds for citizenship and nationality, as in positive belonging and inclusion with associated rights and duties or negative nonbelonging/exclusion. In some cases the state is coded and structured as male, while the nation, to be protected, is coded as female, with consequent gender imagery (Zalewski and Parpart 1998; Parpart and Zalewski 2008).

The growth of the modern military state has been very closely associated with the formation, organization and modernization and management of national armies. The modern state has become a major controller of violence, and a major producer of violence, injury, fear, torture and death. The extreme case might appear to the destructive machinery of the state under the Nazi regime of the Third Reich. However, there are many other examples of mass persecutions by states, para-states and counterstates in recent history, in the Soviet Union, China, Southeast Asia, East and Central Africa, the Balkans and elsewhere. One of the greatest series of state violences in the 'postwar' period is the US bombing of Cambodia (Kampuchea). In order to destroy sanctuaries where Vietnamese had fled for safety, the US began secret bombing in 1970, killing an estimated 150,000 Cambodians by more than 500,000 tons of bombs, more than three times the tonnage used against Japan in the Second World War, and creating over a million refugees. Following this, Pol Pot and the Khmer Rouge took over in 1975, with the 'killing fields' over the next four years claiming an estimated 1.7 million people.

Interstate, and inter-para-state, warring and war-related times and places also provide the contexts for many other actually or potentially violent and violating individual and collective practices—by corporations, by privatized security forces, by organized crime, in arms trading, in the sex trade, all dominated by men, with particular social structures and forms of organizing. In short, warring and war-related times and places provide contexts for many other actually or potentially violent and violating gendered practices. This includes the clearly and persistently gendered practices of corporations and privatized security forces, foreign policy and diplomacy, arms trading, extraordinary rendition and incarceration, atrocities during and after wars, torture, the sex trade, corruption and financial exploitation, organized crime and kidnapping, rape and sexual assault, even peacekeeping and various legal apparatuses. In such ways war and militarism are not simply gendered contexts for other practices but can also be seen as extended gendered practices in themselves.

These practices are all dominated by men with their own particular social structures and forms of organizing. They operate primarily through men's collective and individual practices, whether hand-to-hand fighting, dropping bombs, pressing buttons, 'domestic' violence, sexual violence, along with intimidation, pressurizing, operating keyboards, trading, managing, working for a living and so on. A crucial area of context and consequence that is heavily dominated by men is torture (Huggins and Haritos-Fatouros 1998). Militarism both depends on these interrelated men-dominated contexts and itself provides contexts for other violent and violating activities, also dominated by men. As such, militarism can be seen as one part of a much wider web of activities of militarism-war-violence complex(es); and thus another reason for examining the obvious, and not so obvious, connections of men and militaries.

There is increasing focus on global transactions in processes of masculinity formation and the centrality of men/masculinity in war and international relations. This entails examining interrelations between various genderings and political economic processes within and between states. Yet even critical studies of masculinity have tended to underestimate or neglect the significance of international relations as sites for the reproduction of men's power and masculinities. This is even though key issues in international relations, such as national, international and supranational power, control and decision-making, typically reflect and reinforce dominant masculine practices, which are expressed both materially and discursively. Resistance continues in international relations to seeing men's practices as gendered and to 'naming men as men' (Hanmer 1990; Zalewski and Parpart 1998; Parpart and Zalewski 2008). Men's practices in international relations are so heavily embedded in social, economic and cultural relations that men's dominant practices are often equated with what is seen as 'normal,' usual, even the official way of doing things. This is evident in the gender neutralization of men's practices in international decision-making. Men's practices are constructed as ordinary, mundane—women's as noteworthy, 'quirky' or worse. However, supposed gender neutrality in policy and policy-making is often premised upon masculinist approaches, as with male homosociality (Hearn and McKie 2008).

In gendering international relations it is important to consider the form, development and location of governmental systems within broad global contexts. There are huge intersections of capital and government, as in the massive use and subsidizing of private businesses by the US state in Iraq and elsewhere, and in the arms trade more generally. There is extensive evidence of huge waste and overpayment to companies, such as Bechtel, Blackwater, Halliburton, KBR and Parsons, and simply loss of, theft of or "unaccounted for" US government payments during the Iraqi War. Over 100,000 corporate mercenaries and other private contractors have operated in Iraq, comparable to the official US military presence (Armstrong 2008). Some estimates place the lost, missing and unaccounted for sums at $23 billion at least. The use of cost plus accounting (CPA—all costs plus an additional percentage) in contract accounting partly explains massive overspends. Parsons had contracts for building 150 health clinics paid at $186 million, of which six were completed (Boorstin and Nolan 2004; Bowen 2009): a graphic example of how some men's domination, and indeed ineffectiveness, may impact on women, children and other men.

In the operation of international relations—in foreign affairs, top level summits, the UN, diplomacy, espionage, terrorism, war, military deployments—it is men who are dominant both in sheer numbers and in the ways and means of doing things. Though much of the operations of international relations is controlled and conducted by men—as politicians, world leaders, diplomats, financiers, civil servants, transnational governmental officials—it is remarkable how such men are rarely named as men. Non-naming of men as men is one way in which men's domination of international relations continues, even though men's domination of international relations, in terms of top governmental actors and power brokers, is overwhelming. Men and their social construction and power are generally left unspoken; they are, in that sense, invisible, an 'absent presence,' perhaps because of their dominance, especially at the highest levels, and within international policy, practice and discourse.

Moving beyond these various silences and partial approaches to international relations involves analyzing the gendering of men more fully. This raises many questions, especially in considering men on a global scale, within and constituting trans(national)patriarchies (Hearn 2009). In many transnational processes, both physical and virtual, particular groups of men are the most powerful actors. The transnational governmental class is very much a male transnational governmental class. The study of ruling elite men is a very fertile research area, both as a collective social group and in individual biographies, be it Bush family dynamics (Messerschmidt 2010) or Putin's body image. It is particular kinds of 'political man' that international relations rules and structures are designed for. Different masculinities and men's gendered practices are observable in the contrasts between the cool urbane diplomat, the sound-bite media politician, the career Eurocrat, as well as by different nationalities and cultures.

Different masculine sexualities are also on display, more or less explicitly. The UK ambassador to the US 1997–2003, Christopher Meyer (2005), begins his autobiography with these lines: '"We want you to get up the arse of the White House and stay there." So spoke the prime minister's chief of staff, Jonathan Powell, in the splendour of one of Downing Street's reception rooms. . . . Trust the blokeishness of New Labour to reduce it to an anal metaphor' (1). The ordinary processes of international relations can be more or less subtly invested with complex and sometimes paradoxical entwinings of sexuality, gender, violence and militarism. Urgent studies and actions are needed on men and men's power in international relations, and its relations to multinationals, international finance, energy policy, sex trade, global representations, transgovernmental machineries and most obviously militarism.

Differential Analyses of Military Violence

Different levels of analysis and explanation of violence, men's violences, are relevant at different levels. Explanations of men's violence in war can refer to the 'outbreak' of war, to the conduct of war, to small group or individual acts of violence, as well as violence deemed 'illegitimate.' It may thus be useful to distinguish social processes of those men involved in doing warring from decision-makers on warring, including politicians and senior 'diplomatic,' security services and military men. Others may be very influential, including arms manufacturers, military suppliers and senior businessmen. Then, there are those men who manage the military and the conduct of military violence: senior military officers, the managers of institutional violence. At the interstate level, as in fighting between men leaders and sponsors of violence, by the men of third parties, as between the US and the Soviet Union, in Central America and Africa, such as in Guatemala, where that in turn led to internal oppression, killing and 'disappearance' of political opponents. The Cold War doctrine of Mutually Assured Destruction (MAD) can be seen as macrorisk behavior of men leaders. As noted, these planned military ventures and violences are enacted largely by men— whether in hand-to-hand fighting, trench warfare, distanced shooting or by remote technology. This gives much room for different explanations of the relationship between the level of male group and individual male/men's relations to violence, from psychoanalytic studies of psychopathic love of violence to explorations of cultural imaginaries of 'the other,' to examinations of group conformity, efficient killing and organized discipline to violence performed with distaste.

Central issues analyzed in studies of interpersonal violence are also relevant for warfare and range from responsibility of the irresponsible man; persistent use of excuses and justifications; use and combination of physical and nonphysical violence; power and control of women; frequency of men's violence to women by 'normal men' (much more so than often supposed), contrasting with the persistent of the repeat offender and men with particular and often multiple psychosocial problems (Hearn 1998b; Pankhurst 2007b). Bringing together analysis of the eroticization of different violences (R. Morgan 1989), such as military violence, terrorism, rape and violence to women in the home, is a key challenge.

Military violence is more or less organized violence, so studying men and military needs to attend to organizations, and organizational violence. At the macro, collective extraorganizational level, there is the impact of structural violations. Violence and violations are closely linked, but not totally determined, by structural power differences, including patriarchal social structural relations; systems of capitalist and imperialist exploitation; and national and cultural exclusions, structural racism and xenophobia. This may involve the reproduction of institutional violations, even of whole societies, including the creation of the conditions for violence. At the meso level, organizations and collectivities can be seen as sites of violence and violation, and constellations of violent/violating, potentially or threatened violent/violating actions, behaviors, intentions and experiences (Hearn and Parkin 2001). At the level of microprocesses and practices, violence and violations by organizations and collectivities can be ways of reinforcing relations of domination and subordination; developing resistance; refining gradations of status and power; facilitating alliances, coalitions, inclusions, exclusions and scapegoating; and forming identities.

Mundane military processes, such as military training, have major impacts upon individuals and groups. Military organizations provide multiple social and psychological resources for reproduction and changing of individual psychologies (Dixon 1976), often around violence, sometimes not. These include the processes of rationalization, distancing, following organizational 'roles,' obeying orders and trivialization through humor. Bomber crews may adopt trivializing, casual, ironic and supposedly humorous phrases, such as 'There goes the cookie,' in continuing their bombing without too much direct thought for the impact of their bombs upon others (J. Smith 1993). In a wide-ranging review of the literature on war, the military, massacres, concentration camps, torture, police, prisons and workplaces, Johnson (1986) sets out some organizational and social psychological processes by which violence is reproduced. The means to this 'dehumanization' include bureaucratic organizing, procedures and rules; isolation of the organization from mainstream moral values and regular external review; and insulation of workers or agents of the institution (Johnson 1986: 188ff.). An important part of these processes is the reproduction of transcendent and mundane authorizations (Kelman 1973): both vague justifications of the expendability of people, and more specific justifications of how stipulated ends will be achieved. Those subject to violence can be constructed as less than human, as numbers, not people at all. Dehumanization is necessary in the complex relations of war, terrorism, violence and sexuality, including the use of rape, and is sometimes done systematically.

Men and militarism can be understood in terms of intersectional structures and agency, and different relations of men to social structures and agency. Men's dominance includes diverse relations of men as gendered individuals to gendered structured relations. While individual men may suffer by millions, men's collective structural power remains undiminished, or is even reinforced. In war, typically, but not always:

> Individual men fight, kill each other, die; yet through this enactment of violence men's class power is reaffirmed. Thus individual men may, sometimes in large numbers, perform individual acts that are not in their own immediate interests, perhaps *even including their own death,*

but which maintain the structured relation of men's collective power over women. (Hearn 1987: 96–97)

'Meanwhile other men may resist this process. In other words, men's agency may or may not be oppressive' (97). Some of the many different forms of 'state labors' (and agentic positions) include: indirect oppressive work, for example, army officers' direction of soldiers; direct oppressive work (for example, killing), implicit oppressive work (for example, routine 'professional' soldiering (especially in peacetime) and bureaucratic administration; anti-oppressive work (for example, 'security leaks' for citizens' rights); the avoidance of work (for example, 'skiving').

In making sense of all these matters, questions of space and place, ground and land, domain and terrain, whether personal bodily space or extended domains of the nation, are persistently important. Much militarism, especially nation-based militarism, is 'international' or 'transnational.' And increasingly this profoundly gendered activity dominated by men reaches beyond the earth through 'the weaponization of space' (Delestrac 2009) and militarizations beyond land. At the same time, there may appear to be a contemporary weakening of the links of dominant, violent masculinity and militarism, within current politics of war, peacekeeping and human rights. However, more likely is that new associations between militarism and masculinism may arise in so-called 'post-militarist' societies. Military geographies, 'the cartographies of violence' (Shapiro 1997), collective violences, are plain to see, if not always to decipher. Transnational relations are a persistent theme, as much military activity is away from 'home,' by definition and ambition.

CONCLUDING COMMENTS

In war and militarism, individual men may suffer, sometimes even by gendercide, but men's collective structural power may be undiminished, even reinforced. Through this, women and children are likely to suffer hugely regardless of their part in such violence and killing. Whether this means more women or more men being killed does not change the fact that it is almost always men doing the killing. Moreover, individual men or groups or collectivities of men may perform individual acts not in their own immediate interests, but which maintain men's collective power over women. Meanwhile other men may resist. Men's gendered relations of power are thus complex, even contradictory. The collective power of men may be understood as maintained by the dispensability of some men, for example, as soldiers in war, even with violence to and killing of women and children, usually as noncombatants.

In light of all these important questions, it might be thought surprising that there is not a wealth of books explicitly on men, masculinities and the military. While there are libraries, archives and vaults full of books and documents giving information, often in huge amounts and detail, on these military worlds, there are relatively few that critically revisit this arena in terms of gendered men, masculinities and men's gendered practices. The obviousness of the connections between men, masculinities, violence, war and militarism should not mean that they escape critical scrutiny. There can be few more urgent tasks than interrogating the taken-for-granted character of male-dominated militarism, whether for the sake of science, political justice or peace.

Theme II
Making Gender and (Re)Making the Nation

4 What Does a Bath Towel Have to Do with Security Policy?
Gender Trouble in the Swedish Armed Forces

Maud Eduards

'If foreign and security policy issues often used to originate from the national agenda, now they must increasingly be based on global challenges.' These are the words of the Swedish foreign minister, Mr. Carl Bildt, in a parliamentary debate on foreign affairs in February 2007 (Statement of Government Policy 2007). In addition, he maintains that international involvement is regarded as an important part of a 'modern security policy.'[1] During the last couple of years, the Swedish Armed Forces (SAF) have taken on the task of both defending Sweden's territorial integrity and disseminating peace and security through battle groups, or rapid response units, outside Swedish borders. According to the former Supreme Commander this new setting requires 'a new kind of soldier' (Syrén 2006). In this far-reaching project for the SAF, gender has an important role to play, expressed jointly by the Minister of Gender Equality and the Minister of Defense as a demand for Sweden 'to live up to our reputation as the most gender equal country in the world' (Sabuni and Tolgfors 2007).

The ministers also claim that women are a resource in the work for peace and that equality between women and men is 'crucial for the Swedish operations to produce results,' that is, to contribute with freedom, security, democracy and welfare to the world (ibid.). It is a great responsibility put on Swedish women as soldiers and officers. They should help in creating a better world and let the name of Sweden gain honor around the globe, as expressed in the national hymn. Hence, the gender equality policy, in the sense of a more even balance between women and men, should contribute to combining Sweden's national and global interests.

The SAF have had difficulties in recruiting women to military tasks, both as conscripts[2] and as officers, in spite of what is being labeled active gender equality work. Already in 1981, the Swedish Parliament decided that women should have access to commanding positions in all branches of the SAF. Despite this the proportion of female regular officers remains low, 4.6 percent in 2008. The number of women doing general military training in 2008 was slightly higher at 5.3 percent.[3] Several reports have shown that a high proportion of women in the Swedish military have been subject to sexual harassment and that they also feel marginalized and discriminated against. While the trend is that the problem is diminishing, still 36 percent of women officers and conscripts reported that they had been exposed to sexual harassment in 2005 (Equality Ombudsman 2006: 15).

GENDER TENSION

There is a significant gap between the statements cherishing the importance of women to the SAF and the daily experiences of the few women who choose to join the organization. This comes to the fore as a set of contradictions: firstly, around difference versus sameness/gender neutrality; secondly, as veneration of women versus sexualized behavior; thirdly, as gender being addressed in relation to women and not to men. My argument is that inconsistencies of this kind undermine women's democratic rights and their possibilities to question military practices and discourses. However, these tensions do not exist in the military sphere alone but are embedded in other social and organizational contexts as well (Eduards 2007; cf. Kesic 2000).

The purpose here is to discuss how these contradictions are being (re) produced within the SAF. In order to show how the bath towel is related to perceptions of Swedish security, the following questions are raised: How do the SAF address problems pertaining to gender equality and women (and men) as soldiers? What conceptions of gender, femininity, masculinity, corporeality and national security dominate? What do these notions imply for women's bodily integrity and agency?

My theoretical starting point is that notions of militarization, men/masculinity and violence are closely interconnected (see e.g., Enloe 1989, 2007; Kelly 2000; Connell 2001; Kimmel et al. 2005; McCarry 2007; Hearn, this volume). I will investigate which forms these links assume in the SAF, and to what degree the military power order is responsive to change. Another point of departure is that gender is performed both in what seems to be organizational details and in the overall defense and security policy. Like renowned feminist researchers in International Relations (IR), I assume that power relations at different levels have to be analytically related (Tickner 2001; Ackerly et al. 2006; Steans 2006). Finally, I do not restrict the analysis to what is being stated, but will also reflect upon what is not being talked about in security policy, based on the idea that interpellation and silence can be mirroring each other—one's visibility, the other's invisibility.

This chapter has three sections. First it looks at how gender is approached in the SAF, inter alia in its plan of action for gender equality. The second section discusses the role of women within the assignment to build peace and security beyond the borders of Sweden, illustrated by the implementation of SCR 1325, a case of sexual harassment in the Swedish Kosovo Force, and the meaning of the code of conduct for personnel abroad. I will conclude by returning to the importance of a bath towel for Swedish security policy. The empirical material is mainly drawn from the SAF, principally from their web page (www.mil.se) and other public documents.

GENDER AS (IN)EQUALITY

The task of the SAF is to defend Sweden's security and military standing in the world, but also to promote democracy and human rights. As equality is part of this work for human rights and liberties, equality also has to permeate the military organization as such, according to the Minister of Gender Equality, Nyamko Sabuni.[4] The objective of the SAF is to promote gender balance as well as reflect the plurality of the Swedish society. The concordance between national values and international interventions is for Sabuni an issue of credibility. Most of the time, though, the SAF talk about being effective. An earlier brigade commander within the Kosovo Force maintains that equality and mutual respect is about operational effectiveness or 'combat value' (Gender Force 2007: 31).

The goal of the SAF to enroll more women is characterized by a tension between presenting women and men as equal and designating them as different. There are no positions for girls, is one argument. At the same time, difference is the most common argument for including more women. A report from 2008 on defense duties in the future talks about 'scarce categories,' i.e., women and Swedish men with an immigrant background (but not Swedish women with an immigrant background), groups that have to be mobilized so that the SAF might mirror the Swedish society (SOU 2008; Petersson 2008). The organization wants persons with different experiences and competencies to join the military, but once inside the organization, everyone must be treated equally (cf. Kronsell and Svedberg 2001). This is the principal argument. Simultaneously, the discourse about equal treatment is constantly being challenged by the idea that the presence of women requires that special measures be taken to accommodate them. This tension is embedded in the SAF and the example that follows, taken from the information material to female military recruits, illustrates this.

What Girls Need to Know

The special aspects of being a military woman are emphasized in different ways by the SAF, such as on the web page 'Gal,' where the equipment of the conscript women is listed:

> big bath towel,
> suitable equipment, for example smaller helmet, shoes and body armour,
> underwear allowance,
> if needed, weapon with shorter butt.
>
> (SAF 2009)

The big bath towel has a prologue. The bits of advice, earlier offered to women who were considering doing military service, comprised the following:

> Initially, many may feel embarrassment by having to share showers with someone of the opposite sex, but there are curtains that allow privacy. The SAF nowadays issues bath towels in two sizes, so ask for a bigger bath towel.

The SAF also stressed that women conscripts should never have to accept negative treatment. In addition, female recruits were advised to set their limits and learn to say *stop* clearly and directly, if they felt that somebody went too far (SAF 2007b).

This is not innocent advice. It comprises a whole world of ideas about gendered power relations, sexuality, responsibility and agency. The gender problem is nicely wrapped, but exposes at the same time real tensions in the military organization. Women tend to be looked at in a degrading way and their bodily integrity is questioned. Here, women are regarded as sexual beings, with a menaced sexuality, and simultaneously responsible for their bodies. Or rather: They are made individually responsible for how men perceive their bodies. But no special admonitions are directed to those (men) who look and harass, no one is telling them to learn to respect women's bodily integrity. No obligations are ascribed to men to control their evidently threatening sexuality, and in line with this thought, also they do not need to protect themselves with a big bath towel.

Nowadays women do not have to ask for a bigger bath towel; it is included. To observe that women will get suitable equipment seems to go without saying. But the fact that this implies a smaller helmet—and not the right size of helmet—reveals that there is a (male) norm: a large helmet. This also goes for the weapon, which thus can be equipped with a shorter butt. The three women's networks within the SAF have all complained over these never-ceasing comparisons; uniforms for women are always the ones made in what are called 'odd sizes.' At the same time there is a fundamental unisex perspective: 'We don't differentiate between the sexes,' as the SAF specialist on personal equipment puts it (*Insats & Försvar* 2008: 32–33). That women might have breasts is not being considered in the design of the uniform (cf. Åse 2000).

PLANS OF ACTION

In the SAF plan of action for gender equality for the years 2006 to 2008, gender equality meant, inter alia, freedom from gender-based violence. One aim was to prevent sexual harassment, in line with the 1991 Act on Equality between women and men. Harassment of a sexual nature would not be tolerated (SAF 2006–2008). One measure was to place female conscripts and officers, if possible, at the same points of service, indicating that too many men in a group might be a problem for a small share of women. Thus, women have to seek protection by being more numerous, and by sticking together in their daily activities. If not, they risk being exposed to sexual harassment. The plan casts women as more vulnerable than men in the organization. However, who the perpetrators might be and how their behavior should be culled was left out of the discussion.

The SAF plan of action for gender equality for the period 2009 to 2011 is a more elaborate document. Initially, differences are seen as positive, something that renders the SAF a more effective, creative and credible authority. Highlighted areas of focus are working conditions, harassment and internal and external recruitment. The SAF present themselves as an organization that pursues gender equality actively, at all levels 'in order to preclude, prevent and manage situations, where harassment and sexual harassment arise.' Regarding measures to be taken by the commanding officer, the shower problem comes back: separate dressing rooms and showers that cannot be looked into (for example, through shower draperies) must be available for 'women and men.' The commanding officer shall also see to it that suitable personal equipment is available for 'both women and men.' In addition, employees should be trained in the subject of gender equality in order to 'be more aware of existing norms, attitudes and values about women and men and how they can restrict us' (SAF 2009–2011).

The Swedish military constructs itself as a gender-neutral organization by talking of 'women and men' or 'persons regardless of sex,' as if existing problems within the organization pertaining to working conditions, parental leave or sexual harassment would be the same for all. In exceptional cases women are spoken to, as when their networks need support or in the wish that their share must grow at all levels. This could be understood as a lack of interest in defining problems regarding the scarcity of women in terms of power and organizational resistance. Men, on the contrary, are not addressed in the plan of action for gender equality. They are only characterized in connection with women, in a sort of balancing where both parts are given the same weight. This approach to sex equality is built, maintains Catharine A. MacKinnon, on the idea that likes should be treated alike and unlikes unlike: 'to the extent that women are no different from men, we deserve what they have' (1987: 33). The reverse meaning is that if women are regarded as different, they cannot have what men have.

The plan of action for gender equality can be regarded as a tool for addressing underlying power relations. However, women and men are seen as uniform, simple categories without an explicit relationship. At the same time, they are always addressed together: women *and* men. Possible differences in conditions and space of action are not touched upon. Presenting the situations of women and men as equal, gender is made trivial, which must be regarded as a paradox in a plan of action for gender equality. The plan seems to be written for a situation when it is not needed and founded on an idea that inequality can be nullified through gender neutrality. Hence, the best equality strategy is seen as not siding with any sex. But as Hillary Charlesworth writes in *Human Rights of Women*, referring to Catharine A. MacKinnon, the law should 'support freedom from systematic subordination because of sex rather than freedom to be treated without regard to sex' (1994: 67).

BEYOND THE POLITICAL

In order for the SAF to stand out as credible, more women must be included in the activities, in Sweden as well as abroad. A greater share of women is also said to make the organization more effective. How many are needed to do the job is not clear. If the SAF would mirror society, there should be 50 percent women and 50 percent men. This is an often used argument for increasing the representation of women (based on justice). However, this argument becomes problematic as the inclusion of women is formulated as a natural aspect of democracy: If women amount to half the population they should consequently compose half the working staff. No attention is paid to inequalities of worth or different interests; presence is a reason in itself.

Another issue not discussed is why women have been marginalized and to what extent notions about women as unreliable, dependent and sexual persist in defense policies and practices. If exclusion from the military is about power relations, 'high politics' and masculine perceptions of security, how can inclusion be free from these notions? As is emphasized by Zillah Eisenstein, inclusion and exclusion cannot be seen as simple opposites (2007: 94). The inclusion of women into the military rests on deeply gendered and corporeal premises. As I have tried to show, the use of big bath towels, smaller uniforms for women and the need for women to stay in company with other women at work are examples of how women's bodies are made an issue in the Swedish context. Women who are not able to defend their integrity, physically and mentally, are assumed to bear the consequences. The opposite position is that women are regarded as a resource, which will bring competence and other experiences to the organization. This also goes for immigrants, who are expected to contribute cultural and language skills (SOU 2008: 118; cf. Petersson 2008). Difference in terms of gender and ethnicity is made a justifying resource as well as a problem.

What I argue is that these simplified discourses of sameness and difference depoliticize the gender problem. No opening is left for discussions about power relations, of conflicting interests or possibilities for changed gender hierarchies. What will happen when this unnamed military power order is exported in the Swedish rapid deployment units? What are the implications of the idea that 'our reputation' should be kept up? These questions will be elaborated in the following.

Mission Peace

> Sweden is a clear voice for women's rights worldwide. The Government attaches great importance to the work of promoting equality between women and men, including women's sexual and reproductive health and rights.
>
> (Statement of Government Policy 2009)

In this debate on foreign affairs, Minister Carl Bildt also announced that the role of women must be strengthened in the task to 'implement increasingly comprehensive and complex peacekeeping and state-building operations' (ibid.). Here, the foreign minister is referring to the SCR 1325 adopted in October 2000. However, as the secretary general of the organization Kvinna till Kvinna writes, the Swedish foreign minister does not mention the importance of women for the promotion of peace in other contexts, like press releases or different political statements (Ag 2008). She points to the lack of credibility regarding gender issues in Swedish foreign policy. My point is to show how women and femininity are ascribed different values in varying contexts and how gender thereby is appropriated for different purposes.

WOMEN, PEACE AND SECURITY

The Swedish government has sanctioned a second national plan of action for the implementation of SCR1325 during the period 2009–2012 (NAP 2009). The aim is to facilitate an active participation of women in peace processes and attend specifically to the protection and the security needs of women and girls. Women are regarded as both actors and victims. Sweden considers itself a leading country when it comes to the implementation of SCR 1325. In order to fulfill this aim regionally and globally the resolution has to be 'fully implemented at the national level.' This implies that the work should 'include both women and men,' that women and men should participate on the same conditions. As regards a strengthened protection of women in conflict situations, an increased participation of women is assumed to contribute to the prevention of gender-based violence, such as men's violence against women and girls. The reasoning in SCR 1325 pertaining to the vulnerability and special needs of women is strengthened by another Security Council Resolution, 1820, from June 2008. Its focus is on rape and other forms of sexual violence in situations of armed conflict that can be defined as war crimes (UNSCR 1820: §4). The Swedish government sees SCR 1820 as elaborating on the aspect of protection in SCR 1325 (NAP 2009).

The Swedish plan of action speaks about a comprehensive view of women in peace support operations. An interesting aspect of the debate in the Swedish Parliament is that this comprehensive view is mainly reduced to imply more women in the SAF (Danielsson 2009). It is as if gender equality in the Swedish military is the best way to promote peace and security. More women officers seem to be regarded as a sign of modernity and peaceful intentions. In this perspective, the boundary between war and peace is blurred. Or, in the words of Vivienne Jabri, 'war comes to be a practice of security' (2010: x). The content of SCR 1325 is a good deal wider: Women should be involved 'at all decision-making levels in national, regional and international institutions and mechanisms for the prevention, management and resolution of conflicts' (UNSCR 1325: §1). The security discourse embedded in SCR 1325 is important for civil society, not least for local grassroots feminist organizations (McLeod, this volume).

The way women are constructed as a group in SCR 1325 is criticized by Laura J. Shepherd for being liberal and essentialist. She comes from a poststructural feminist perspective and emphasizes the problem with femininity being tied to peace, as in the title of the resolution: women, peace and security. The problem is that women are defined to be in need of protection, with the state as the imagined provider of security. Men are not mentioned in the resolution. Gender signifies women, not men. Shepherd doubts that the resolution can be successfully implemented because of its specific gender mainstreaming approach (L. Shepherd 2008). Christine Sylvester, who has reviewed Shepherd's book from another IR position, expresses the hope that Shepherd will reread SCR 1325 and realize that this is 'exceptional politics,' not only disappointment (Sylvester 2009). Debra Bergoffen argues in a similar spirit that an important aspect of the resolution is that it rejects a sex-neutral concept of humanity and that 'women's rights are recognized as essential to the project of securing peace and justice' (2008: 91–92). However, in this debate Shepherd shows, in an interesting way, how the discourse of women and peace tends to be made into a fixed, depoliticized project. It is already decided what women's conditions look like and how 'feminine' qualifications have to be utilized, a thought that catches on the SAF approach to women soldiers as specific.

Sexual Harassment

Kosovo is regarded as a trouble spot, where Sweden has been present since 1999 with one battalion in KFOR, a NATO-led international force responsible for establishing and maintaining peace and security in the country. Of the 40 women in the Swedish Kosovo Force of 2003, eight reported their male colleagues for sexual harassment. One case was taken to court by the Equality Ombudsman, but the young woman lost it. She was accused, by the spokesman of the SAF, of having problems with cooperating. This is the usual case: Reported men get away without any sanctions. The head of staff of the SAF has excused these men's behavior by saying that they have been abroad many times and 'do not stick to Swedish values.'[5] In other words, harassment behavior is not contained within Swedish male sexuality, it belongs somewhere else.

Female soldiers and officers who call attention to sexual harassment embody the failure of the perpetrators to behave in an equal and respectful way. Men who harass and assault women break both with the traditional task of the soldier to protect 'women and children' and with the modern image of Sweden as the most equal country in the world, thereby challenging the image of social unity as well in the military organization as in the nation. That gender can be disrupting is also a theoretical point of departure in the investigation following the Kosovo case:

> the majority (the men) becomes conscious about its own culture when somebody else, i.e., a woman, comes into the group. Men can become afraid of losing their culture. The effect is that the difference between the majority and the minority is exaggerated. Men show which culture holds sway, and under which conditions women can take part. (SAF 2003: 2)

Here, there is an awareness that homosocial bonds between men are reinforced by the presence of women, and that women must adapt to the prevailing culture. In this interpretation women's presence seems to reproduce rather than challenge a traditional linking of military, masculinity and violence (cf. Enloe 1989: chap. 3). Sexual harassment and assaults against women in one's own organization can be seen in a similar light. Women are degraded and excluded from certain operations as a way to confirm the norms and culture of the majority group.

The investigation suggests continued training opportunities in order to 'bring round the attitudes of individuals, and their view of sexual harassment' (SAF 2003: 2). The reasoning about gender, men's actions and culture leaves no trace in the recommendations. Problems related to power and collective action are reduced to the need for individual learning and enlightenment, which can be interpreted as another way to depoliticize gender power relations.

International Conduct

The same gender-neutral policy as in the plan of action for gender equality appears in the code of conduct (valid from January 2004) directed towards personnel on international missions. The introduction states that Swedish personnel has a 'good reputation globally' and that everyone has the responsibility of keeping up this reputation. As regards discrimination, buying sex, sexual assault, sexual harassment and pornography, the instruction states that Swedish law must be followed, which means that such activities are not permitted during service abroad (Network for Ethics and Codes of Conduct 2004).

The explicit intentions behind the code of conduct are related to the crisis management activities of the EU and a road map for implementing SCR 1325. The need for guidelines should also be seen in light of increasing violence, assaults against women and prostitution in areas where peacekeeping forces under UN command operate (Whitworth 2004; Puechguirbal 2007; Hebert, this volume). According to the code of conduct, formulated by the Swedish Civil Contingencies Agency, departing staff has to subscribe, inter alia, to being 'aware that I have a power position in regard to the local population, and I will not make use of my position in an inappropriate way' (Swedish Civil Contingencies Agency 2009).

Since 2007, the SAF has also had ethical guidelines, similar to those of the Civil Contingencies Agency (SAF 2007a). Here, assignment personnel are being addressed in a familiar 'You' but the essence of the documents remains the same. All staff on international missions must commit themselves not to take advantage of their position of power, to profit on others or to buy sexual services, etc. However, the subject—the you—is neither ascribed a sex nor is the meaning of power defined. On the other hand, the SAF arrange courses on these issues, something that can be regarded as a way for the state to take responsibility for the sexual behavior of Swedish staff abroad. To sum up, the guidelines can be interpreted as stating not only that sexual violence must be checked, but also that Swedish soldiers abroad reproduce the reputation of the nation.

WHO IS PROTECTING WHOM?

In these three examples—the implementation of SCR 1325, the Kosovo affair and the code of conduct—gender and corporeality are intertwined. The unequal sex/gender relation is made invisible, either by naming no one or by a focus only on one part, the subjected—and acting—women. Men are an implicit meta-category in the documents. Important questions pertaining to intersections of gender, security and armed conflict are left unanswered, since they are not made negotiable or political.

The three examples also illustrate that the national is placed beyond critical scrutiny, beyond politics (Pettman 1996/2002: 48–49; Eduards 2007). Simply put, the national perspective tends to hide other political controversies. Thus, for example, men are safeguarded by the SAF from being pinpointed as the bearers of masculine, ethnically Swedish, military culture—a culture that does not protect women. This is what Iris Marion Young (2003) would call an example of 'the logic of masculinist protection,' the idea that women and children are offered protection in exchange for support of national security policies. This bargain is dangerous, according to Young, since it (re)produces asymmetric relations between protector and protected, and undermines democratic norms and practices. The notion of protection is central to the way a state forms its international security considerations; in fact, it can be seen as reproducing the state's identity as masculine. The masculine protector relegates the protected to subordinate and exposed positions (Wadley 2010).

The issue of sexual vulnerability of women in SCR 1325 takes the form, within Swedish foreign operations, that 'the other women,' who live in war-torn areas, have to be taken care of by peacekeeping Swedish women. Local women should be freed, or with the legendary formulation by Gayatri Spivak, 'white men are saving brown women from brown men' (1993: 92). The difference from colonial times, which Spivak speaks of, is that now also white women, as soldiers and officers, should act as liberators. That these white women risk being subjected to violence and harassment in the international arena—by their own countrymen—is not part of the national concept. The problem can be formulated as a duality: The bodies of women serve as targets for various sexual attacks in parallel to being made symbols of freedom, democracy and equality.

Women are included in the Swedish national defense but requested to adapt; they need to balance between a cooperative, heterosocial subject position and a threatening sexualized one. Women are also expected to act in the field of tension between what is considered feminine and what characterizes a (male) soldier. If women participate on the same conditions as men, they risk crossing current notions of femininity. Certain achievements are demanded from the (male) soldier, others from women. This also goes for the small things, or as an earlier project leader of the Network of Women Conscripts formulates the contradiction: 'If a girl is too slow in running she is no real soldier. If the same girl is too fast she is not a real woman' (*Insats & Försvar* 2008: 35; cf. Cohn 2000).

BATH TOWELS AND SECURITY

With women's increased military presence, the construction of gender has become more complex and malleable. When gender boundaries are increasingly understood as blurred and ambivalent, the more important it seems to reproduce sex and gender as two fixed categories, either as the same or as different. Women and men are kept apart behind a rhetoric of gender neutrality, as if gender is not of importance any longer. The binary and essentialist discourse of sameness and difference—that feminist theory has tried to abandon for decades—is evident in military practices.

Women, who earlier were regarded as too good for the horrors of war, are now taking part in military operations both in the US, Great Britain, Sweden and other countries and in the peacekeeping missions of the UN. Women in the rapid response units are expected to act as benevolent and understanding 'sisters,' to defend women in other countries, nota bene women that are 'with us.' Internally, however, women should defend themselves with a bigger bath towel and through working together, avoiding at any price to be treated as sex objects. I see the bath towel as a symbol of the gender tensions within the organization: Women are designated as being different; they are sexualized and addressed separately.

At the same time, the new soldier is presented as fair-minded and equal, an expression of Swedishness as acting for peace and democracy in a troublesome and globalized world. A good representative of the military should safeguard the country's security interests without alluding to masculine values, such as physical and emotional strength, violence and aggressiveness (cf. Whitworth 2008). As the new soldier also can be a woman, gender troubles are in a paradoxical way disarmed. To the extent that women and men are related to each other the linking term is 'and.' In that way two separate but inseparable categories are reconstructed, categories that can be filled with a new and more 'modern' content—and still appear the same.

Identifying war with masculinity and peace with femininity is a simplified way of framing the world in terms of given value hierarchies. Kimberly Hutchings emphasizes that '[t]he crucial characteristic that is shared by all masculinity discourses is that they are not feminine' (2008: 401). In her view, the notions of masculinity and femininity as two stable and exclusive categories must be challenged. Otherwise there is a risk, in the words of Ann Tickner, that the association of women with peace in a male-dominated society 'contributes to the devaluation of both women and peace' (2001: 59). But what we see today in global politics is indeed different, Hester Eisenstein (2009) would argue; women's work and feminist ideas are exploited, but in the interests of the global elite. I would say that the same goes for transnational actions for peace and war in the name of human security. Women and feminism are used to legitimate military action. As Kelly Oliver writes: 'Selective appropriation of feminism and concern for women have become essential to imperialist discourses' (2007: 39).

The gendered logic of Swedish security policy could be read as if women in the military life are ascribed both an individual shame for their corporeality and special obligations against other women as a collective. In addition, they are held responsible for the preservation of the national self-image. On the other hand, men are not addressed by the SAF. Silence is here an implicit norm, at all levels. Gender, masculinity and femininity are constructed in ways that restrict women's bodily integrity and agency. Ultimately, the question remains whether democratic values and gender equality are compatible with militarized peacekeeping.

NOTES

1. *Svenska Dagbladet*, 6 November 2007, 'Kan vi hjälpa till så ska vi göra det.'
2. The conscription-based Swedish military service was replaced by a contract system on 1 July 2010.
3. *Dagens Nyheter*, 27 December 2008, 'Rekordmånga kvinnor väntas mönstra 2009.'
4. *Svenska Dagbladet*, 29 September 2008, Interview in advertisement from the National Service Administration.
5. *Dagens Nyheter*, 16 April 2004, 'Åtta kvinnor anmälde trakasserier.'

5 Friendly War-Fighters and Invisible Women
Perceptions of Gender and Masculinities in the Norwegian Armed Forces on Missions Abroad

Torunn Laugen Haaland

The gendered practices of military organizations are a main theme in feminist security studies. The Nordic countries are particularly interesting cases in the context, since these countries are perceived as being in the international forefront when it comes to gender equality. Furthermore, their military forces have played a significant role in UN peacekeeping, and have therefore obtained an image as more prone towards peace than war, at least compared to the armed forces of larger countries such as the United Kingdom, France and the United States. However, this image needs closer scrutiny. In this chapter we will explore the extent to which these images of the Nordic societies and their militaries are in sync with the internal perceptions of gender and masculinities in the Norwegian Armed Forces (NAF). After a brief presentation of some basic facts about women in the Norwegian military, I will first analyze to what extent, and how, these women, and the women encountered in the deployment areas abroad, are referred to in military sources. Second, I will examine expressions of masculinities in the same sources.

Analyses of the gendered practices of military forces have often underlined that the deployment of peacekeeping forces does not necessarily enhance the security of local women. Instead they may in fact represent an additional threat due to an increase in prostitution and trafficking in human beings; the sexualized violence and sexual harassment by military personnel; the spread of sexually transmitted diseases; the abandonment of local women and children by military personnel; and changes in local gender dynamics brought about by the actions of military and civilian personnel in peace support operations (Higate 2004; Whitworth 2004; Martin 2005; Koyama and Myrttinen 2007: 25). Based on this evidence, some draw the conclusion that armed forces are largely unsuitable for peacekeeping tasks since 'militarized peacekeeping results in greater insecurity for far too many people, women and men, who through the exclusionary practices of militarism and armed intervention become targets of sexual abuse and racist violence' (Whitworth 2004: 186). This image is clearly at odds with the Nordic perception of how their militaries act in peacekeeping operations. The main argument put forward in this chapter is that military peacekeepers are not idealistic peace activists whose prime motive is to bring peace and stability to people in distress in different parts of the world. Their core expertise rests with their ability to inflict violence. On the other hand, military forces are not necessarily characterized by an uncritical promotion of violence, misogyny, homophobia and racism, as claimed by for instance Whitworth (2004: 3). Based on material from the NAF, it will be argued that the military remains a deeply conservative institution with regard to how they perceive both women and men within their own ranks, as well as local women and men in their deployment area, and that this conservatism influences how military operations are conducted.

Before entering into the discussion, a few remarks should be made about the primary sources on which the chapter is based. The data consist primarily of documents produced in connection with Norway's participation in military operations abroad, primarily UNOSOM (Somalia); UNPROFOR, IFOR, SFOR and KFOR (all former Yugoslavia); and to a lesser extent ISAF (Afghanistan). More precisely, the sources consist of (a) contingent reports, usually written at the end of a deployment by the contingent commander and his staff summarizing their experiences and lessons learned; (b) memory books, composed by the forces themselves on a voluntary basis;[1] and (c) communications (letters, reports, etc.) between Norwegian Headquarters Defense Command in Oslo and other parts of the armed forces at home, the Ministry of Defense or forces deployed abroad (Haaland 2008: 51–55).[2]

Since the sources were produced for distinctly different purposes, they emphasize different aspects of the same experiences. They also have certain systematic biases that must be taken into consideration. The purpose of the contingent reports was to ensure organizational learning within the military. Knowing that these reports could be read by higher-ranking officers, and thus have an impact on future careers, authors would tend to emphasize their successes rather than their failures. These reports are thus likely to present a (too) positive picture of military experiences. The purpose of the memory books was to create a collective memory by a group of people who had lived together and formed strong, but often temporary, relationships during their deployment. They are more informal than the contingent reports, but since they were to be brought home and perhaps read by girlfriends, wives and parents, a certain amount of self-censoring is likely. These books do not necessarily reflect how the troops remember these events; they rather reflect how the troops would like their joint experiences to be remembered. Consequently, they should be read 'not as innocent tales of reality, but as strategic interventions' (Woodward and Winter 2007: 65). Finally, Headquarters Defense Command's archival sources cover various official inputs in the decision-making process inside the military organization. The sources have two common features: First, they are written sources, which means that even though they are internal, they are reporting devices for fairly public consumption; second, their authors were almost exclusively men.

THE INCLUSION OF WOMEN IN THE NORWEGIAN MILITARY

The military remains one of the most male-dominated sectors in Norwegian society, which is otherwise characterized by broad female participation in public life. On a global scale, the percentage of women who are educated, work outside the home and are economically independent is very high in Norway. One implication of that is that the traditional military family, consisting of a male breadwinner with his wife and children constantly on the move to new locations, is losing ground. Nevertheless, in 2010, women constituted about 8.5 percent of military personnel in the NAF (NAF 2011). This reflects a small increase compared to the last couple of years, but the overall percentage has remained fairly stable over the last 20 years, even though the increased recruitment of women has been a political goal since the mid-1990s. At the top of the military hierarchy the percentage of women is much smaller.[3]

Women have participated in Norway's military deployment abroad since the end of the Second World War, and in recent years, women constituted between 6 and 12 percent of the military personnel in Norwegian units abroad, depending on the type of unit deployed (Norwegian Ministry of Defense 2007: 12–13). A majority of these women served in medical and other support functions, and this was fairly uncontroversial. Their entry into other roles has been more contested. Arguments put forward against this development are, for instance, that women would not be able to endure the physical strains of these operations; they would not be able to negotiate with male officers from the local forces without harming relationships between the UN and the host nation; troop morale would suffer if women had to share rooms with their male colleagues; women would be looked upon as sexual prey by male officers who were forbidden to have contact with local women; women could not be relied upon in crises; and male comradeship would be endangered by feelings of jealousy (Norwegian Contingent Commander UNIMOG 1990; Norwegian Contingent Commander UNIFIL 1992; NAF Headquarters Defense Command 1992; Karamé 2001). However, in the last couple of years, Norwegian military leaders seem to have recognized that female soldiers can be especially valuable in foreign deployments. A commonly used argument is that female soldiers enhance the ability to build trust in the female local population (Haakonsen and Jansen 2010).

However, negative attitudes towards women in the armed forces in general, and in international deployments in particular, are hardly extinct. In

2007, the editor of *Norges Forsvar*, a magazine produced by a prominent military lobbying group, repeated many of the traditional arguments against female participants in combat units, quoting anonymous officers stating that military platoons with female members were destroyed by feelings of jealousy and a perceived need to protect the women (*Norges Forsvar* 2007a: 14–15). Female participants also endangered the units by not being taken seriously by 'tough warriors in Afghanistan and most people' (*Norges Forsvar* 2007b: 24–26). The military leadership quickly rebutted these views, but the articles nevertheless indicated that negative attitudes towards women in the military did exist in the NAF (see also Gustavsen 2011).

PERCEPTIONS OF WOMEN IN NORWEGIAN DEPLOYMENTS ABROAD

Throughout the 1990s, male-dominated Norwegian units abroad had roughly three forms of contact with women: (a) there were a few Norwegian women soldiers in the forces; (b) they had contact with local women when on duty as UN and NATO soldiers; and (c) they had contact with local women during their spare time. In general, it seems fair to conclude that these contacts left very few traces in the material I studied. Starting with the female privates and officers who were part of the Norwegian forces abroad, the contingent reports and correspondence to and from Headquarters Defense Command do not contain any reflection on gender issues. For instance, with one notable exception, none of the contingent reports referred to difficulties regarding men and women working together, or difficulties regarding relations between Norwegian female soldiers and local actors. Also, none of the reports referred to any advantages of having women in their units. In fact, they were completely gender neutral (or gender insensitive).

In the informal accounts in the memory books, the gender of female soldiers was recognized and commented upon to a greater extent. In the early 1990s, these books were quite informal and much attention was devoted to stories of drinking and partying, as may be expected when people of a certain age tell stories about their life. Having very little contact with women in general, the comments about the female soldiers in the books seemed to reflect that the men greatly appreciated the few females present. They were typically referred to as having 'a good smile for everyone.' Sexist comments were very rare.

During the second half of the 1990s, these books changed character and became more formal. There were fewer stories and pictures referring to partying and more focus on military exercises and soldiering. Attention to the gender of the participants became rare. Female soldiers were not singled out in the presentations, but referred to in the same way as their male colleagues. One typical example read: 'Marianne is the only "girl" in the platoon . . . She is absolutely "one of the boys"' (NORLOGBN/IFOR 1996/97: 94 [memory book]). Most books contained a brief and informal presentation of each platoon or company, which usually consisted of informal stories about experiences inside and outside camp. Sexist remarks about women did occur, for instance, in relation to sexual encounters at home or during leave, but they were rare, and certainly not more frequent than could be expected in informal accounts from an almost all-male group of men in their early twenties. In general, the memory books indicate that while sexist attitudes towards women might have existed among the troops, they were not put down in writing. Offensive and crude language rarely occurs.

Contact between the Norwegian forces and the local population in the deployment area was another subject receiving scant attention in the material produced by the military forces. The formal contingent reports focused mainly on internal and technical matters. Topics such as the relationship between the forces and the home organization, the quality of their equipment and also (seemingly) trivial details such as purchases of new office furniture dominated the reports. Accounts of contacts with the local population were rare, and accounts of contacts with local women were close to nonexistent. That being said, there can be no doubt that Norwegian forces aided local civilians through, for instance, the field hospital in Tuzla in Bosnia. When the Norwegian forces in Bosnia changed from support to first-line units in 1997, the local situation was mentioned and described in some detail under the heading 'Threat Assessments,' focusing almost exclusively on the military forces in the area. Assessments of the gendered implications of different operations were also nonexistent. Operational assessments rarely went beyond rather narrow accounts of, for instance, the number of guns confiscated or the forces' ability to calm a crowd at a given moment. A broader societal assessment of the consequences of the military operation was simply lacking in all types of reports.

The only type of contact between local women and Norwegian soldiers that was regularly reflected in the contingent reports was the type of contact that resulted in listing the number of troops treated for sexually transmitted diseases. Throughout the 1990s, this phenomenon was typically referred to as a health hazard for the Norwegian troops. As troops were confined to camp most of the time in the mission area, visits to prostitutes mostly took place during so-called '60 hours,' that is a short leave to a nearby larger city. According to the army's own statistics, the percentage of personnel who reported having purchased sex during a mission decreased from 30–40 percent in the 1980s to less than 10 percent in the late 1990s (Lysaker and Håbjørg 2002). Military sources never expressed any concern for the female sex workers; their focus was exclusively on the well-being of the Norwegian troops. The sources thus confirm that the NAF had what Sarah Martin (2005) and others have identified as a 'boys will be boys' attitude towards the sexual exploitation of local women. In some operations, such as UNIFIL, contact with the local population in the operational area was closer, and resulted in several marriages between Norwegian soldiers and local women (Karamé 2001; Stømmen and Lerand 2005). Such marriages also occurred in later contingents in the Balkans. This type of contact with local women was not referred to in the military sources.

Much like the contingent reports, the memory books focused on the internal life of the units. References to contact with the local population were infrequent; but did exist. First, all books contained pictures showing Norwegian soldiers talking to local men and sometimes women, and playing with local children. Second, some books contained a brief overview of the main events that had taken place during deployment. Women were not referred to in this context. Last, even though the memory books often referred to partying and heavy drinking during leave, visits to brothels or buying sex were rarely mentioned. Here, many explanations are plausible. As already mentioned, these books were to be accessible by wives, girlfriends and mothers. Secondly, buying sex is morally condemned in Norwegian society, and the reputation of the military as well as the participants could be tarnished if these practices were openly referred to. However, comments in memory books sometimes hinted at such visits. For instance, one memory book contained a picture of a female sex worker wearing parts of a Norwegian uniform (Telemark kompani 1999 [memory book]).[4]

I found no accounts of misconduct or violent behavior committed by the Norwegian troops towards Norwegian or local women in any of the sources. This does not prove it has never occurred. In the early 1990s, the armed forces investigated accusations against Norwegian officers for having had sex with underage girls during a UN mission. The investigation concluded that the local women had not been underage, but that the behavior of the Norwegian officers could undermine the standing of the UN forces in the area.

Two main conclusions can be drawn from the preceding discussion. First, Norwegian women who participated in these operations were invisible in the formal military sources. They were not mentioned in positive or negative terms. This indicates that the general approach of the armed forces was to treat women as 'one of the boys.' If they had an impact on the running of military operations or social life in the camp, this was not reflected in the reports. In the informal memory books, the women were more visible, not least because the books contained pictures of the participants. Their femininity was occasionally recognized and commented upon, but more often they were presented as 'one of the boys' in these sources as well.

Second, assessments of the gendered consequences of military operations were completely absent in official reports. This is hardly surprising, since little attention was paid to such issues in general before the adoption of SCR 1325. However, a study of the Norwegian PRT unit in Meymahne in Northern Afghanistan found that gender assessments were still lacking in 2009 (Andreassen et al. 2009). The study found that the Norwegian military personnel had almost no contact with Afghan women. All sources for assessment of the security situation in the province were Afghan males, and the question of whether women's security situation might be different from that of the men was not taken into consideration. Norwegian military personnel explained that they had been taught not to make contact with women since this could lead to local men 'losing face' and to the women being punished. It seems safe to conclude that the behavior of Norwegian military personnel reinforced local power structures in which women were subordinated to male control. It should also be noted that military personnel did not condone the treatment of Afghan women: They were more likely to be appalled by it but having been told that any contact between Afghan women and Western men was banned, they felt that there was nothing they could do. The first Norwegian gender adviser was deployed to Afghanistan in 2009, perhaps partly as a result of the mentioned report.

EXPRESSIONS OF MASCULINITIES

The second topic that will be addressed here concerns expressions of masculinities in the sources. Masculinities are 'those behaviours, languages and practices, existing in specific cultural and organizational locations, which are commonly associated with males and thus culturally defined as not feminine' (Whitehead and Barrett 2001: 15–16). In her gendered analysis of peacekeeping forces, Sandra Whitworth argued, 'part of what goes into the making of a soldier is a celebration and reinforcement of some of the most aggressive, and most insecure, elements of masculinity: those that promote violence, misogyny, homophobia, and racism' (2004: 3). In this section I will analyze to what extent such expressions of masculinity can be found in the material from the NAF. I will also discuss to what extent 'soft' peace support missions are inherently in conflict with perceptions of masculinity in the military, even in a small and 'peace-loving' country like Norway.

Sandra Whitworth notes that national myths portray Canada as a selfless middle-power. Participation in UN peacekeeping operations not only fits this myth, it consolidates it. Norway has traditionally belonged to a group of similar states that seeks to endow its military forces with a soft image. In the early 1990s, Norway's military engagement in foreign operations would often be embellished by references to idealistic motives. When the UN operation in Bosnia was handed over to NATO in 1995, Norway recognized that a more robust image was needed to gain military prestige as well as political goodwill within the alliance. Consequently, its contributions changed from support units to more robust forces. Since political support to NATO (and the EU) could not easily be wrapped in humanitarian language, the idealistic motives behind the Norwegian contributions were somewhat toned down.

Nevertheless, if there is such a thing as a national imaginary construction of the male Norwegian soldier, I would argue that its defining characteristic is that the Norwegian soldier is an average representative of the male population of a certain age. He is the wholesome boy living next door, who dons the uniform for a limited time before returning to civilian life. A common expression of this national construct is to emphasize that Norwegians are good soldiers because their largely civilian values make them able to handle difficult situations with flexibility and common sense, not because of their toughness or bravery in combat.

To what extent are these public perceptions in line with expressions of masculinities inside the military organization? First of all, the sources show that perceptions of peace support operations, and perceptions of the ideal skills and qualities of the operation's personnel, varied between different parts of the organization. Starting with the military organization at home, idealistic motives were not mentioned and peace support operations remained quite unpopular throughout the 1990s. This was not because they were deemed unworthy of support, but because they removed focus and resources from the armed forces' main priority, which was the development and maintenance of combat skills. Experiences from peace support operations were seen as having little relevance in this regard. High-intensity missions, on the other hand, offered opportunities to gain prestige and to modernize the units' materiel and equipment. Another characteristic of the views expressed by the military organization at home was a strictly instrumental approach to these issues. Decisions were not value based or concerned with the legitimacy of the mission at hand: They were focused on available capabilities and maintaining and developing the war-fighting capacities of the armed forces.

Formal reports from the field were more diversified, but had some of the same characteristics. A preoccupation with war-fighting became more noticeable in the field reports after NATO took over the UN operation in Bosnia. Instead of reporting about the overall quiet, but nevertheless difficult, situation at hand, the Norwegian rifle companies in SFOR II and III emphasized that they had conducted exercises in platoon and company attack (Norwegian Battalion in SFOR II 1997; Norwegian Battalion in SFOR III 1998). As for personal qualities held in high esteem by the forces in the field, I found that commonly praised qualities were firstly the ability to endure boredom, monotony and unpleasant (but not dangerous) physical conditions; secondly, a good sense of humor and being good at keeping up spirits; and, thirdly, personal drive and initiative. These qualities were praised in both formal and informal reports and throughout the period under scrutiny. The emphasis on endurance and good spirits rather than toughness and courage may of course be explained by the type of mission these troops were engaged in. In a war, that may well have been different.

These findings are only partly in accordance with other studies of military masculinities. For instance, Frank Barrett found that 'the image of masculinity that is perpetuated [in the US Navy] involves physical toughness, the endurance of hardships, aggressiveness, a rugged heterosexuality, unemotional logic, and a refusal to complain' (2003: 81). John Hockey's (2003) study of a British infantry unit found that many of the same qualities were held in high esteem: Endurance, stoicism, sexual athleticism, aggression and loyalty to ones' mates were important expressions of masculinities. The most notable difference between these descriptions and those found in the Norwegian sources was that aggressiveness was not a commonly praised quality. It was rather the need for restraint and control that was emphasized. For instance, in the first KFOR (Kosovo Force) contingent, the mission commander commented on two shooting accidents in the battalion and warned against what he called 'Rambo tendencies' among officers and privates (Norwegian Contingent Commander KFOR 1999). However, the pictures in the memory books present a slightly different image. From the early SFOR period onwards, the memory books contained many pictures of soldiers and officers with camouflage paint on their faces, sitting on tanks and holding guns in their hands. There were pictures of soldiers with children and old women as well, but the combat units apparently preferred to pose with their weapons displayed. The memory books from the UN period had few such pictures, which indicated that a cultural shift had taken place.

I also found few expressions of aggressiveness or violence. The forces in the field nevertheless had a very clear perception of themselves as military men and women. They did not see themselves as 'helpers in uniform'; they were military forces and the basis for everything they did was their military skills.[5] There was, however, a distinct difference between the UN operations and the NATO operations. Somewhat simplified, in the UN operations, civilian skills, knowledge of the UN system and a problem-fixing mentality were highly valued, and respect for military hierarchies was quite lax. In the NATO operations, reports placed a greater emphasis on order, discipline and military skills.

Several studies have argued that there is an inherent tension between what soldiers perceive as the real army geared towards combat and the nonaggressive and even effeminate army engaged in peacekeeping operations (Harris and Segal 1985; Miller and Moskos 1995; Winslow 1998; Røkenes 2004; Withworth 2004; Sion 2006). Frustrations caused by this tension were expressed in both contingent reports and memory books from the NATO period. So-called sharp missions were always welcomed as an opportunity to relieve tensions and practice what the forces saw as their real skills. For example, an infantry unit in SFOR, which was assigned as an immediate reaction force for SFOR's (NATO's Stabilization Force in Bosnia) highest military commander but spent most of its time on static guard duty, typically referred to potentially sharp operations as 'the icing on the cake' (*rosinen i pølsa*; SFOR II 1997: 104 [memory book]).

The KFOR books also contained comments about the discrepancy between training back home and the tasks at hand in Kosovo. The personnel had trained for war, and adjusting to social patrols and static watch duty was not always easy. One anonymous contributor wrote: 'The war promised us by TV2 did not exist; the dogs were our only enemy' (KFOR I 1999: 52 [memory book]). As in SFOR, soldiers and lower-rank officers got bored. Kosovo was seen as different from everything they were used to. The frustration caused by this estrangement was balanced by the good moments, which consisted mostly of military activities like confiscating weapons, demonstrating firearms and escorting with loaded weapons. A common theme was that this operation was not really a soldier's job. As the years went by, the troops also found it increasingly difficult to see the overall purpose of their mission: 'We look forward to the end of this disastrous NATO mission . . . Our platoon has done more than could have been expected, and better than what is expected of professional soldiers. So our bosses at the top, who benefit from our efforts, should be pleased' (KFOR VII: 98 [memory book]).

Such complaints were rare in the reports and books from the support units in the UN operations. In these operations the prime cause of frustration seemed to be feelings of powerlessness, particularly in UNPROFOR, which was an operation with strict limitations on the use of force. An incident in November 1993, in which Norwegian medical personnel tried to reach a mental hospital that had been abandoned by its staff, illustrates this. After a strenuous trip, the troops were not allowed to pass through a Serb roadblock eight kilometers from the hospital. One of the participants described the situation as follows: 'It felt unbelievable. We were representatives of a world organisation and we were stopped by five lousy and half drunk soldiers sitting around a campfire at their control post. It was as if Captain Hook had stopped an aircraft carrier' (NORMEDCOY I 1993: 58 [memory book]).

Other negative characteristics of military masculinities, according to Whitworth, are racism and homophobia. Remarks of such kind were once again rare, but other studies have found that Norwegian officers formed negative attitudes towards the local population during their deployment (Mæland 2004). Thus, a significant finding in the material I studied was that such problems were hardly touched upon in the contingent reports. This may indicate that the armed forces were reluctant to recognize and deal openly with difficulties that arose in their relations with the local population. Another possible explanation is that such matters were addressed by procedures and routines that were not reflected in the written sources.

CONCLUSION

In the sources examined in this chapter I found relatively few references to the masculinities that Sandra Whitworth claims are those that go into the making of a soldier: those that promote violence, misogyny, homophobia and racism. (Due to limited space I have not discussed expressions of homophobia, but the tendencies are the same: Some examples can be found in the memory books, but they are rare.) The most valued qualities of a good soldier were rather endurance, a good sense of humor and personal initiative. A significant finding was that aggressiveness was hardly ever mentioned as an important quality among Norwegian military personnel abroad. Nevertheless, a 'friendly war-fighter' is to some extent a contradiction in terms.

This conclusion naturally raises the question of whether these sources reflect the realities of the Norwegian military. I have little doubt that negative remarks about race, women and homosexuals are much more frequent among troops on the ground than what is reflected in written sources. A recent study of a combat unit in training before deployment to Afghanistan found that sexist comments about women were quite frequent (Totland 2009). However, the fact that men in their early twenties talk about having sex with women is neither surprising nor a phenomenon exclusively found in the military. The fact that sexist and racist comments are not openly expressed in the sources of this study may at least indicate that such views are not encouraged, or condoned, in military training and education. On the other hand, the sources seem to indicate that the military organization pay less attention to 'soft' and untechnical aspects of its operations compared to matters regarding equipment and materiel.

Another question that arises is to what extent these negative traits are distinctly military. I would argue that so far there is no evidence that misogyny, racism and homophobia are more frequent in the military than elsewhere in the Norwegian population. As Paul Higate (2007) has pointed out, sexual exploitation of local women in peace operations is not only a military practice, but applies to civilian aid workers as well. Furthermore, a recent study of the implementation of SCR 1325 in the Norwegian PRT in Northern Afghanistan found that civilian aid workers were just as ignorant of gender issues as their military colleagues were (Andreassen et al. 2009: 92). In that sense, the public image of the Norwegian soldier as the boy next door holds true. It is still a fact that the boy next door may be both sexist and racist, but in Norway there is no evidence to support the claim that such attitudes are more prominent in the armed forces than in the rest of society.

However, some expressions of masculinities were distinctly military. Most notably, the military self-image was tightly knit to war-fighting skills, mastery of weapons and discipline. These qualities distinguished the Norwegian military men from their civilian counterparts both at home and abroad. Last but not least, the military culture is completely dominated by men in the sense that women are invisible and have to adapt to male norms in order to be accepted. Being 'one of the boys' is unanimously presented as the highest praise that can be bestowed to a female soldier. It goes without saying that many women will not feel at home in this environment, and therefore choose another occupation.

Finally, to what extent does military perceptions of gender and masculinities make them unsuitable for peacekeeping? The sources present a more diversified picture than 'the binary universe of absolutes,' which is a common framework for analysis of the military and peacekeeping (Higate 2007: 102). Norwegian officers emphasized the importance of maintaining individual war-fighting skills, but at the same time stressed that they were careful not to scare children during weapon searches, and that local needs for firewood were mapped after the search was over. Evidence of their complete disregard of gender issues was much more conclusive. Even though small steps are taken to change this, military masculinities remain deeply at odds with ideas such as gender mainstreaming of military operations. Yet, the answer to this problem may not be to turn militaries into humanitarians or to wrap the deployment of military force in humanitarian phrases. The effectiveness of military forces ultimately rests with their destructive potential. If that potential is not required, there should be no reason to send military forces in the first place. It is in the question of how military forces choose to inflict violence and the considerations made in planning and assessment procedures before and after military operations where insights from feminist research can be influential.

NOTES

1. The making of memory books is an institutionalized practice in Norwegian units serving abroad. The entire force contributes to the book by writing friendly descriptions of each participant. In addition, the books often include greetings from commanders at all levels, short stories about memorable events and a great number of pictures from the mission. Some of these books are available in the libraries at the Norwegian Defense University College, the Army's War Academy and the Armed Forces' Defense Museum. Others have been lent to me by their owners.
2. Norwegian Movement Control/UNPROFOR 1992.
Norwegian Movement Control/UNPROFOR 1992–1993.
NORMEDCOY Bosnia, Kontingent I, 1993–1994.
NORMEDCOY Bosnia-Herzegovina, Kontingent II, 1994.
NORLOGBAT I, Bosnia/Herzegovina 1994–1995. Full kontroll.
NORLOGBN III, IFOR I, Bosnia-Herzegovina, oktober 1995–juli 1996. Fra FN til NATO.
NORLOGBN IFOR, Bosnia-Herzegovina 1996–1997. Underveis.
SFOR I, Det norske bidraget til Nato-styrken i Bosnia-Herzegovina, januar–september 1997.
SFOR II, Det norske bidraget til Nato-styrken i Bosnia-Herzegovina, oktober 1997–mars 1998.
SFOR III, Kontingent april til september 1998.
SFOR IV, Kontingent oktober 1998–mai 1999.
Telemark kompani, Kontingent V, Januar–juli 1999.
The Last of the Nordic Peacekeepers, FYROM 1999.
KFOR I kontingentbok. Det norske bidraget til Kosovo Force aug 1999–apr 2000. Veien mot fred.

KFOR II kontingentbok. Det norske bidraget til Kosovo Force apr 2000–sep 2000. De neste stegene.
   KFOR Kontingent VI. 15. juli 2002–15. januar 2003. I riktig retning.
   KFOR Kontingent VII, 15. januar 2003–15. juni 2003. Langt på vei.
3. In 2010, the two highest ranking women in the NAF were one rare admiral and major general. This accounts for almost 10 percent. However, the percentage of women at the levels of colonel and brigadier was much lower and there were no women at the levels above major general.
4. The phenomenon is also addressed by Strømmen and Lerand (2005: 322–323).
5. Maren Tomforde found that 64 percent of the German soldiers and officers who participated in SFOR in 2003 defined themselves as 'helpers in uniform' (2005: 578).

6 The 'Rotten Report' and the Reproduction of Masculinity, Nation and Security in Turkey

Alp Biricik

> In my attempt to expose the dynamics of militarism and militarization in Turkey, the ultimate challenge has *not* been in the *invisibility* of the military and its power, but the discrepancy between its strong presence and visibility, and the lack of critical analyses of this strong presence. I kept returning to a single central question: How is it possible that the military as an institution and 'military-nationhood' as an idea have been so omnipresent, yet a discussion of militarism and militarization so absent?
>
> (Altinay 2004b: 3; emphasis original)

'Homosexual Referee Wants His Whistle Back' was the headline of *Fanatik*, a popular sports newspaper in Turkey, when the Board of Referees in Trabzon, a city in the northern part of Turkey, did not renew a male football referee's working license in relation to his military service (Can 2009). In the beginning the media, in the name of protecting the referee from any harm, did not reveal his name; a few days later Halil İbrahim Dinçdağ, the 33-year-old football referee who had directed 105 football matches since 1996, had to come out 'live' on a TV sports show and tell the story behind the scandal (Telegol 2009).

Sometime ago, Dinçdağ applied and received the so-called medical report, often referred to as a 'rotten report' (*çürük raporu*) or 'pink discharge paper' (*pembe tezkere*) in public,[1] that exempted him from the mandatory military service. The report is given to men who have mental or/and physical disabilities. During the annual license renewal process, the board reviewed Dinçdağ's health records, including the 'rotten report,' and denied renewal of Dinçdağ's referee working license. In their decision, the Board of Referees addressed Article 25 of the Turkish Football Federation's regulation (Türkiye Futbol Federasyonu Merkez Hakem Kurulu 2009: 12). Someone cannot become a football referee if he is exempt from military service due to health reasons (Birch 2009; Çakır 2009). The debate that followed in Turkish newspapers and TV channels was intense. Soon, the discussion turned to the question of whether it was actually possible to have a homosexual man direct football matches. However, throughout these discussions critical questions regarding the medical report per se were never raised.

Even today Dinçdağ struggles to gain back his rights. In this chapter, my aim is not to explore how Dinçdağ received the report, but to examine the military institution's procedures and military medical professionals' practices in 'rotten report' cases through the narrations of other male applicants who are involved in the process in Turkey. I argue that the production of the 'rotten report' is a violent practice of the state. Thus it simultaneously produces security, nation-state-building discourse, and strengthens the notion of 'ideal' manhood symbolized as 'the protector-heterosexual-male-citizen.'

In the first section, I discuss militarism in the everyday culture of Turkey, drawing upon an empirical study carried out in 2006.[2] Then, I outline the so-called medical procedures and practices carried out by military doctors who perform the task of establishing whether a potential conscript to the Turkish Army is indeed 'rotten' (i.e., homosexual) and should be exempt from doing his military service.

A WELL-KNOWN SAYING IN TURKEY: 'EVERY TURK IS BORN A SOLDIER'

Article 72 in the Constitution of the Republic of Turkey states that military service is mandatory for every Turkish male citizen (Constitution of the Republic of Turkey 1980).[3] The service is symbolically regarded as paying back 'the debt to the nation' (*vatan borcu*; Başaran 2007). Along with circumcision, first sexual intercourse with a woman—referred to as 'becoming national' (*milli olmak*), getting married and setting up a business, military service is perceived as a rite de passage for 'becoming a real man' (Sinclair-Webb 2000; Helvacıoğlu 2006: 35–36; Biricik 2009; Selek 2009). Each rite of passage is celebrated with extended parties where family members and friends gather and celebrate the occasion. Since the 1990s, farewell ceremonies for young men on their last day before entering into conscription have become regular cheerful events in the cities (Varoğlu and Bıçaksız 2005: 585). Completing one's military service on time is often a sociopolitical and economical must for any young man in Turkey. Traditional families consider military service a respectful social element and would not permit their daughter to marry a man who did not complete his military service. Employers prefer to recruit men who have completed military services (Biricik 2008).

Male conscription is a practice whereby the relationship between the individual Turkish male and the Turkish state is regulated and maintained. Military service not only makes the 'manly man,' but it also functions as a system of surveillance in controlling the order of 'proper' male citizens

(Başaran 2007) and inevitably male bodies. For instance, any man who has not completed the military service on time, will not be allowed to leave the country. He will be arrested by the border control even if he has a valid passport and a visa (Biricik 2008). Furthermore, as will be shown in this chapter, it also has a very concrete disciplinary function of defining 'real' masculinity.

PERFORMING SECURITY AND THE MALE-CITIZEN-PROTECTOR OF THE TURKISH STATE/NATION

In Turkey, militarism is a pervasive practice in all spheres of everyday life: politically, socially, economically and in the educational system (İnsel and Bayramoğlu 2004; Çınar and Üsterci 2009). Historically, the Turkish Armed Forces have been considered as the most prominent guardian of Kemalist ideology[4] (Zubaida 1996; Altınay 2004b), with the mission to protect the country's borders (*Misak-ı Milli*) as of the Lausanne Treaty in 1923. The military coup d'états in 1960, 1971 and 1980 forged strong relations of trust between civil society and the military institutions.[5] Thus there is a widespread notion of the Turkish soldier as the 'Protector of the Nation' against both internal and external enemies. For instance, the internal enemy, mainly the Kurdish Workers' Party (PKK), has, in effect, been at war since 1984 with the Turkish state. This ongoing internal conflict has strengthened the heroic image of the young Turkish male as the conscripted soldier who risks and also loses his life for the sake of internal cohesion of Turkey. During the peak years of the conflict, 1989 to 1994, the funerals of Turkish conscripts and officers oftentimes erupted into sites of extreme nationalist 'celebrations' or 'performances.' Outwardly, the Turkish Armed Forces have also played a special role as an integrative force vis-à-vis Europe and the US. Turkey has been a member of NATO since 1956, thus the Turkish Armed Forces can be seen as representing the Turkish nation in the NATO forces in international military operations on foreign soil, such as Kosovo, Bosnia-Herzegovina, Somalia, Iraq and Afghanistan (Varoğlu and Bıçaksız 2005).

Militarism is an integrated part of Turkey's educational system. One concrete example of this is the fact that since 1926, there has been a mandatory course in high school known as *Milli Güvenlik* (National Security), teaching all girls and boys 'to be proud members of a military-nation and obedient citizens of the Turkish state' (Altınay 2004a). The course, taught by military officers, aims to endow the students with a basic knowledge of military service. Thus, it focuses more on the boys who will join the military soon after graduation. Girls are reminded that they must be ready to assist the military forces in armed conflict, in case of emergency (ibid.). The building of the nation in Turkey is thus clearly connected to militarism and gender. In his analysis of the concepts of militarism and nationalism in Turkey, Tanıl Bora notes that 'in all textbooks, the military has been represented not only as the savior in the war of Independence, but also the purest symbol of national identity' (2004: 68).

The military institution as security provider in Turkey can also be seen playing an important role in the country's economy. Since 1961, the Armed Forces Trust and Pension Fund (Ordu Yardımlaşma Kurumu [OYAK]) has provided old age economic security to its 205,000 members. Each member pays a 10 percent compulsory fee of their income. Today, the fund has shares in more than 40 companies and is considered one of the top 10 investors in Turkey (Akça 2004).

THE MEDICAL PROFESSION AS GUARDIANS OF TURKISH MANHOOD

> This first stage in selection is mainly to find out if the applicant knows Turkish, and whether he speaks it well or badly, but it is also to check his appearance. Well, I mean, we have had stutters, some with huge boils, some with asymmetrical faces and others with flat feet. Sometimes they are bald, or color-blind, or cross-eyed, or dwarfs. We get rid of them straightaway. We are very keen to have people with as normal an appearance as possible. It is not that we are seeking for good looks; we just do not want anything abnormal. (Birand 1991: 15)

The description of the selection criteria for entering military schools depicts how every individual body is crucial; the body is much more than just a young person standing in front of a state representative, a military commander in this case. In the commander's eyes, the male applicant's 'healthy' mind and body signify conditions of normality that represent the healthy Turkish nation. Although the interview with the commander was held two decades ago, in this section I argue that a similar approach still reigns today in the Turkish military institutions.

During the drafting procedures, every applicant must complete a series of standard health examinations since the authorities need to know if the draftees are suffering from any bodily or mental disorders. The medical checkup procedure is held under the supervision of three military medical doctors and it involves simple medical techniques such as calculation of the proportion of weight and height and measuring blood pressure. As I have mentioned earlier, if the person is deemed to have a serious physical or mental disorder, he can be exempt from the military service by applying to the affiliated military institutions to prove that he is 'unfit' for military service.

Today, there are no provisions in the Turkish legal system that prohibit homosexual men from entering into military service (Anıl et al. 2005). However, in the Health Regulation for Turkish Armed Forces (Article

17; 'psycho-sexual disorders'), the sexual 'behavior' of the draftee is dealt with. The article states that if the applicant has a sexual behavior disorder 'explicitly seen and diffused all over his life,' it must be determined by medical observation and documentation. The main purpose of the medicalization process is to verify 'any possible negative effects' on the military order (Türk Silahlı Kuvvetleri Sağlık Yeteneği Yönetmeliği 1986). These two stipulations, 'explicitly seen' and 'diffused all over his life,' have become instrumental for draftees who wish to be exempt from conscription. In effect, they have set up strategies for how to qualify as performing a genuinely 'deviant' sexuality, as defined by the military medical professionals. Such disobedient performances require their own tactics and techniques that are produced or defined, and then reproduced or performed in close negotiation with the militarist 'medical gaze' (Foucault 1963/2003). How these negotiations are carried out in practicality will be further described in the following.

To start the procedure, the applicant should visit the military conscription department and ask to be consigned to the military hospital. In this process, which may last from one day to one week, the applicant meets white-collar military staff to complete paperwork but at this stage he does not have to state his sexual orientation. Having been consigned to the military hospital, during the standard checkup the applicant requests consultation with the psychiatric department due to his sexual orientation. In the following process the applicant gets an appointment with the psychiatry department and meets the psychiatrists. Depending on the applicant's gender/sexual performance (Butler 1990) and the negotiations with doctors—quite similar to Kandiyoti's concept of 'patriarchal bargain' (1994)—the first consultation plays a key role in determining the next steps towards receiving the 'rotten report.' The sessions with the psychiatrists may last up to 40 minutes. According to my informants, consultation visits may occur up to 12 times a month.

During the consultation sessions, the military doctors may require the applicant to complete a number of psychological personality tests, such as the Minnesota Multiple Personality Inventory (MMPI), the Rorschach inkblot test, the Incomplete Sentence Test or the House-Tree-Person test (HTP).[6] In addition to these tests, the medical authorities may send the applicant to the surgical section of the military hospital in order to perform a rectal examination. The rectal examination may last from one minute to three minutes. During the examination, the doctor may ask the applicant to squeeze his anal muscle. The belief is that it is possible to determine whether a person has had repeated anal sex by looking for loss of anal muscle control. Needless to say, it is highly doubtful whether there are any scientific findings supporting this hypothesis. The anal examination is a practice performed by a professional in the name of state security, masculine cohesion and legitimacy. To me, it symbolizes a form of 'penetration.' The individual becomes an object, examined and humiliated by a penetrating militarized state ideology, objectified by a professionalized medical gaze. In representational terms, this particular practice, almost ritualized by its standardized nature of how it is performed, represents the need to safeguard masculinity. The idea of masculinity (in singular terms) must be kept safe from attack (i.e., reinterpretation or redefinition). The attacks are assumed to be located outside the body/nation. In order to sustain and protect male/national honor (assumed to be situated inside the body), the body/nation must not be 'opened' (by penetration). Penetration equals the symbolic breakage, which threatens to transform the 'normal/ideal' male body/nation from its dominant subject position to a vilified position, equaling the position of passive femininity and the female body.

In some cases, authorities may require at least two photographs taken during sexual intercourse with another man where the applicant must be seen in the 'passive' role, or in other words depicted as 'the feminine.' Of course, the military psychiatric staff knows well that they cannot certify the 'pathology' of the applicant by using material props, such as the photos. However, they collect them anyway as evidence of distorted masculinity, as evidence of 'moments of explicit deviancy.' In representational terms, the photographs of sexual intercourse become determinant proof. Moreover, as some of the interviewees noted, the so-called evidence is collected as a way for the military medical doctors to secure their future careers should there be an investigation of 'fake' medical reports of men seeking ways of exemption from military service.

Following the consultation sessions, the applicant is sent to the medical committee for the final decision. However, in some cases, if the committee is not satisfied with the results, the applicant may be obliged to stay at the psychiatry sections of military hospitals from one to three weeks. At the psychiatric sections, the applicant will undergo further medical observation in special sections, referred as 'pink' sections by the informants. Sometimes, and even if the applicant has completed all these procedures and examinations, the final decision may be postponed a year or two. Every year, the applicant may be obliged to undergo all described medical examinations once again in order to determine if there are any changes in the applicant's health condition; however, the process cannot be prolonged more than three years. Once the medical committee has come to a decision, the applicant's diagnosis is sent to the police and registered in all military conscription departments.

According to a survey in 2005 (Lambda-Istanbul 2006) on 399 lesbian, gay, bisexual and transgender persons in Turkey, 27 out of a total of 215 gay or bisexual men applied to have the rotten report. Six of them were rejected in their first step of application by the white-collar military authorities and they were not consigned to the military hospital. Twenty-one applicants faced degrading inhuman and illegal regulations. Six men were required to submit photographs taken during sexual intercourse (i.e., being penetrated by another man) and 13 of them had to undergo rectal examination. Seven of the 21 did not qualify as homosexual by the military hospital authorities: The major reason given was that they were 'not effeminate enough.'

PREPARATIONS, PERFORMANCES AND STRATEGIES

Almost everyone I interviewed had learned about the existence of the so-called 'rotten report' from friends or they had read about it in the newspaper. Kemal, the very first person in his circle of friends to receive the 'rotten report' in the early 1990s, said:

> I heard it early in my childhood that they were not letting fags join the military service. This is what we heard most but we did not know really whether that was really true [...] I missed the opportunity for paid military service because of my age [...] I met a high officer from the army. He told me that if a man's forefinger was disabled, or if his weight and height were in inappropriate proportions, then he could not join the military, or if you were extremely homosexual. You were not allowed to enter the military system if you were transvestite.

Collecting information from friends who had received the 'rotten report' earlier is a crucial strategy for the interviewees for two reasons. First, hearing about the experiences of others, one starts to form an idea as to how one should perform the gender role to qualify as unfit for the military service. Second, the applicant learns about the possible risks and advantages involved during and after the report process. Throughout our conversations, all interviewees considered the military service to be a waste of valuable time during their most productive years. This was said for those who planned to have a business career. All were well aware of the oppressive nature and hard disciplining structures of the military institutions and felt that it would damage them both physically and psychologically. Cemal, who after a three-year-long struggle with the authorities finally received 'extremely homosexual' diagnosis, remarked on the absurdity of it all:

> The military service is terrible. You have to wake up and sleep all together at the same time. You have to obey whatever they say, like a slave, even when they beat you, you cannot stop them. Once my brother told me that one of his military commanders punished a pair of boots for ten years! Can you believe this? They punish people, shoes, everything.

Murat wanted the report after having completed the one-month basic military training. After his first-year application round with the military medical staff, he was diagnosed as having an 'antisocial personality.' The following year, he was diagnosed with 'homosexuality.' Murat talked about the strict discipline and violent punishment system in the military institutions:

> I was supposed to do military service for 18 months. After I entered the military (unit), I felt that I had come to a concentration camp. It was like a movie [...] I had to wake up like a robot [...] I had to weed the grass on the garden and collect the cigarette butts at four o'clock in the morning [...] Military service crushes your personality.

For all interviewees the examination procedures and all the rest they had to submit themselves to in order to receive the 'rotten report' were indeed considered stressful. However, even more stressful was finding out how to perform a type of sexual/gender performance that would fit the medicalized notion of deviancy upheld by the authorities. Listening to the experiences of their friends guided them as well as drawing upon their own personal experiences of homophobia in everyday life. In other words, the interviewees knew the rules of the game. They knew the power games acted out in the 'heteronormative matrix' (Butler 1990). If their audience found the performance believable, they would successfully receive the 'rotten report,' thus be officially labeled as 'the deviant other'—the nonmale according to Turkish national military standards.

Depending upon the applicant's choice of strategy, these gender performances had different variations on the overarching thematic, 'male homosexuality.' Their performances could, for example, vary between performing 'the feminine' or 'the masculine' that bespeaks the patriarchal cultural codes of gender constructions. I argue that the main reason behind these gendered and sexualized bodily performances is a challenge either to fit or reconstruct the image of 'homosexual man' in the eye of the military medical doctors. In other words, the applicants use gendered and sexual strategies to receive the report in a shorter period of time. One key element of these performances is being (in)appropriate to the militarist medical gaze. As discussed earlier, the medicalization process firstly aims at determining the risk of deviant sexual acts taking place within the ranks that might disrupt the discipline and the military order. Consequently, in this theater of differently gendered personas, the military doctors set out to investigate the applicants' possible 'pathology' by focusing on three specific levels. First, the physical appearance of the applicant's genitals and his sexual practices; second, the applicant's self-image, called his 'gender role stability'; third, his socioeconomic and educational background. Kemal chose the act of feminine homosexuality, in a 'lady performance.' He describes his preparations and how, in the meeting with the militarized medical notion of homosexual man, this monolithic image is being challenged:

> I knew that I had to go there deeply effeminate. I absolutely went to the hospital like a transvestite. I shaved all my body hair, I put on makeup but I did not inject any hormones (for growing breasts). I got a wig from an artist, a skirt from another artist, a pair of shoes from another. I made up my hair, my clothes were quite expensive. I wore real jewelry.

> I knew that it would make a difference if I looked like a lady [...] The doctor looked at my testicles and he said, 'They look strong but why don't you have breasts?' And I said 'I have started to take some hormones, they will grow soon.'

As explored earlier, the practice of upholding the idea of normal masculinity as a symbol of Turkishness is bound to be full of contradictions. What is the overall script that would help the medical staff maintain their connection to 'science'? It seems that to some military doctors being a homosexual man would mean being trapped in an abnormally sexed male body that is in the process of transformation into 'the feminine other.' Playing into this script, the applicant would sometimes inject his body with hormones to start growing breasts. This strategy could work as a way to receive the 'rotten report' in a shorter period of time. Cemal said:

> I think it was some time between 1993 and 1995, my cousin had to take some hormones to grow his breasts and dress up before the consultation. Then he went to the health examination like a woman, he got rid of his body hair. Then I helped a friend of mine, he also injected hormones [...] He had to go to the military hospital like a woman.

However, in some cases, the physical change of the applicant's body was still not found to be 'adequate' enough to qualify as being truly deviant. Performing 'like a woman' could be just as effective and is therefore used as another strategy. To put it differently, sexing the body by transposing it into 'the form of the female other,' will not automatically be considered essential proof for the medical staff of the military. Based on the interviewees' experiences, it seems clear that a social gender performance must accompany 'the patriarchal bargain'; thus it is more essential than the physical or bodily aspect. However, as mentioned already, this gender performance often provokes violent retaliation. Performing the feminine other, that is, a gay feminine man in a highly militarized masculine space such as the military hospital, recalls homophobia, and inevitable violence, sometimes sexualized violence. Nuri, diagnosed as 'extremely homosexual,' said:

> Before I went there (to the military hospital), I thought a lot about this case and I prepared myself for the scenario. My friends told me to act. They said that if I took the process in a submissive mood, I would have hard times [...] I started to practice my role in front of the mirror at home. I was acting like a woman. One of my friends taught me how to insult people if I had to face any problem there because he said that during the hospital visits, the soldiers would try to tease and abuse me. Hence he taught me how to handle the issue. Because when you go there, you are alone and they don't let your friends enter.

Bedri had to stay for 10 days at the military hospital for observation. The first year, he was diagnosed as having an 'anxiety disorder.' The following year, he was more successful and received the 'rotten report' as he was diagnosed as 'extremely homosexual.' Bedri tells about how the experience shaped his gender performance and his strategy of resistance to the abuse:

> The soldiers in the military were horny. If they could have caught me, they would try to fuck me. One of them even said, 'I have all the keys (of the hospital room), I am horny, come and fuck with me or at least suck my dick' [. . .] I was trying to keep on reading books to protect myself but this time I was looking like an alien because my role was to act the fag to the doctors and the depressed patient to the soldiers.

Performing deviant sexual behavior was also taught to heterosexual men. Cemal mentioned that he coached five of his heterosexual friends to receive 'the report' and trained them how to behave like an 'effeminate gay man.' In his words:

> There was a book about homosexuals in those days. In the book, there was a list of words, gay slang words. First, I gave them the list and they studied the words. I told them to use these words during the consultations. For instance, if the doctor was supposed to ask them how they were earning money, I told them to say *berdeli koli kesiyorum* (I'll have sex for money). I explained to them that they should first reply to the doctor's questions in gay slang, and if he asked them for their meaning, they should explain it in (proper) Turkish.

Performing 'the self' as a masculine man, as some interviewees mentioned, was another strategy to deal with the categorizations during the so-called medical consultations at the military hospitals. Erhan, after his first visit to the military hospital, rejected submitting photographs and only agreed to complete the psychological tests. He said:

> For the report, I did not put on makeup or dress like a woman. I don't practice such things in my daily life anyways. I think this was the mistake. If I had put on makeup, etc., the result could be different. I think they didn't expect to see a straight-looking gay man; they wanted to see a homosexual man dressed up like a woman, even a transsexual. They wanted to see the proof that I was practicing the woman.

After a monthlong struggle, he was diagnosed under the psychiatric category of 'borderline personality' but at the same time found 'fit' for completing military service. Hence, he was nevertheless conscripted and completed the service working in a white-collar position. I argue that Cemal's gender/

sexual performance passed as a straight-looking man, which does not disturb the discipline of military order. His outlook is considered masculine 'enough,' and therefore manly enough, in the medical gaze.

Threatening military discipline was also used as a strategy to receive the rotten report. Hasan's story highlights another form of violence after his struggle with the military doctors on the rectal examination and the photography issue. Similar to Erhan, he rejected completing these tests; furthermore, he menaced the doctors by claiming that he would disrupt the discipline:

> I told the doctor, 'I have problems with authority, when I see the soldiers here with their uniforms, I can hardly stop myself, I want to fuck with them. For instance, during the lunch break, I met one of the soldiers, and I am going to meet with him at the weekend for fucking.'

After this response, he was diagnosed under the category of 'neurotic adaptation' and sent to two other military hospitals to determine his possible future impact on disrupting the discipline in the military ranks. After having had a face-to-face consultation with the medical doctors in the third military hospital, he received the report in one day with the diagnosis, 'extremely homosexual.'

Nine interviewees who received the report described their sense of relief afterwards. However, the social drawbacks and overall ramifications of receiving the 'rotten report' are not to be underestimated in Turkish society. Receiving the 'rotten report' means that one is stigmatized for life; to some, it means entry into a world of exclusion, in particular, in the labor force. Ali, who was exempt from doing military service after having successfully performed, in his own words, 'the effeminate gay,' reported that after the military doctors had learned that he had graduated from medical school, they were not as abusive to him throughout the process of examinations. Ali received the report in a very short time—in one and a half days he was diagnosed as 'transsexual.' However, Ali's description illustrates how the state's punishment for inability or refusing to maintain the militarized masculinity of Turkishness can be inflicted:

> When you have a 'rotten report,' apparently you agree to exclusion. It means you cannot work in white-collar jobs or work as an expert at the universities. Even if I pass the necessary exams to enter a university as an academician, they will recognize the related code of the rotten report on my documents and I will lose all my gained rights. They will kick you out of the institution immediately.

There are in fact no legal restrictions in Turkey regarding homosexuality. Similar to the football referee, Dinçdağ, case discussed in the introduction, there are vaguely drawn legal restrictions for men's access to the labor force who have not accomplished their military service. During job applications, however, 'specific' medical conditions such as 'homosexuality' can be acknowledged as a deviant qualification.

Article 48 in the Law for Civil Servants organizes the conditions for civil servant recruitment in Turkey and states that eligible male applicants should not have any military service requirements. In other words, they should have fulfilled their service or at least postponed it. In the complementary Article 53, although bodily disabilities of applicants' are not considered as a disadvantage, mental disabilities (without any concrete definition) are acknowledged as a disadvantage. Under these conditions, it is often possible for authorities to assess an applicant who has his rotten report as ineligible during job interviews or recruitment (Devlet Memurları Kanunu 1965).

CONCLUSION

In order to avoid military service in Turkey, there are limited possible solutions: One can escape, declare himself as a conscientious objector,[7] which is still not officially recognized by state authorities, or try to receive the medical report that I have examined in this article. By exploring the rotten report cases, I have examined some struggles of men who tried to resist the destructive mechanisms of militarism and their reflections regarding the notion of the 'ideal/normal' man in Turkey. However, there is still more to discuss. Hence, I suggest that anyone who wants to explore gender/sexual matrices in Turkey, especially if the question is raised by a social scientist, should start by interrogating the nationalist and militarist discourses, which are deeply embedded and materialized in various forms and structures of everyday life in Turkey.

As I have outlined, by studying the practices and institutions of conscription in Turkey, one can begin to uncarth the power–knowledge nexus in relation to the ideational aspects of state security-masculinity and 'the Protector of the Nation.' The medicalization process involved clearly shows us the interconnectedness of the state institutions, such as the military, the police department and the medical profession at the military hospitals. I argue that all these institutions are crucial spatial machines of the state that have the effect of empowering the militarization of everyday life. It is an ongoing machinery for the reproduction of a militarist-masculine national identity in every generation, representing the continuance of the rationalist modernization project of Turkey. The medicalized/bureaucratic processes involved when determining deviant sexuality are built upon a rationalist notion of knowledge and power. As long as the 'rotting' process continues, it will hinder a democratic development of society as it forecloses any discussion that explores the interplay between patriarchal power relations, misogyny and homophobia.

Since the mid-1990s, the rotten report issue has been on the agenda of LGBT, feminist and antimilitarist groups in Turkey with particular emphasis on the interplay of militarism, gender and sexual politics. The efforts have been limited but valuable (Biricik 2009). It is believed that Turkey's integration process within the European Union will bring significant changes to the 'democratization' of patriarchal structures, as well as new positive regulations in everyday life. More importantly, the democratic integration process is considered to be a positive development since it is likely to weaken the dogma of heteronormativity by advancing a discussion on sexual politics and the need to strengthen citizenship rights in Turkey. However, I argue that such a sociocultural and economic transformation, as part of Turkey's 'modernization and Westernization' process, will bring new discussions onto the feminist and antimilitarist agenda. In particular, the question is how this new 'Western democratic power' of Turkey will articulate militarism and what ideal characteristics of the citizens should be strived for and played out in everyday life.

NOTES

I am grateful to Erika Svedberg and Özlem Ezer for their comments on earlier versions of this chapter.
1. The 'rotten report' is not an official name given by the Turkish state.
2. This chapter is a summary of my research study held with 11 men who identified themselves as *gey* or *eşcinsel* and who received, or tried but failed, or were refused 'rotten reports.' Although *eşcinsel* literally means *homosexual* in Turkish, since early 1990s' discussions on the sexual politics, gay and lesbian groups have regarded the term 'homosexual' as a scientific term. Today, *gey* and *eşcinsel* are commonly used by gay and lesbian people to express their sexual identities. The semi-structured and face-to-face interviews were held in April 2006 in Istanbul. All the interviewee names were changed with pseudonyms. For an extensive discussion, see Biricik (2008).
3. Article 72 states, 'national service is the right and duty of every Turk. The manner in which this service shall be performed, or considered as performed, either in the Armed Forces or in public service shall be regulated by law' (Constitution of the Republic of Turkey 1980). Furthermore, the Military Service Law of 1927 states, 'according to the regulations of this law it is compulsory for every man who is a subject of the Turkish Republic to do military service.' Thus, men, from 1 January onwards in the year they turn 20, are obliged to do their military service. Depending on the educational status of the person, duration of the military service may vary. If the person has not obtained any higher level of education (e.g., bachelor's), he should serve for 15 months as a regular soldier. If the person has completed his university degree, he can be conscripted for six months, as a regular soldier, or for 18 months as a military officer with a higher rank depending on his will. Paid military service (*Bedelli askerlik*) is the only way to complete the military service in a shorter period. In this process, workers who acquire residence permits in other countries can do their military service for 21 days by paying a certain amount of money (Constitution of the Republic of Turkey 1980; Başaran 2007; Biricik 2008).
4. Since the foundation of the Turkish Republic in 1923, six disciplines of Kemalist ideology—republicanism, popularism, secularism, revolutionarism,

nationalism and statism—powerfully direct the country's politics (Zürcher 2003).
5. For instance, the total number days under martial law between 1923 and 1987 are 25 years, 9 months and 18 days, which represents 40 percent of the whole republic's regime since its foundation (Üskül 1989: 23).
6. As Başaran notes, 'HTP is a projective test and is not deployed as widely as MMPI in medical inspections. In these tests, one is asked to draw a house, a tree and a person (he can add more figures to these, but these three are required) and to interpret what s/he has drawn. In the picture, if there is no chimney on the house (believed to symbolize a phallic object) or if there is a hedge around the house (believed to signify vulnerability of the person), the doctors may use these test results as indicators in support of their decision regarding one's homosexuality' (2007: 70).
7. The number of conscientious objectors in 2010 reached 80 people, including a few women (Savaş Karşıtları 2009).

7 Men Making Peace in the Name of Just War
The Case of Finland

Pirjo Jukarainen

All-male conscription has been constitutional in Finland since its national independence in 1917. Today, almost 100 years later, we see how in practice this has meant that defense and military matters are masculine concerns. Every male Finnish citizen is liable for military service starting from the beginning of the year in which he turns 18 years old until the end of the year in which he turns 60. The institutionalized male 'duty to protect' has not only been a way to secure manpower for the national defense, but part of a norm system forming Finnish national identity. Normative politics of military masculinity has thus been at the center of nation building (of similar politics in South Africa, see Conway 2008). What is interesting is that the deep belief in the solidity of the conscription system has further institutionalized male peacekeeping agency in international missions. The masculine 'war heroism' or rather, honorable defense, has been practiced both at home and abroad. On the international scene the male national defender is carrying a glorious name of peacekeeper. However, this hardly entails just 'keeping' peace, but being involved in active peace building, if not peace-enforcement, in warlike environments, such as Afghanistan.

One aim of this chapter is to show how the gendered idea of masculine military protection can extend to the international spatial scale and in what way this is problematic. Mostly due to a long tradition of conscription in Finland, Finnish military activities abroad do not drastically differ from the national defense, but function as a kind of 'extended defense,' the extension of the Nordic neutrality idea into peacekeeping missions in faraway places. I argue that the conscript's duty to protect and the masculine heroism it contains face problems of justification in contemporary peace building environments. Furthermore, I argue that there is a gendered objective underlying both the national defense of Finland and Finland's international peacekeeping engagement, coming from Just War theory. This, I argue, makes it especially problematic from a more critical feminist point of view. Traditional gender constructions of male and female as opposites in relation to security come alive once again, like the Phoenix bird, in the shapes of an honorable male protector and a weak female protected.

Men Making Peace in the Name of Just War 91

In the mid-1990s, Charles C. Moskos and James Burk envisioned an almost glorious future scenario of righteous military work: 'The ideal form of a national military, associated with universal male conscription, masculine virtues, and national patriotism, has been transformed into a 'high-tech' professional armed force, providing military power for temporary international coalitions' (Moskos and Burk 1994: 145). Their description fits the Finnish case quite well as Finland has an all-male conscript army with a high level of engagement in international military cooperation. Defining military crisis management/peacekeeping as 'military refresher course abroad' (reservist training) in the military language illustrates the Finnish way of thinking.[1] This discourse poses a challenge to the justification of the female military peacekeepers presence in 'tough, warlike places' and denies the operational need to deploy them in new type of peace building missions.

With a feminist approach I analyze how the Finnish soldiers and defense officials reason and justify Finland's military activities in the contemporary twenty-first-century security environment. I claim that the Finnish soldiers' geopolitical construction of *both* the national defensive space *and* international crisis management space are both based on the gendered, Aristotelian principle of Just War, with masculine war heroes and to-be-defended (female) civilians. The empirical materials of my analysis are twenty-first-century issues of Finnish military journals (*Ruotuväki*—semimonthly bulletin of the Finnish Defense Forces; *Sinibaretti*—magazine of the Finnish peacekeepers association; *Sotilas*—journal of the military officers trade union; the independent journal of *Suomen Sotilas*; and *Kylkirauta*—journal of the cadet's association) and occasional military officials commentary texts in two major national newspapers (Aamulehti 2010; *Helsingin Sanomat*) and *Suomen Kuvalehti* magazine. This material has provided me with a rich source in terms of the language and the jargon used by defense intellectuals when reasoning about Finnish defense and international military engagements.

CONSCRIPTION AND CONSTRUCTIONS OF MALE DUTY

In comparison to other European countries as well as two of its neighbors (Sweden and Germany), Finland has been slow to change the all-male conscript system. Furthermore, unlike other countries, Finnish peacekeepers are predominantly (80 percent) not professional soldiers but voluntary reservists trained as conscripts. Thus, in the case of Finland, there is a large men's reserve from which to recruit soldiers to international missions. Most likely, this is one of the reasons why there are so few women in Finland's international military activities. Since the country's first mission to the Suez in 1956, a total of 32,000 Finnish citizens have taken part in international peace operations, of these, around 500 were women. I claim that conscription is the key reason behind the gender imbalance in defense and military crisis management in Finland. The Finnish model of masculinity resembles the Machiavellian soldiering-citizenship, where practices of the civic militia are both necessary to the existence of the republic and a much-needed ingredient in the creation of virtuous manhood (Snyder 1999: 24–25). In other words, part-taking in international peacekeeping operations is helping Finland to uphold this model.

The large reserve of men is one major obstacle to Finnish women proving themselves and the worth of their capabilities in international missions. There are today several thousands of female reservists; nevertheless, women's participation as soldiers in the military is marginal. Of the military officers, 2 percent are women officers. Annually, only 1 to 2 percent of all conscripts are female. In 2009, women's share among the volunteers in peacekeeping operations was slightly higher at 4 percent. However, the relative number of women has decreased during the last 20 years. In the mid-1990s, 15 to 17 percent of the applicants were women; in recent years their share has been less than 5 percent. This can be explained by the fact that in 1991, when the first female peacekeepers served as medics in peacekeeping, military service was not a requirement for recruitment. In 1995, women were given the opportunity to do their military service, and since then all personnel in military crisis management must have prior training in the armed forces.

Following the opening up of the military service to women in 1995, there were a couple of years of a 'transitional period' when a number of women without military training were recruited to peacekeeping missions. Their position was precarious, to say the least. For instance, from the Macedonia UN PREDEP operation, it was reported about a group of young reservist men from Finland, dressed in T-shirts with the initials V.Ä.S.Y. The letters equated a pejorative saying in Finnish: *Vittuun ämmät YK-joukoista* (translated 'Fuck off, biddies/women from the UN troops'). Women peacekeepers themselves have reported that the attitude towards them has changed for the better, as women now are also fully trained combatants.

And still, soldiering in Finland is predominantly a male practice as it remains a duty only for men. If a Finnish man totally refuses to complete all the service—armed or civilian—he will be sentenced to a maximum of 197 days in prison. This practice has been criticized for being a human rights violation by both Amnesty International and the United Nations Human Rights Commission. The question of whether the obligation to serve actually extends to missions abroad is not judicially clarified, but rather confused. According to the recently renewed Conscription Act[2] the duty to defend is indeed limited to the national territory of Finland. At the same time, in the new act on Finnish Armed Forces (FAF),[3] participating in international military crisis management is one of the three main duties of the defense forces (military defense of the country and providing support for other authorities being the other two duties). Still, conscripts or reservist trainees may not be ordered to take part in operations abroad, including military training, since this requires the written approval of each individual soldier who is sent on a mission. The will to risk one's life in (post)conflict zones is created by means of moralizing language, not by legal coercion. In the materials studied for this chapter, going to Afghanistan is said to be an equally heroic and just way to fight for peace as it is to be prepared for defending the Finnish homeland.

In Finland, as in Sweden, the overall defense policy was based on the idea of nonalliance in peacetime, aiming for neutrality in case of war. A neutral country avoids provoking armed conflicts but it has every right to protect its own country and population from any aggression. As the nonaligned state could not count on external military support, it needed to be self-sufficient in terms of defense capabilities. Further, as the defensive tasks were and still are gendered, the system of all-male conscripted army got justification, too (Kronsell and Svedberg 2001). International operations in the form of traditional peacekeeping extended this gendered principle of a neutral country defending itself. Traditional peacekeeping affirmed the idea of the justified defense because it positioned the neutral power at the center of a global security context. Even if the practices of international operations have changed to active peace building it is still emphasized that Finnish soldiers use arms only for defense, only for self-protection.

> From experience is well known that Finnish peacekeepers have a very high threshold to use lethal arm power. In addition to peaceful and neutral approach this has perhaps been the main reason why only two Finns have fallen in peacekeeping operations as victims of belligerent fire. (Salonius–Pasternak and Visuri 2006: 38)

The reverse side of the defense narrative has been the fact that activity—even when prolonged—has done more to strengthen the status of the peacekeeping country than facilitating sustainable peaceful development in the local context. Despite this, Finns speak proudly about themselves as a previous 'peacekeeping superpower' sending large reserves, large numbers of military men abroad. This was previously supported by concentrating on UN missions (or operations with a UN mandate) and setting the activity within the framework of other Nordic neutral countries (Vesa 2007). The fact that Finnish military has not had any clear exit strategies during operations further confirms and illustrates how the main idea has been more to practice national foreign policy objectives than anything else (Valenius 2007: 510). To Finland, peacekeeping could very well be a matter of just being present 'to settle the dust' as an adequate enough achievement. An article published in the journal *Sinibaretti* (the Blue Barett), describes the Finns' presence in the UN-led Lebanon operation (1982–2001) as a 'prolonged refresher course' (Rauhanturvaajaliitto 2001). Brigadier General Juha Kilpiä (2006) characterizes volunteering reservists' crisis management tasks on a leading national newspaper *Helsingin Sanomat* likewise as a 'one-year-refresher course abroad under challenging conditions.' Or, as worded by former Commander-in-Chief Juhani Kaskeala: 'International crisis management and defense of the home country are different sides of the same coin. Finland uses mainly reservists for both tasks' (Kaskeala 2006: 2).

National military defense forces have in other words been strengthened by international peacekeeping opportunities as they have offered the opportunity to train Finnish conscripts and officers in real warlike circumstances. In his preface in a book on Finnish peacekeeping, former Minister of Defense Seppo Kääriäinen, remarked aptly: 'We do international military cooperation because it supports also the development of national defense (Kääriäinen 2006: 2). We get such international experience and know-how, which is not elsewhere available. Peacekeeping and national benefit go together.' However, to include engagement in international peace missions as a 'natural' part of Finland's overall security thinking has also been questioned. We might want to ask ourselves what the difference actually is between a traditional Finnish defense and taking part in contemporary peacekeeping/crisis management. Former commander-in-chief (1994–2001) General Hägglund asked: 'What would happen to the will to defend, if it should be justified by crisis management?' (Hägglund 2007: 23). However, according to the next commander-in-chief, Admiral Kaskeala (2001–2009), there was no difference. To Kaskeala, international crisis management and national defense were different sides of the same coin (Kaskeala 2006).

THE JUST SOLDIER IN WAR AND PEACE

The so-called Just War principle has guided both the justification of the reason for going to war (*jus ad bellum*), and the means used during war (*jus ad bello*). Warfare itself is justified if it is conducted in order to protect civilians. On the other hand, the civilian immunity principle must be respected during the course of war. This immunity is both a matter of right and duty. Civilians must have a right to remain unarmed, plus there is always a duty to protect civilians as the war is fought on account of them. This principle is problematic because there remains an implicit gendered division between protector and protected. The embedded silence on gender in Just War theory means that the term *civilian* is not a gender-neutral concept (Sjoberg 2006a: 18; 2006b).

Ilan Zvi Baron has described Just War theory: 'According to the tradition, a war is just if the criteria of just cause, right intention, proper authority, last resort, effectiveness, proportionality and discrimination are met' (2010: 217). Aristotelian reasoning is based on the idea of linking citizenship and going to war. According to Aristotle, it is glorious to die in battle, and become a hero citizen—a person to be remembered. A resemblance to this thinking may be found in Finland's foremost nationalistic and romantic writer, nineteenth-century poet Johan Ludwig Runeberg. Still today, the honorary march of the Finnish Defense Forces, *Porilaisten marssi* with Runeberg's lyrics, is played at military funerals when lowering the coffin.[4] In Finnish national culture, there is a strong tradition of honoring war heroes and especially the victims of the last war which took place almost seventy years ago.

> Sons of a race whose blood was shed,
> On Narva's field; on Poland's sand; at Leipzig; Lutzen's dark hills under;
> Not yet is Finland's manhood dead;
> With foemen's blood a field may still be tinted red.
> All Rest, all Peace, Away! begone!
> The tempest loosens; lightnings flash; and o'er the field the cannon thunder
> Rank upon rank, march on! march on!
> The spirit of each father brave looks on as brave a son.
> (*Porilaisten marssi*, the March of the Pori town; English translation from Norman 1904: 70)

The very same patriotic tune is found in the Cadet's Oath. The wording has remained the same, emphasizing masculine honor, although for more than a decade now female cadets have also pledged the oath. The wording of the oath speaks of the duty to defend as closely tied to manly honor:

> In front of the Cadet flag, soldier's supreme virtues fidelity, manhood, honor and comradeship I promise to sacrifice my work and life to the Fatherland. During the time of being cadet and thereafter let my insignia be Finland's freedom and national prosperity. May the memory of our fathers be sacred to me, and the soldier's honor my guiding star. Let my thoughts, motivations and goals be always noble and high-minded. (Kadettivala, the Cadets' Oath; author's translation)

Recently, theories of Just War have added the phase of postwar (jus post bellum), principles for postwar settlement. The idea is that there is no real peace without justice (Bass 2004). The question is: Can this peace be just from a gender perspective? In 2008, as Finland published the National Action Plan, 2008–2011, for the implementation of SCR 1325 a more critically minded discussion started of what possible gender implications Finland's international military operations might have. Until this time there was hardly any talk about possible benefits of including women personnel in peacekeeping operations. In the discourse of national defense officials (in publications, briefs and talks) there have not been any analyses of the gendered nature of conflicts. For example, in an official publication, commemorating 50 years' history of Finnish peace building efforts, there is a female soldier on the cover but in the text there is neither any mention of women combatants nor of the gendered aspect of conflicts (see Salonius-Pasternak and Visuri 2006). The case of Norwegian peacekeeping missions, represented in this volume by Torunn Haaland, shows a similar invisibility of possible gender aspects on peacekeeping.

That the Just War principle is based on the protector–protected dichotomy also entails that civilian adult men and older boys would normally be considered as potential combatants and therefore not included among protected civilians. The Srebrenica massacre, when thousands of men were killed, took place literally in front of the watchful eyes of Dutch peacekeepers. This is often mentioned as a horrible consequence of the gendered nature of Just War. The gendered Just War principle of civilian protection had excluded military-age men and boys 15 years or older and consequently they were not evacuated but should have protected themselves (e.g., Zarkov 2002; Carpenter 2006). Instead it is women, small children and elderly men who represent the defenseless civilians, whose protection justifies traditional peacekeeping, crisis management or humanitarian interventions.

Just War theory has a long history, and its principles have been institutionalized in international law. (Sjoberg 2006a: 27). This, in turn, implies that the gendered protector–protected dichotomy also influences the practices of international peace building organizations like the UN that rely heavily on international legal principles. In general, in the UN discourse on gender mainstreaming equates the term *gender* with women, and women are given the role of protected or a civilian role of working for conflict resolution and peace; women's possible combatant role is largely dismissed. There is indeed an opening up of broadened security thinking in general, of new types of war, in Kaldorian terms, and on security in terms of human security. However, as noted by Tarja Väyrynen (2004), although this has contributed to a discursive space for thinking about gender, this space has not been fully utilized by the UN.

GIRLS IN CANTEENS VERSUS MEN IN ARMS

In Finland the gendered justification of international peacekeeping has recently been related to the operation in Afghanistan. This discussion became hot in 2007 when some people thought that the 'place had become too bad' for the Finnish troops. Minister of Defense Häkämies had a different opinion and caused a minor sensation with his statement: 'It just does not work that Finland applies only canteen tasks in crisis management.' His wording underlines that Finns are not only in supportive, feminine, auxiliary roles, but capable of masculine combat duties. Minister Häkämies found it daunting that Finnish troops might withdraw from the Afghanistan operation once the conflict situation had become more challenging. He compared it to being unethical, in Christian terms, irresponsible to his fellow men: '[i]t is easy to say, let's take our boys away so that nobody will die. [. . .] As easily we can say, let's end all the missionary work' (quotes from Lappalainen 2007: 23).

What was gendered in the statement of Minister Häkämies was making the comparison between the military crisis management and missionary work in the context of the Just War principle. The national defense and international military operations comprised—to say it in gendered terms—a 'brotherhood of arms.' The talk of canteen tasks referred to the Soldier's Homes, recreational centers inside garrisons, which in Finland have been maintained by the women's voluntary defense association since 1918. Canteen tasks, hence, referred to auxiliary duties, tasks of female civilians. The irony of this statement is that in reality it is often the nonmilitary (i.e., 'civilian') workers who actually precede the military troops and also often remain even after the withdrawal of the military, at least in the most well-to-do organizations. This was, for instance, articulated in the recently published Finnish national strategy for civilian crisis management. Indeed, civilian tasks, instead of hindering, actually enable the withdrawal of military troops when they aim at rebuilding the post-conflict state's own measures of security.

The gendered aspect of the previous episode is strengthened by knowing the fact that at the time, female soldiers were not preferred to serve in Afghanistan. According to Elli Flén—one of the rare exceptions who worked as an information officer in Afghanistan in 2007—this informal ban indeed was a general policy of the defense sector in mid-2000. Military women were considered to pose a security risk and have no possibilities to work there efficiently. And still, Officer Flén received an excellent evaluation of her service and reported being needed several times when, for example, approaching local Afghan women (Flén 2010).

Following Finland's SCR 1325 National Action Plan, the discourse has begun to shift slowly. It seems that in a Finnish context, establishing an action plan helped to set in motion analyses of international military operations from a wider gender perspective, inducing the imaginations to go beyond gendered stereotypes of masculine-military agency, on the one side, and feminine-civilian victimhood on the other. In a report produced by the military in May 2009 and signed by Commander-in-Chief Puheloinen, there is mentioning of the Nordic SCR 1325 Military Observation Team in Afghanistan in quite derogatory ways. However, already in 2010, the same commander-in-chief, in the regional newspaper called *Aamulehti*, called for more women to serve in Afghanistan (Pääesikunta 2009; Aamulehti 2010).

IS THERE AN HONORABLE PROTECTOR?

The postbellum acts of international peacekeepers in contemporary conflicts are often in contrast with the noble principles of Just War. For instance the UN fact-finding mission on the Gaza conflict in 2009, after investigating

36 incidents that took place during the period 27 December 2008 until 18 January 2009, found that both Israeli forces and Palestinian militants committed war crimes and breaches of humanitarian law and that the justification of their acts were questionable (Human Rights Council 2009). Likewise, the so-called traditional wars have also compromised the principles of Just War. Alexander B. Downes claims that democratic states are the ones who have most often killed noncombatants (people not carrying or using weapons) during interstate wars and this does not even consider collateral damage suffered by civilians when military targets are destroyed (Downes 2007). In Iraq and Afghanistan more civilian than combatant deaths have been reported (Sjoberg 2006a).

The operational safety of expensively equipped combatants has always been a priority in modern wars; safety of the locals—whether civilian or soldiers—have come in second place. Soldiers move between safe clusters, confinement areas, under armed escort. The description of the situation by Corporal Jani Heikka, a duty officer in the Afghanistan Provincial Reconstruction Team (PRT) is very illustrative. When in Afghanistan, Corporal Heikka never visited any place that was not behind camp walls or barbed wires, but for the purpose of vacation. Heikka described a typical scenario of everyday life during the mission: 'I can see the misery outside through the tiny windows of the *Pasi* [nickname of the armored vehicle] but have no particular longing to get any closer' (Tuominen 2008: 6). Ironically this, however, collides with the fact that PRT groups should be 'detachments of civilian and military workers whose task is to assist Afghan Government officials to enable safe environment for the humanitarian aid and reconstruction' (ibid.). In peacekeeping, peace (truce, formal peace agreement) may have an intrinsic value at the expense of monitoring human rights. In military interventions, victory itself can be more important than preventing civilian casualties (Marlies and Kaldor 2005). Now when civil society works more and more as a battlefield, the fundamental justifying principle of Finnish defense or international crisis management, the protection of civilians, becomes less and less plausible (Downes 2007; Eck and Hultman 2007).

The honorability of the military subjectivity also deserves a closer look. Today's combat forces and their auxiliary services are more often formed by private companies, which work on a commercial base, literally for the money (Scahilla 2007), rather than in the name of masculine honor for the protection of innocent civilians, women and children. Interestingly, the privatized militaries have been called in gendered terms: 'whores of war' (Pitzke 2007). The same label is oftentimes given to militant women involved in violent actions. Women in military or paramilitary forces are criticized for behavior outside the limits of traditional gender roles, and the language of the critique is sexualized. Either they are viewed as bad women because they sleep with men, or if they do not sleep with men, they are labeled lesbians and therefore also bad women (see Sjoberg and Gentry 2007: 7). Interestingly, the shaming involved here is hitting on both female combatants as well as private military companies; they are feminized, sexualized and made to feel shame. It is a classic disciplinary measure of somebody who is seen to deviate from the normal and acceptable—in this case in the area of military/war practices. Finnish women who have served in international military operations have reported the same kind of pejoratively sexualized language. They too are put into two categories: whore or lesbian (Jukarainen and Terävä 2010).

WHAT IF THE HONORABLE PROTECTOR IS RETURNED IN A COFFIN?

As we have seen, Finnish peacekeeping operations are often seen as reservists' training grounds, as military refresher courses abroad or as authentic training fields with the purpose of ameliorating Finland's national defense. Behind the rhetoric is—in terms of Just War principles—that the to-be-protected civilians are the ones staying at home waiting for the 'refreshers' or 'international trainees' to return home honorably. Needless to say, not all Finns are ready to silently accept this outlook and are doubtful regarding the utility of sending soldiers to violent conflicts elsewhere. In Finland, people who express such feelings of doubt have been blamed to be victims of the so-called 'zinc coffin syndrome.' This is a condition whereby they are considered gutless and irresponsible. Major General Paavo Kiljunen (2006) described the concept 'zinc coffin syndrome' as not being able to handle defeat, and he had found it in political as well as in the general public discourse. In the weekly periodical *Suomen kuvalehti,* a military officer stated that: 'Our Parliament has zinc coffin syndrome–an absolutely paranoid fear of losses' (Lindholm 2008: 50). The message is that we must be prepared to accept the return of combatants in coffins, which would be a sign of national heroism and not a national disease. It must be tolerated that Finns sacrifice themselves for the nation also outside the territory. Crisis management is described as national defense extended to transnational space. The use of the concept 'zinc coffin syndrome' in the debate indicates that military activities abroad are framed as having both national legitimacy and binding force, irrespective of the risks and losses involved.

Also in Canada there have been critical discussions about the continuation of NATO operations in Afghanistan, where Canada has sent around 2,500 soldiers. Since 2002, 83 Canadian combatants have lost their lives on duty. The Canadian Broadcasting Company (CBC), publicized on the Internet basic information on all; their name, age, military ranks and units, portraits of them dressed in uniform, the time and exact geographical location where they died. There is no additional private information; the information given has the purpose of being the military's public tribute to a fallen soldier who fought for the nation. The cartographic location of death reconstructs and extends the nation onto an otherwise foreign territory.

The corpse of the fallen soldier marks symbolically the incorporation of this faraway land into the national security space. As if echoing this, in his memorial speech for a Finnish peacekeeper killed in Afghanistan in 2007, Senior Chaplain Aurén said:

> When Petri Immonen returned from vacation back in Finland to the Maimana military base, he sent an SMS to his peacekeeper comrades where he said, maybe a bit humorously [...] 'Finally I returned home.' [...] Within a few weeks he had gotten so acquainted with his new duty in Afghanistan, he had adapted and placed himself at work in foreign conditions in such a way, that one can say, he was there like at home. [...] Now today and at this moment returning home means that [...] we bring the deceased peacekeeper brother to the homeland of Finland, [...] to be buried into the earth of the Fatherland. [...] We only keep asking, why do some of the best men move into eternity so sudden and all too soon?[5]

Similar to the publicizing of the death reports in Canada, this publicized memorial speech is part of the process of (re)creating a national narrative anew, of men defending the home country far away from home. The death of a soldier is constructed foremost as a national sorrow and *home* means the nation, not the family. International Relations (IR) scholar Laura Sjoberg's work (2006b: 907) suggests a way out of this gender and war straitjacket, where traditional gender constructions are making humankind constantly re-create wars: 'In a world where men did not have to prove their masculinity by fighting wars to protect women, the global political arena might look increasingly peaceful rather than increasingly bellicose.' Sjoberg's ideal—albeit utopian—world would be the one, where the real effects of the physical and structural violence of war to all people (not only civilians) would get more attention than the heroic narratives of justified wars with their gendered immunity principles.

PROBLEMS OF MASCULINE PROTECTION

Today, Finland's partaking in international peacekeeping missions is no longer as self-evidently honorable and heroic as it perhaps once was. Now, the process of winning the 'hearts and minds' of the civilians through peace building measures, both in the conflict zones and at home, is more uncertain. The main problem appears to be that wars emanate out of, and gain magnitude from, situations of states' structures collapsing. Thus the wars are asymmetric; there are no clear national opponents. The new wars are postmodern, privatized and virtual (Kaldor 2006). In fact the deepest problem of the Just War principle lies in its close framing with territorial nation-states. John Williams asks aptly: 'Can one be a "combatant" in the name of transnational political project that cannot be accommodated within the dominant contemporary geographical framework, and can one claim the authority of acting in the name of the leaders of such a project?' (2008: 598). But there remains always the difficult question of the justice, duty and morale of the military. Critical academics like geographer Derek Gregory (2004) claim that justification of military interventions is done in order to conquer the other; Afghanistan, Palestine and Iraq have become cultural others, the barbaric and the uncivilized ones, who are taught and disciplined by military means. And yet, in other places like Rwanda, civilians were left to fend for themselves in the midst of genocide. In Juha-Antero Puistola's words: 'the price of a foreign peace may be too high in the home country. For the voters peacekeeping must often be marketed with humanitarian reasons' (2008: 49–50).

The second problem is that militaries in peacekeeping missions 'remain, in some respects, refugees of traditional concepts of masculinity' (Dittmer and Apelt 2008: 70). Until recently, female peacekeepers in Finland were seen as a liability and a security risk instead of as a valued human resource. Cordula Dittmer and Maja Apelt report a similar attitude among Germans in the Afghanistan ISAF operation. Female soldiers have been protected against the cultural and religious 'other,' the Afghan and 'Islamic' male (Dittmer and Apelt 2008: 73). Thus, paradoxically, Finnish peacekeeping efforts contribute to the strengthening of a traditional male security subjectivity as they reproduce the same deplorable patriarchal gender regime that was used in the rhetoric to morally justify the launching of the military intervention in the first place.

In the Finnish case the equality of the conscription system should be put under clear scrutiny. Every year around 70 percent of Finland's young men do the military service. In public opinion polls, the general all-male conscription enjoys high, although somewhat declining, support among citizens. According to the recent 2010 survey of the Advisory Board for Defense Information (ABDI), 60 percent of the Finns supported retaining the general conscription for men (since 2009 the number in support of conscription was as high as 70 percent).[6] In a recent national youth survey, *Nuorisobarometri 2010*, 40 percent of all 15- to 29-year-old respondents considered male, as opposed to male *and* female, conscription to be unequal (Jukarainen 2010). Clare Snyder (1999) sees that the ideal of the manly citizen-soldier contains a problematic interconnection between gender, military service and citizenship. Men's engagement in civic and martial practices constitutes them as masculine republican citizens. Simultaneously, women's exclusion from the same practices contributes to the dominant construction of femininity: Women traditionally engage in practices constitutive of 'republican mothers' rather than citizen-soldiers (cf. Stiehm 1982; Elshtain 1995). According to Snyder, the citizen-soldier tradition—in all its chauvinism and totalizing conformity creating aspects—is particularly problematic when it is linked to national identity building. When civic identity is produced through military service it makes nationalistic military conquests more likely because it forces people to identify themselves as a member of one people or a nation in opposition to an 'enemy' against whom one wages war (Snyder 1999: 2–9).

Kari Laitinen has analyzed the reasons behind this strong belief in the conscription system in a Finnish context. Two main arguments are common. First, there is the idea of needing a large reserve army to be capable of defending the large territory of the country with its geopolitically difficult position next to (former Soviet) Russia. Here, the horrible war memories of the Winter War (1939–1940), which was fought successfully, on the Finnish part, along the massively long border of 1,300 kilometers/807 miles, makes the utility of being able to quickly mobilize a big army clear to all. Second, conscription has been seen as equalizing men with different social status; after the bloody civil war following Finland's declaration of independence, the army constituted in practicality an educational institution, which helped to taper bitterness and confrontation (Laitinen 2006). Heroic historical narratives of the 'boys next door' waging war together are still common in the popular media, literature and films. In other words, conscription is viewed as a guarantor of universality; of maintaining an all-male will to defend the nation, thereby also creating a bond between all ordinary men. Torunn Haaland describes a similar kind of friendly civilian warrior image in a Norwegian peacekeeping context (see Haaland, this volume).

Finland's national defense and its international military operations alike are based on Just War thinking with gendered protector/protected categories in the image of the honorable male protector and the weak female protected. Conscription is the major institution behind the gender imbalance and gendered division of labor when it comes to security. The Finnish model resembles the Machiavellian soldiering-citizenship, where practices of the civic militia are related to a virtuous man-citizen. In the case of Finland, there are in fact several thousands of women reservists (volunteers); however, women's share among soldiers and peacekeepers is still marginal. In the political discourse military women have been considered to pose a security risk in patriarchal conflict environments in faraway lands. We might ask ourselves, to what extent is Finnish peacekeeping actually contributing to the resurrection of male dominance and the legitimization of an all-male military institution? All this can be seen as problematic considering the need of gender-sensitive peace building in contemporary conflicts. Finland has committed itself to implement SCR 1325, something that also involves increasing the number of female peacekeepers and gaining an understanding of how security is gendered. Without a thorough gender analysis and reform of the national security sector this implementation stands to fail. Traditionally gendered Just War theoretical reasoning has lost its applicability.

NOTES

1. Refresher courses are lawfully binding (based on the Conscription Act 1438/2007). Courses aim to train and maintain reservists' preparedness and combat readiness. Courses can take up to 100 days for commissioned officers, up to 75 days for noncommissioned officers and special trained crews and up to 40 days for the other crew.
2. Conscription Act 28 December 2007/1438.
3. The Finnish Armed Forces Act 11 May 2007/551.
4. The same honorary march serves as the ceremonial march for the president of the republic of Finland.
5. Aurén (2007).
6. ABDI (2009).

Theme III
Institutional Practices and Traveling Concepts

8 Analyzing UN and NATO Responses to Sexual Misconduct in Peacekeeping Operations

Laura Hebert

Hundreds of allegations of sexual exploitation and abuse have been brought against UN peacekeepers over the past five years, tarnishing the organization's reputation and placing the operational effectiveness of its peacekeeping missions at risk. In contrast to the UN, NATO has been praised in recent years for the absence of sex abuse allegations against its personnel and for its leadership role in instituting policies to prevent human trafficking. NATO officials, however, have tended to underplay the legacy of NATO complicity in fueling the problem of sex trafficking in the Balkans and have overstated the extent to which its policies represent a departure from anti-misconduct measures put into place by the UN.

A flurry of 'gender mainstreaming' reforms have been undertaken by both the UN and NATO in the wake of the adoption of SCR 1325 on Women, Peace and Security,[1] which affirms the urgent need to address gender-specific harms endemic to war-torn societies and to incorporate a gender perspective in all stages of peacekeeping operations. Following on 1325, Security Council Resolution 1820 calls specific attention to the problem of sexual violence in armed conflict, and sets out the obligations of combatants and other parties to conflicts, including international peacekeeping and humanitarian personnel, to take all necessary measures to prevent sexual violence, protect civilian populations from all forms of sexual violence and ensure accountability for perpetrators.[2] UN and NATO reforms that build on these resolutions may be interpreted as signifying the consolidation of the transnational norm of 'gender justice' that recognizes women as equal citizens entitled to full respect of their human rights—a norm that the UN has played a pivotal role in diffusing. In this chapter, building on a feminist constructivist perspective, I instead argue that a comparative analysis of UN and NATO responses to sexual misconduct committed by peacekeeping personnel reveals the uniformly shallow approach to gender that informs these organizations' policies and practices. Irrespective of the advances that have been made globally in legitimizing the norm of gender justice, the gender-related policies instituted by UN and NATO officials have primarily served to mollify member concerns about the effects of misconduct allegations on the reputation and operational effectiveness of the organizations, while the gender hierarchy that perpetuates gendered relations of exploitation and violence has remained untouched.

GENDER AND SECURITY: COMPARING THE UN AND NATO

The UN and NATO share the core objective of defusing security threats, though the strategies they employed to fulfill this objective differed significantly in the decades following their creation. As a collective security organization, the UN's purpose was to build peaceful relationships among member states through instituting laws and standards governing international relations, promoting development and establishing dispute resolution mechanisms. Although Chapter VII of the UN Charter allows for the use of force to respond to breaches of peace, Cold War rivalries weakened the enforcement powers of the UN and set the organization on a path of a near exclusive reliance on noncoercive measures, with the deployment of peacekeepers to conflict zones evolving as a way for the UN to remain a relevant actor in maintaining international peace (Karns and Mingst 2004: 306). The first operations authorized in the 1940s and 1950s established the parameters of UN peacekeeping, including the requirement that missions have the consent of the parties to the conflict, that operations be governed by the principle of neutrality and that peacekeepers be unarmed or lightly armed and authorized to use force only in self-defense (Gareis and Varwick 2005: 100–101). As a consequence of these rules of engagement, peacekeeping has long been considered a 'soft power' form of military intervention, removed from the combat function soldiers are trained to fulfill.

In contrast to the collective security orientation of the UN, NATO is a collective defense organization originally formed to deter a Soviet nuclear attack against America's European allies. Technological innovation and the nature of the US–Soviet standoff diminished the prospect that retaliation against a Soviet attack would take the form of traditional infantry combat, historically the arena in which idealized masculinity is put to the test. As articulated by Liora Sion, infantry combat is perceived by soldiers as 'the only "real" military service, real in the sense of doing a physical and dirty job that involves direct confrontation with enemy and therefore with danger' (2006: 460) Nonetheless, it is difficult to imagine a more 'hard power' military environment than one centered on the threat of massive nuclear warfare.

In the post–Cold War era, both the UN and NATO have adapted to shifts in the nature of security threats in order to remain relevant. For the UN, it has adapted in part through progressively expanding the complexity of its operations and the mandate granted to peacekeepers. As the Chapter VII missions deployed to the Democratic Republic of the Congo (DRC) and Darfur illustrate, peacekeepers may be authorized to use all means necessary to ensure the implementation of peace agreements and the protection of civilians and mission personnel. At the same time, UN peacekeepers increasingly perform nonmilitary tasks, including the delivery of humanitarian aid and post-conflict reconstruction. UN peacekeepers therefore confront contradictory developments: an increased danger associated with the move towards more 'hard power' combat situations and the stretching of peacekeeping to encompass more 'soft power' tasks—leaving the image of UN peacekeeping more muddled than ever.

Following the end of the Cold War, NATO struggled to reestablish an identity and mission in the absence of a Soviet threat. In the 1990s, NATO's key function appeared to be picking up the slack for a European Union ill equipped to accept responsibility for regional security. But NATO missions in Bosnia-Herzegovina and Kosovo served to reinvigorate the organization and transformed how its members interpret their security objectives. The 9/11 terrorist attacks gave further impetus to institutional restructuring and expanded its role in the management of conflict crises. NATO's leadership of the International Security Assistance Force (ISAF) in Afghanistan signals its entrance into territory more familiar to the United Nations. Although NATO forces are operating in a violent, uncertain environment that frequently demands use of force, ISAF's reconstruction activities signal a dramatic departure from the institution that existed at the time of the Warsaw Pact. For an organization created to respond to the threat of nuclear attack, the arguable softening of its operations has triggered a debate among military analysts about whether it is truly possible for soldiers to be both peacekeepers and warriors (Nash and Hillen 2001).

For both organizations, geopolitical changes have created openings for the reconstitution of gender arrangements in relation to personnel decisions and military operations. Nonetheless, a review of UN and NATO responses to the problem of peacekeeper misconduct reveals that a superficial approach to gender has prevailed. Even in efforts to promote gender mainstreaming to improve operational effectiveness, 'gender' is reduced to 'women' and policies remain informed by stereotypical expectations of the role of men and women in conflict situations.

UN PEACEKEEPING AND SEXUAL MISCONDUCT

In May of 2004, a report on the DRC, titled 'Sex and Death in the Heart of Africa,' appeared in the British newspaper *The Independent* (Holt and Hughes 2004). The article was striking not for its coverage of the rapes that are routinely perpetrated by combatants, but rather for its revelations of sexual violence and exploitation by peacekeepers serving with the UN Mission in the Democratic Republic of the Congo (MONUC). Of more than 30 girls in a camp for internally displaced persons in Bunia interviewed for the article, half admitted to having sexual relations with peacekeepers in exchange for food. A follow-up article offered more specific details of the forms of abuses allegedly perpetrated by peacekeepers in the DRC, including the operation of a child prostitution ring at the MONUC airport in Bunia, the rape of minors by Nepalese and Uruguayan peacekeepers and child pornography and sex shows organized by Moroccan soldiers in Kinsangani (Holt 2004).

The Independent articles were far from the first media reports alleging misconduct by UN peacekeepers. Complaints of child prostitution and sexual harassment against local women surfaced during the 1992–1993 UN mission in Cambodia (UNTAC).[3] The UN has long battled accusations that peacekeepers serving with the UN Protection Force (1992–1995) and the UN Mission in Bosnia and Herzegovina (1995–2002) fueled prostitution and sex trafficking in the former Yugoslavia (Hranjski 1994; Thompson and Ferguson 1997). And claims of sexual impropriety, from the solicitation of prostitutes to gang rape, were brought against UN peacekeeping personnel in nearly every mission deployed between 1992 and 2004, including in Somalia, Mozambique, Haiti, Sierra Leone, Kosovo and East Timor. Most of these allegations were denied by the UN, actively suppressed[4] or dismissed as 'isolated events' involving a 'few bad apples' (Roth 2005).

A change in attitude among UN officials began to occur in 2001 when a preliminary report by the UN High Commissioner for Refugees (UNHCR) and Save the Children Fund UK revealed that children in refugee camps in Liberia, Guinea and Sierra Leone had been sexually abused by aid workers and UN peacekeeping personnel (UNHCR 2002). Shortly thereafter, the UN established the Inter-Agency Standing Committee Task Force on Protection from Sexual Exploitation and Abuse in Humanitarian Crises, mandated to institute guidelines for eliminating sexual abuse and exploitation by UN personnel and improve the well-being of women and children living under conditions of conflict and humanitarian crisis (UN 2002). This was followed by the Secretary-General's decision in October 2003 to issue a bulletin on 'Special Measures for Protection from Sexual Exploitation and Sexual Abuse,' which clarified the specific acts comprising serious misconduct for UN staff and called on non-UN entities and individuals cooperating with the UN to adhere to proper standards of behavior (UN 2003b).

These measures indicate the UN's acknowledgment of the abuses occurring within its peacekeeping operations. Rather than taking immediate action to prevent abuses or hold perpetrators accountable, UN officials focused instead on preempting the damaging effects of future allegations of impropriety. Following the release of the UNHCR/Save the Children report, the Department of Peacekeeping Operations (DPKO) drafted public information guidelines instructing field personnel to underscore to the media the UN's determination to eliminate sexual misconduct in its missions. According to the guidelines, UN personnel are to emphasize the UN's zero-tolerance policy, identify the steps undertaken by the UN to prevent or respond to cases of misconduct and highlight the need to accurately report the facts and dispel rumors. Mission personnel are cautioned that '[e]ven if the number of actual incidents is small, the negative publicity these cases generate tarnishes the image of the United Nations in general and of peacekeeping in particular' (UN 2003a).

Irrespective of its preemptive efforts, UN officials were caught off guard by the media offensive in 2004 that exposed the disjuncture between the gender justice norm being promoted by the UN and the practices of those serving as its agents of peace and security. Over time, the UN leadership has come to recognize that sexual misconduct is by no means unique to MONUC, as indicated by Secretary-General Annan's decision in July 2004 to appoint the Jordanian Ambassador to the UN, Prince Zeid Ra'ad Zeid Al-Hussein, as his adviser to address sexual exploitation and abuse throughout UN peacekeeping missions. In his 2005 report to the UN, Zeid singled out UN rules and norms that have exacerbated the problem, including the privileges and immunities accorded to different categories of peacekeeping personnel; the absence of guarantees from troop-contributing countries that allegations of misconduct will be pursued through national mechanisms; the weak accountability of mission leaders for the personnel under their authority; and the underrepresentation of females in peacekeeping operations (UN 2005). A number of policy changes have since been instituted by the UN, including the establishment of a Conduct and Discipline Team in the DPKO in November 2005 responsible for overseeing cases of misconduct and the deployment of gender advisers to field missions. Renewed attention has also been given to predeployment and in-mission training on gender issues.[5]

For its peacekeepers to be responsible for perpetrating gender-based abuses clearly undermines the UN's role as a global standard setter in the advancement of women's human rights. The UN has therefore tried to compensate for its historically slow response to peacekeeper misconduct through drafting new policies and creating new committees, permanent bodies and 'point' individuals in order to quell doubts about its commitment to eradicating sexual misconduct. Nonetheless, military and civilian staff continue to be ill informed about the UN's zero-tolerance policy, internal reports confirm that some mission managers have failed to create an environment intolerant of misconduct and the UN has had negligible success in convincing troop contributing countries to investigate and discipline peacekeepers accused of misconduct (R. Murphy 2006: 536; Stecklow and Lauria 2010; UN 2010: 13–18). Moreover, it is perhaps indicative of the UN's organizational culture, in which personnel tend to blunt information that reflects negatively on the institution, that both increases *and* reductions in allegations have been interpreted by the UN as a sign of the success of its efforts. In the Secretary-General's May 2006 report on the status of investigations into sexual misconduct, the substantial increase in allegations in 2005 compared to 2004 was attributed to 'greater awareness and use of reporting mechanisms' (UN 2006). In a later press release, the

UN attributes the fall in allegations against mission personnel in Liberia to 'its progress in its preventive efforts and the establishment of its Conduct and Discipline Unit' (UN 2007b). Whichever way the statistics fall, it is apparently a win-win situation for the UN.

NATO AS A MODEL FOR THE UN?

While the fallout from the DRC scandal continues to cast a shadow over UN peacekeeping operations, NATO has been commended in recent years for its 'aggressive' and 'proactive' response to the problem of sex trafficking in zones of conflict (Allred 2006; Office to Monitor and Combat Trafficking in Persons 2007). Human trafficking has been framed by NATO officials as a social problem that exacerbates insecurity and undermines the effectiveness of NATO operations (NATO 2004b). Under the leadership of the United States and Norway, and influenced by developments surrounding the adoption of the UN Convention against Transnational Organized Crime (UN TOC) (UN 2000b) and its protocol relating to trafficking in persons (UN 2000a), NATO initiated consultations with troop contributing countries and anti-trafficking organizations in the fall of 2003, which culminated in the institution of a zero-tolerance policy on human trafficking during the meeting of NATO Heads of State and Government in Istanbul in June 2004. The policy specifically calls on NATO allies to (a) report their progress in fulfilling the anti-trafficking standards established under the UN TOC and the trafficking protocol; (b) ensure that personnel participating in NATO operations have received training on the nature of trafficking, its human rights and security implications and their obligation to refrain from engaging in or facilitating human trafficking; (c) provide support 'within their competence and respective mandates' to aid host countries in combating human trafficking; (d) establish provisions explicitly prohibiting contractors from engaging in or facilitating human trafficking; and (e) periodically review the implementation of anti-trafficking efforts (NATO 2004a). NATO supporters acknowledge that this policy leaves vague important definitional questions (Allred 2006: 15). Nonetheless, NATO's efforts have been characterized as 'very comprehensive' and 'efficient,' and an example for the UN to follow (NATO 2004b). As argued by Keith Allred, '[w]ith American and NATO troops severely limited from engaging in any conduct that facilitates human trafficking in areas where they deploy, there is hope that the demand for trafficked women will begin to dry up in those areas. There is no reason that UN peacekeepers cannot use the same techniques in areas where they deploy' (2006: 17).

NATO's admission that the deployment of military operations is linked to sex trafficking and its subsequent imposition of a zero-tolerance policy are signs of the gradual diffusion of the norm of gender justice. But it is premature to be congratulating NATO for the progressiveness of its gender-related policies. Even when condemning the link between soldiering and trafficking, the organization has managed to distance itself from its role in the rise of trafficking in Bosnia-Herzegovina and Kosovo. As human rights experts have documented, it was only following the deployments of UN and NATO missions in the 1990s that the Balkans became a major destination for trafficked women from Eastern Europe, with international personnel generating a demand for sexual labor that has greatly profited transnational criminal networks over the past decade (Godec 2010; Mendelson 2005). Nonetheless, NATO leaders tend to stress that NATO is not alone in having contributed to trafficking and minimize the complicity of their personnel. As remarked by Nicholas Burns, US Ambassador to NATO, 'all of us as member states will do everything in our power to make sure that our soldiers, *unwittingly, to a very great extent*, have nothing to do with this problem' (NATO 2004b; emphasis added).

Three additional issues undermine NATO's anti-trafficking policy. First, its substantive impact remains unclear, in part because NATO has taken a hard line against trafficking while approaching prostitution as a matter of national discretion. In conflict environments, high levels of criminality and poverty are associated with a rise in coercive means used to procure prostitutes and decreased opportunities for women to engage in nonsexual economically productive labor. For NATO personnel to be allowed to patronize prostitutes in such an environment runs a high risk of the organization being associated with trafficking; it also reinforces the association between military masculinities and sexual access and 'success,' exacerbating the gender stereotyping of both males and females.

Second, although NATO created the position of Senior Coordinator on Combating Trafficking in Human Beings in 2007, the first two individuals who served in this capacity—John Colston and Jiri Sedivy—simultaneously served as the Assistant Secretary-General (ASG) for Defense Policy and Planning, in which they held responsibility for informing NATO policies on urgent issues that have nothing to do with trafficking, such as terrorism and weapons of mass destruction (NATO 2007a). Not unexpectedly, the senior coordinator hasn't as much as made a public statement on NATO's trafficking policy since 2008. With Hüseyin Diriöz's replacement of Sedivy as ASG in 2010, it is unclear whether the position of senior coordinator remains active. NATO's failure to establish a dedicated oversight body on trafficking raises significant questions about the organization's commitment to the policy's implementation.

Third, supporters of the policy have ignored the narrow focus of NATO's engagement with the problem of personnel misconduct. As demonstrated in UN missions, sexual misconduct takes varied forms, including not only involvement in trafficking, but also rape, sexual harassment and using the promise of food or a job to solicit sex. NATO personnel are increasingly performing duties that bring them into daily contact with local communities, presenting the same challenges faced by UN personnel. NATO officials may not yet have come under fire for allegations of misconduct beyond trafficking, but it is unclear whether this is because of the strength of its policies or because issues concerning women and gender are so thoroughly marginalized within the institution.

As with the UN, strong rhetoric by NATO's leaders has not translated into strong action. Officials from both organizations have been quick to underscore the limited options that are available to punish peacekeeper misconduct, since the ultimate responsibility rests with troop contributing countries to pursue criminal sanctions against their nationals (UN 2003a; NATO 2004b). Even if internal investigations conclude that a peacekeeper has engaged in serious misconduct, the only punitive measure available to the UN and NATO is to repatriate the individual. If a state chooses not to pursue investigations or prosecutions, or chooses not to disclose how it handled the allegations, officials have little recourse. Neither institution has proven willing to refuse troop contributions from countries whose soldiers have committed misconduct or to exert pressure on states to pursue prosecutions. Instead, state confidentiality is upheld, making it nearly impossible for outside observers to track allegations or assess the effectiveness of efforts to reduce incidence rates.

This is more than a simple case of the UN and NATO deferring to the will of member states. As I argue in the following section, policies aimed at preventing peacekeeper sexual misconduct will inevitably remain reactive as long as a 'thin' approach to gender mainstreaming prevails. Yet for these organizations to adopt a deeper approach to gender mainstreaming disturbs traditional gender norms that inform and are informed by the long-standing privileging of militarized sovereign states in the international system, generating considerable resistance among those who have a stake in the maintenance of the (gendered) status quo.

GENDER MAINSTREAMING AND THE THREAT OF FEMINIZATION

International women's mechanisms such as the Convention on the Elimination of All Forms of Discrimination Against Women (UN 1979) and the Beijing Declaration and Platform for Action (UN 1996) acknowledge that realizing women's *lived* equality requires challenging the gender norms that perpetuate the power of men over women and legitimize violence against women. This requires implementing strategies that interrogate the relational construction of femininities and masculinities, expose the processes behind sociocultural tolerance of male exploitation and abuse of females and engage males and females alike in resisting and transforming harmful gender norms. The concept of gender mainstreaming, which speaks to each of these objectives, is ubiquitous in UN documents, speeches and programs. As defined by the UN Economic and Social Council (ECOSOC), gender mainstreaming refers to:

> the process of assessing the implications for women and men of any planned action, including legislation, policies or programs in all areas and at all levels. It is a strategy for making the concerns and experiences of women and men an integral dimension of the design, implementation, monitoring and evaluation of policies and programs in all political, economic and societal spheres so that women and men benefit equally and inequality is not perpetuated. (UN 1997)

Secretary-General Ban Ki-moon has praised the UN's progress in raising the organization's commitment to gender mainstreaming, improving the monitoring of women's involvement in peace processes, and working with member states to institute gender machineries at the national level (UN 2007a). But the impression of activity in this area is contradicted by the informal, underresourced and uncoordinated nature of gender-related efforts within the UN, and persisting confusion over the meaning and purpose of gender mainstreaming (Nduka-Agwu 2009; Rao 2006).

ECOSOC's definition of gender mainstreaming builds on an understanding of gender as relational, learned and changeable. But this acknowledgment of the complexity of gender relations hasn't filtered into UN policies and programs, including in the peacekeeping arena. The 'Gender Resource Package for Peacekeeping Operations' put together by the UN to gender sensitize peacekeepers, for example, acknowledges that gender does not refer exclusively to either men or women, 'but to the relationship between them, and the way this is socially constructed' (UN 2004: 1). Moreover, it observes that men and women confront different social conditions and are socially positioned differently within particular societies, which shapes the expectations and circumstances they encounter in conflict and post-conflict environments. Yet, even when acknowledging the social construction of gender, the manual replicates the association of men as protectors, political actors, and agents and targets of combat violence; and women as reproducers, providers of household needs, and victims of sexual assault and rape in non-combat settings (UN 2004: 2). The multifaceted processes underlying gender conformity and resistance are obscured. Furthermore, proposed solutions to gender inequality primarily take the form of adding women in to existing structures and environments, rather than transforming the structures and environments themselves.

A guiding assumption informing UN peacekeeping policies is that integrating women into existing structures will ultimately have a transformative effect. But as long as women are expected to conform to existing structures in order to be deemed acceptable and nonthreatening to operational effectiveness, these efforts will inevitably remain manifestations of changes *within* the gender hierarchy as opposed to changes *of* the gender hierarchy.

The latter requires sustained attention to the values, attitudes and behaviors that are at the root of gender-based harms. This is not possible unless male allies of gender mainstreaming are fully engaged as partners in resisting the gender status quo; for example, working toward dissolving the association between gender and the characteristics and roles within military systems that are most valued and devalued.

The measures prioritized by the UN to date to respond to sexual misconduct are indicative of an administrative, damage control approach that fails to address the need for structural changes. Imposing curfews and 'no-go' areas may limit opportunities for sexual exploitation and abuse, but these policies also take the occurrence of misconduct as inevitable—that is, they reflect an expectation that, if given an opportunity, soldiers *will* exploit. Such an approach infantilizes peacekeepers, perpetuates a monolithic approach to men and masculinity and reinforces the misconception that containment is equivalent to prevention. Induction training offers an opportunity to interrogate gender norms; but gender is not uniformly addressed across peacekeeping missions and, when addressed, the amount of time allocated is usually minimal, ranging from 30 minutes to two hours (Lyytikäinen 2007: 9). And instituting zero-tolerance policies and improving investigative procedures may be crucial for challenging the normalization of gender-based violence; but if mission leaders themselves hold gender-biased attitudes or choose to prioritize the reputation of soldiers under their command over the security of community members, changes in policies and procedures are meaningless.

NATO's approach to gender mainstreaming is just as superficial as that of the UN. In the early 1960s, senior female service officers from NATO countries began meeting to discuss how women could be more effectively integrated and utilized in NATO forces. Their efforts eventually led the Military Committee (MC), NATO's highest military authority, to establish a consultative committee in 1976 with the purpose of facilitating information sharing between NATO members on the representation of female military personnel and issues affecting women's ability to perform effectively in the armed forces (Garcia 1999). The Committee on Women in NATO Forces (CWINF) met formally only once a year, for a maximum of five working days (NATO 2007b: 8). Nonetheless, for 20 years it was the only body in the organization directly addressing women's roles and status. In 1997, the MC agreed to create the Office on Women in NATO Forces (OWINF), run by two staff members, in order to allow for greater continuity in NATO's support for the integration of women (Garcia 1999). The establishment of these bodies was the result of many years of hard work by women serving in NATO's armed forces. The CWINF and the OWINF, however, focused not on gender mainstreaming, but rather on the integration of women in NATO forces through increasing the representation of female military personnel, ensuring female military personnel enjoy the same personal and professional opportunities as their male colleagues, and improving the quality of life of female personnel.[6]

In May 2009, the MC made the decision to replace the CWINF with the NATO Committee on Gender Perspective, while the OWINF was renamed the NATO Office on Gender Perspective. According to the MC, these changes were made to support the organization's objective of integrating 'the gender perspective into all aspects of NATO operations,' in line with Security Council Resolutions 1325 and 1820 (NATO 2009). The responsibilities of these bodies now include facilitating information sharing on gender mainstreaming within NATO, among NATO members, and between NATO and other relevant international organizations and agencies; providing advice and support on gender mainstreaming to the MC; and gathering information on the progress of member states in implementing Security Council Resolutions 1325 and 1820 (NATO 2009). The changes made, however, appear to have greater symbolic than practical significance. Like the bodies they replaced, the NATO Committee on Gender Perspectives meets once annually for a maximum of five working days, while the NATO Office on Gender Perspectives is run by only two staff members, one of whom is an administrative assistant rather than a gender specialist. As with its anti-trafficking policy, the limited dedicated support the NATO leadership has directed to these gender mainstreaming bodies inevitably constrains their ability to have a substantive impact on NATO policies, planning priorities and operations.

From a feminist constructivist perspective, there is nothing surprising about the failure of the UN and NATO to go beyond a surface approach to gender mainstreaming in the security arena, even when these institutions (particularly the UN) position themselves as women's rights standard setters. Although IR scholars have made clear that states are not 'black boxes' that are uniform across time and place, common markers nonetheless distinguish states from other political entities, including their ability to harness the resources to wage war and preserve peace (Tilly 1990: 12). Prior to the mid-twentieth century, sovereign statehood was guaranteed only for those states that possessed the capacity to defend their sovereignty. Following World War II, however, sovereign statehood was granted to states through international recognition, whether or not they were fully capable in the modern sense (Jackson 1990). Since the period of decolonization, rapid militarization has occurred throughout the global South, attributable less to the practical urgency of state survival and more to global environmental processes and pressures that have come to define the symbols of legitimate statehood. Militaries, as described by Eyre and Suchman, 'no longer build modern nations, but rather, the world political and social system builds modern nation-states, which in turn build modern militaries and procure modern weaponry' (1996: 82). Military systems have not remained static. They have adapted to changing domestic and international environmental pressures and circumstances, including the shifting nature of security threats and technological developments that have altered strategic calculations and recruitment needs. But what largely remains unchanged is that military systems continue to function as 'muscular,' virile, masculine symbols of state power, irrespective of women's gradual integration into armed forces (Peterson 1992b: 48; 2010: 23–24). Thus, for organizations such as the UN and NATO that rely on member states for their military capacity, to take gender and gender mainstreaming into account is to threaten the military institutions that have been constructed as emblematic of sovereign statehood and substantive membership in the international society of states—a move inevitably resisted by their constituent states.

Even with the rise of robust Chapter VII missions, peacekeeping continues to be characterized as a softer form of military power, with contemporary operations mainly requiring soldiers to perform a peace support rather than combat role. Although peacekeeping forces may serve a function distinct from national military systems, peacekeeping is ultimately inseparable from traditional militaries. Given the human and financial constraints facing most military systems, creating and training peacekeeping forces detached from military contingents serving national security interests is not a feasible option (Dandeker and Gow 2004: 12). Even in countries where the threat of interstate war is remote, the priority is placed on preparing soldiers for the potential of combat situations and then 'training down' in order to 'cater to the needs of missions in which a more restrained use of force is appropriate' (Sorenson and Wood 2005: 11). Nonetheless, concerns persist among military leaders that the 'peacekeeping ethos' will filter into national military systems and erode combat capabilities (Boëne et al. 2004: 416). The failure of political and military leaders to take gender seriously in the security arena is thus neither the result of accidental oversight or lack of appreciation of the complexity of gender construction. Rather, attempts to penetrate military systems and culture in order to deepen the gender justice norm and prevent gendered exploitation continue to be frustrated by the fear of feminization—the fear at the heart of concerns that the peacekeeping ethos will taint national military systems. To expose the gender norms that inform (and are informed by) militarism is to exacerbate the perceived threat participation in peacekeeping missions poses to national military strength and preparedness.

The norm of gender justice has sufficiently penetrated the security arena such that it can't be ignored or overtly rejected, thus the recognition by the UN and NATO that their reputations and operational effectiveness are damaged by allegations of sexual misconduct. It can, however, be co-opted through the adoption of policies that invoke the appropriate language and give the impression of substantive change but that instead blunt its transformative potential. As long as the fundamental association between security threats, military capacity and the masculine soldier ideal persists, we can expect that gender mainstreaming will continue to take the form of integrating women into already-defined masculine structures and efforts to address peacekeeper sexual misconduct will remain palliative rather than preventive.

CONCLUSION

Given the mutually constitutive relationship between gender and military systems, to achieve the consolidation of the gender justice norm will require the disembedding of the entrenched gender norms that have informed dominant notions of security, dating back to the very origins of the modern system of states. To reduce security to the military capability of states to protect themselves from the (assumed-to-be-inevitable) organized violence of other states reifies the destructive human and technological capabilities of military systems as the logical, *natural* response to the dangers of human interaction. It also, by its very taken-for-grantedness and assumption of inevitability, informs the socialization of individuals into the gender roles, and the expected characteristics and capabilities associated with these roles, most suited to harnessing collective social resources against external security threats. Rather than alleviating potential dangers, however, the association of idealized masculinity with the ability and willingness to employ violence to ward off threats, and the association of idealized femininity with the reproduction of 'soldiers' and the 'home' in need of protection, serves to perpetuate these very threats. To expose the construction behind gender identities, to shatter as myth the monolithic masculine ideal behind interpretations of humans as intrinsically violent and egoistic, is to call into question the privileged social positioning of military systems as preservers of nationhood. But even the most optimistic of feminists among us remain enormously skeptical of the prospect of military systems being displaced from their privileged position across societies or of militaries of the future functioning as agents of social justice rather than agents of violence.

NOTES

1. S/RES/1325 of 31 October 2000.
2. S/RES/1820 of 19 June 2008.
3. According to Barbara Crossette of the *New York Times* (1996), Bulgarian peacekeepers serving with UNTAC earned such a poor reputation that locals commonly referred to them as 'Vulgarians.' In response to a letter sent by locals to the mission protesting against the inappropriate behavior of its peacekeepers, Yasushi Akashi, UNTAC's Special Representative to the Secretary General is widely quoted as having replied that 'boys will be boys.' See also Martin (2005) and Whitworth (2004).
4. For example, an investigator employed by DynCorp, a private American security company that handled the contracts of US officers working for the international police force in Bosnia, was fired for writing a report detailing

sexual abuses by UN peacekeepers (see McGrory 2002). A former UN human rights investigator also accused the UN of suppressing his inquiry into the role of Romanian, Fijian and Pakistani officers in enslaving Eastern European women in brothels in Bijeljina (see Lynch 2001).
5. The *Gender Resource Package for Peacekeeping Operations*, for example, is intended to institutionally clarify the meaning of gender and gender mainstreaming, reiterate the significance of adopting a gender perspective in peacekeeping operations, and offer peacekeeping personnel guidance in this area (UN 2004).
6. See the "Committee on Women in the NATO Forces" website at www.nato.int/issues/women_nato/index.html.

9 A Gendered Protection for the 'Victims' of War
Mainstreaming Gender in Refugee Protection

Jane Freedman

Media reports of widespread rape and sexual violence during recent conflicts (such as that in the Democratic Republic of Congo [DRC]) have brought public attention to the question of war and gendered violence. But less attention is often paid to the question of how to protect the victims of such violence, including those who are displaced or exiled as a result of conflict. The issues of gender-related persecution and violence against women have been put onto the international agenda, largely thanks to lobbying by feminist NGOs and transnational networks. In the Beijing Platform for Action, the section on women and armed conflict includes a strategic objective to provide protection and assistance to refugee women. There is a question, however, of how successfully this agenda setting has translated into effective policy-making and policies that will increase the protection of women who are displaced as a result of conflicts. For nearly twenty years, since the early 1990s, the United Nations' High Commissioner for Refugees (UNHCR) has identified 'refugee women' as a policy priority, and yet despite this prioritization of concerns with women refugees and gender issues in the asylum and refugee process, 'implementation continues to be slow and ad hoc' (Baines 2004: 1). This implementation failure can be attributed to the difficulty of transmission of the goals of gender-sensitivity through all of the various bureaus and representatives of a large bureaucratic organization such as the UNHCR, but also, and more importantly to an unwillingness of those within the organization to really engage with the gendered causes and effects of displacement and with the roots of violence suffered by refugee women. This chapter will examine the way in which the concept of gender has been adopted within the UNHCR and the processes that have been put in place to mainstream gender within refugee protection activities. As a traveling concept, the meaning of gender mainstreaming will change in each institutional setting, and the success of implementation will also be dependent on institutional characteristics (see the introduction to this volume). The path dependencies created by institutionalization of norms mean that it is often difficult to introduce a real change in thinking in these institutions, for example, in order to interrogate the construction of gendered identities and norms relating to war, peace and security. In this chapter we will consider the way in which this concept of gender mainstreaming has 'traveled' into the sphere of refugee protection. How far has the concept of gender mainstreaming really been integrated into refugee protection activities? And has this concept been modified as it has traveled into an international organization? How far has mainstreaming managed to move policies to protect women beyond a mere focus on vulnerable groups, and to integrate a gendered understanding of the global processes that produce refugees, and of the protection needs of these refugees? As other chapters in the book also show, we will argue that too often 'gender' in these circumstances is interpreted as meaning 'women,' and that this equation takes away the real power of gender mainstreaming as it was originally conceived by feminist activists.

PUTTING GENDER ON THE MAP OF REFUGEE PROTECTION

For a long time, any consideration of gender issues was absent from discourses on refugees. This absence relates in part to the circumstances surrounding the drafting and adopting of the 1951 Convention Relating to the Status of Refugees, which together with its 1967 protocol remains the major international convention regulating refugee protection (Freedman 2007). It can be argued that the 1951 convention, like other international human rights conventions, was written from a male perspective and that the situations of women were ignored. As Bunch maintains, 'the dominant definition of human rights and the mechanisms to enforce them in the world today are ones that pertain primarily to the types of violations that the men who first articulated the concept most feared' (1995: 13). Thus violations and persecutions pertinent primarily to women are often left out of the spectrum of those that are considered valid as reasons for granting refugee status.

The neglect of the issue of gender in the 1951 convention can be seen as an important factor leading to a failure to take into account the protection needs of women asylum seekers and refugees. Moreover, difficulties in mainstreaming gender in asylum and refugee policies and practices can still in part be attributed to this limited definition and understanding of who is a real 'refugee.' Gender was not put on the agenda of refugee protection in any meaningful sense until the 1980s (Hyndman 1998), on the basis of growing international pressure to take account of questions particular to women refugees and asylum seekers. In particular campaigning by transnational networks of women's organizations put pressure on the UNHCR to recognize the need to consider gender issues following growing public awareness of gender-based violence and persecutions against refugees. One of the first signs of the issues of gender in refugee crises becoming visible was during the massive forced migrations from Southeast Asia in the early 1980s. The plight of the boat people was reported worldwide, and particular attention was paid to the vulnerability of women on the boats, who were at risk of sexual violence and rape if the boats were attacked by pirates. At the same time, it became more and more difficult to ignore women refugees in other areas of the world, particularly because of the sheer numbers of women in refugee camps, and because of the practical questions relating to distribution of food and other aid. Models of aid distribution that took the household as a unit of analysis came under question. The number of women-headed households within these camps, for example, made models of resource distribution that targeted men with the idea that this would then be distributed to the rest of their household unworkable. Various issues like these gradually entered the international consciousness and coalesced to provide a focal point for the start of transnational activism in support of a more gender-aware approach to refugee issues, which gained momentum at the World Conference on Women in Nairobi in 1985. At the Nairobi conference, hundreds of representatives from refugee women's associations attended the parallel NGO forum. Following this conference an International Working Group for Refugee Women was set up, creating a network of national groups aiming to push the UNHCR to take action.

The UNHCR responded to this international pressure by appointing a Senior Coordinator for Refugee Women in 1989. Baines recounts that when the first woman to take up this post, Anne Howarth-Wiles, arrived in Geneva she had a rather cold welcome with few resources at her disposal and 'little enthusiasm amongst her co-workers' (2004: 44). In an interview with Baines, Howarth-Wiles describes her initial experiences:

> As soon as she arrived, it became obvious to her that most UNHCR staff were reluctant to embrace a gender perspective. Most believed that international refugee instruments and practices applied equally to men and women and were therefore non-discriminatory. A policy on refugee women was considered unnecessary. (Baines 2004: 45)

As argued in the following, interviews with UNHCR staff today indicate that although the organization has officially adopted gender mainstreaming, this belief that international refugee conventions and instruments are in fact nondiscriminatory and that there is no need for targeted action on gender is still present amongst some staff today.

Despite this initial reluctance to engage with issues of gender, the senior coordinator managed to impose a campaign involving the development of a policy on refugee women, together with training programs to raise awareness of the issues involved both inside and outside of the UNHCR. Initial policies and programs focused on women refugees, rather than on the relational issues of gender in refugee programs. This focus on women could be argued in some contexts to further marginalize women by targeting them as a separate group and so essentializing their difference and ignoring the relational aspects of gender that affect both women and men. By the end of the 1990s, the focus within the UNHCR was moving away from one that was specifically on women, and more towards gender-based policies and programs. This coincided with efforts to incorporate gender mainstreaming in all UN operations. Gender mainstreaming can be seen as a 'traveling concept' that has moved from its origins in feminist theorizing and activism into various institutional settings. However, these institutions construct and utilize the concept in differing ways. In the case of the UNHCR, research for this study suggests that the adoption of gender mainstreaming as an approach may paradoxically lead to gender slipping off the agenda, as it becomes dissolved within other concerns. Interviewees at UNHCR headquarters pointed to the fact that although mainstreaming could have advantages in that it should remind all UNHCR employees of the need to consider gender in all aspects of their work and not merely to relegate it to a separate 'women's issue,' in effect without the dedicated effort of an individual or group devoted to bringing gender issues to the forefront of policies and programs these issues might easily be ignored.[1] They argued that many of those employed within the organization still ignored questions relating to gender or women's rights and were sometimes reluctant to integrate these questions into their general work, feeling that they had more important priorities.[2] Thus although gender mainstreaming is an officially accepted target for the UNHCR, there is still a long way to go before this mainstreaming really becomes effective and is transformed in practice into equal protection for men and women asylum seekers and refugees. The difficulties involved in mainstreaming gender arise both from national and international responses to forced migration, including obstacles within the organization of the UNHCR and difficulties with the way in which gender is interpreted in the context of refugee protection.

REFUGEE WOMEN: AN 'UNKNOWN' ENTITY?

Two of the difficulties in adopting and implementing policies to ensure equal protection for men and women asylum seekers and refugees are the diversity of situations implied by forced migrations and the lack of accurate data on some refugee populations. In fact, the lack of accurate gender-disaggregated statistics on forced migrants has led some to overstate the proportion of women refugees in an attempt to draw greater attention to their situation. Oosterveld, for example, claims that: 'The faces of refugees are overwhelmingly female: women and children represent eighty percent of the world's twenty seven million refugees and displaced people' (1996: 570). This type of claim is used to try and reverse a previous invisibility of women in research and policy-making and to press for further national and international actions. However, a basic problem with these statistics is that they conflate 'women and children'[3] into one single category, thus obscuring even further the real nature of the statistical differences between men and women. The amalgamation of 'women and children' into one category of 'vulnerable' refugees is an important feature of the representations of women refugees in humanitarian actions, representations that can be argued to have major impacts on the way in which gender is treated in issues of refugee protection (Rajaram 2002). According to the UNHCR, women make up about one half of the total populations of concern to them (UNHCR 2007). Women are the majority in some refugee camps resulting from mass influx situations following wars and other conflict situations where men will be those principally engaged in fighting and women will be more likely to flee. Although, as Carpenter (2006) argues, the category of women and children should not be used interchangeably with that of civilians, as in contemporary wars many men are also civilians and women may also be combatants. On the other hand, women have historically been less represented amongst those seeking asylum in industrialized countries. Statistics that are available show that in Europe, for example, women make up only about one-third of the total asylum claimants (Bloch et al. 2000; Freedman 2007).

INTERNAL CONSTRAINTS ON GENDER MAINSTREAMING

Despite the UNHCR's adoption of gender mainstreaming, 'implementation continues to be slow and ad hoc' (Baines 2004: 1). As a traveling concept, the meaning of gender mainstreaming will change in each institutional setting, and the success of implementation will also be dependent on institutional characteristics. The seeming inability to put into practice much of the discourse on gender and women refugees must be seen in part as a result of internal difficulties and crises with the UNHCR's own organization. Unlike most of the other UN agencies, it is an agency which is dependent on donor funding, with up to ninety eight percent of funds coming directly from national governments (Väyrynen 2001). These funds are renewed annually, creating a particular dependence on donor states. This means that donor states can have a large degree of control over the UNHCR's agenda, and that in some cases the agency might be seen to prioritize these state's interests over those of asylum seekers and refugees (Crépeau 1995; Hammerstad 2000). These pressures from states have led to what some have argued is a change of direction from the UNHCR, moving from a function of protecting refugees to one of controlling them in the interests of donor states. In these conditions, the policies followed by UNHCR must resonate with the agenda's of its donors, and particular issues such as introducing gender mainstreaming may be pushed down the policy agenda of the organization in favor of more popular priorities.

In addition, Väyrynen (2001) highlights the problem of earmarking of UNHCR's funds, which has had notable impacts in relation to the comparative availability of funds for projects in Africa and in Eastern Europe, with African countries often falling to the bottom of the lists of priorities for donor states. These particular motives for distribution of funding may have impacts on UNHCR's ability to adequately fund activities and programs that aim at promoting gender equality or extending adequate protection to women refugees. This is both because many of the women who are most in need of protection find themselves in geographical regions that are not considered a priority by donor states and so do not receive much funding, or because gender equality programs that are seen as long-term investments with often intangible or only marginal results are not favored by the UNHCR staff who have to decide how the scarce budgets should be spent.

UNHCR must also be viewed as a huge bureaucracy[4] and one that holds tremendous discursive and institutional power over refugees. This power can be seen to take away possibilities of agency from refugees and displaced people, limiting their participation in any form of planning, implementation or management of operations (Baines 2004). This critique might be particularly relevant to operations designed to overcome gender inequalities, which are often designed and implemented without any input from women and men refugees themselves as to what their needs or desires might be, and that can be criticized for their framing of women merely in terms of their vulnerability. Although there are clearly staff in the UNHCR who are committed to mainstreaming, it could be argued that there are insufficient key individuals in positions of responsibility who are pushing for mainstreaming. Some UNCHR employees interviewed for this study pointed to the continued need to persuade and remind their colleagues (and in particular their male colleagues) of the needs for integrating a gendered approach into their work. They also highlighted the problem that in much of UNCHR's work in the field, and particular in situations of extreme conflict and crisis, the majority of the protection officers are male, and thus may not always be sensitive to gendered needs.[5] This lack of female staff, particularly in emergency situations and in dangerous areas, may be a result of the 'deep structures' of the organization that make little concession to the reconciliation of work and family, as Rao and Kelleher have shown for other organizations (Rao and Kelleher 2002).

Without wishing to advocate a position that implies that only women can be sensitive to gendered aspects of policy-making and implementation, it does seem that the balance of men and women working within an organization will have some impact on the way in which gender is considered, and that in the case of the UNHCR women are still underrepresented both at higher levels of the bureaucracy and in field operations.

WHAT PROGRESS IN GENDER MAINSTREAMING?

So what have been the substantial changes that have resulted from the UNHCR's attempts to take more account of specific needs of refugee women and to integrate and mainstream gender in its policy-making and activities in the last two decades? In 2001, the Women's Commission for Refugee Women and Children (WCRWC) carried out an assessment of the results of 10 years of implementation of the 1991 *Guidelines on the Protection of Refugee Women* (UNHCR 1991). This assessment concluded that the guidelines had succeeded in raising awareness among UNHCR staff and partners of women's specific needs and interests, but that overall the implementation of the guidelines was 'uneven and incomplete, occurring on an ad hoc basis in certain sites rather than in a globally consistent and systematic way' (WCRWC 2002: 2). The report cites barriers to implementation, including a lack of female UNHCR staff, which is a serious obstacle both to obtaining information from refugee women and to addressing the specific protection issues they face. It argues further that insufficient participation of refugee women themselves in decision-making is also a serious barrier to the full implementation of the guidelines (WCRWC 2002). A consultation exercise that the UNHCR organized with some refugee women came to similar conclusions that despite progress in some areas, women refugees often still lacked access to food and other basic resources, and that they were not adequately protected against sexual and gender-based violence. One issue raised was the continuing failure to provide refugee women with their own personal documentation, such as their own food ration cards. The distribution of these cards to male 'heads' of families led to particular problems because it increased women's dependency and thus the protection problems that they faced. In places such as Guinea, where individual ration cards were not provided, some refugee women and girls were forced to exchange sex for food. 'Most refugee women participants agreed that food would be distributed more evenly within families if ration cards were distributed to refugee women and they were equal partners in the development and implementation of food distribution strategies' (UNHCR 2001: 19). The consultation exercise criticized the way in which refugee women were often left out of camp-planning and decision-making processes. Women in Guinea, for example, 'felt they were left out of planning, designing, implementing and even evaluating programmes for refugee assistance' (UNHCR 2001: 26). This exclusion of women from planning and implementation was a contributing factor in lack of access to basic resources.

These criticisms of the implementation of UNHCR policies on refugee women and on gender are consistent with other analyses of UNHCR's actions, in particular refugee situations in which they intervene. Many of the criticisms stem from an underlying understanding and construction of the relationship between the refugee and the UNHCR/NGO bringing aid as one between helper and victim, with no possibility of collaboration as equals being envisaged. Relations of power that start off as highly unequal may be made even more so by the way in which aid is administered. In the context of management of refugee camps, for example, UNHCR and other aid agencies have been criticized for promoting unequal power relations between aid workers and refugees and for encouraging types of dependent behavior on the part of refugees (Harrell-Bond 2002; Hyndman 2000). It is argued that the nature of aid given out develops a patron–client relationship within which powerful and competent aid workers distribute aid to the 'helpless' refugees. Even the conditions in which refugees tell their stories and register their claims for protection with the UNHCR authorities in a camp can be seen as reinforcing power inequalities. Often they may be forced to wait hours in a queue in the sun before gaining access to a UNHCR official. And when they do get access to a UNHCR official to relate their stories, they are themselves frequently forced into a reaffirmation of their victim status. As Ratner (2005) comments, refugees often feel the need to tell stories about their own 'powerlessness' in order to gain certain advantages from UNHCR officials or from other aid agencies, benefits such as extra food rations, child support or even third country resettlement. This reappropriation of stories of powerlessness and victim status can be seen as a form of agency on the part of refugees who adapt their strategies for survival to the dominant representations created by those providing aid to them: 'The refugees have to tell stories of "powerlessness" to invest in their future and ironically, the disempowering experiences that got them in their hopeless situations in the first place, become a strategic tool for survival in the form of a utilitarian narrative that is far from a powerless act' (Ratner 2005: 19).

These unequal power relationships within which refugees are constructed as 'vulnerable' or 'helpless' victims may have particular resonance in the case of women refugees, reinforcing gendered constructions of women's powerlessness and lack of agency in certain societies. We will discuss in the following the way in which representations of refugee women have perpetuated particular understandings and constructions of the specificities of these women's situations, which may serve to essentialize women's experiences and to diminish the understanding of the differences in their positioning dependent on class, ethnicity, age and other factors. As with other refugees, however, women may in fact exercise a very particular kind of agency in reappropriating and mobilizing these representations for their own benefit. Thus the way in which they are treated as victims may be used to help their own personal survival strategies. In some camps, for example, women may actively use the stories of sexual violence which they have experienced as a pragmatic strategy for improving their own situation (Ratner 2005).

However, despite these possibilities of reappropriation of the discourse of 'victimization' to further personal survival strategies, the overall effect of the highly unequal relationships between UNHCR and refugees has been that of removing refugees from the decision-making and planning processes concerning the organization of their lives and their protection. This is in many cases particularly problematic for women as they are generally already positioned in a subordinate position with relation to these processes in their own societies, and so relationships with UNHCR and other aid agencies can act to reinforce local gender inequalities and mechanisms of domination. Further, important physical and material barriers may exist to women's participation in planning such as lack of childcare facilities to enable them to participate in meetings. Unless all of these factors are taken into consideration by UNHCR staff, then gender equality in any camp planning programs will remain illusory.

Another explanation for the difficulties in implementation of UNCHR's gender policies and programs in refugee camp situations is highlighted by Baines and Harrell-Bond, who point to the way in which goals of cultural sensitivity may undermine efforts to implement gender equality policies. Harrell-Bond points particularly to the way in which the aim of cultural sensitivity has led humanitarian agencies to encourage traditional methods of solving disputes within refugee camps. This method of favoring traditional methods of negotiation and arbitration can reinforce the power of those already dominant in any society or population and can give license to many kinds of oppression by the camp elders (Harrell-Bond 1999). As these elders are generally older men, their judgments may well reinforce unequal gender relations among refugee populations. Baines also points to the way in which resistance to gender equality policies within the UNHCR has sometimes stemmed from the ideal of universalism, which is used to deny the validity of treating women as a separate category. This type of recognition can be 'associated with privileging one group over another in a zero-sum game' (Baines 2004: 63). In parallel with this claim to universalism, however, exists a discourse that locates the roots of gender inequality and practices of domination or oppression within the realm of cultural values and norms of the country of origin or of the host society:

> Gender equality then, is regarded by some staff as a cultural imposition, undermining the principle of non-intervention embedded in UNHCR culture. That gender equality is perceived to be a Western-feminist imposition is defended by staff who maintain a certain cultural relativism in their belief systems, despite their loyalty to principles of universality. (Baines 2004: 63)

THE WOMEN AT RISK PROGRAM

The Women at Risk Program is one of the ways in which the UNHCR has sought to respond to the needs of women refugees, and particularly those in refugee camps around the world. The program was introduced in 1988 following recommendations emanating from the third World Conference on Women in Nairobi in 1985. It is a program that aims to identify women in refugee camps who are at extreme risk of harassment, physical or sexual violence and to fast-track their removal and resettlement in one of the seven Western countries that have agreed to take part in the program. The criteria state that exiled or displaced women who have been identified as being at extreme risk should be eligible for immediate resettlement whether they have formally been recognized as refugees or not. The problem, however, is how to identify those women 'at risk.' It is a term open to varied interpretation and is subject to the personal biases of those involved in selecting women for the program. The problem of definition and selection is particularly acute when a large number of women can be identified as potentially at risk. Pittaway and Bartolomei quote one director of a refugee camp in Africa who comments that: 'Every woman in this camp has been raped. Do you want to resettle them all?' (Pittaway and Bartolomei 2003: 91). In addition to the criteria established by the UNHCR to qualify for this program, the countries that accept these refugees for resettlement may also have their own criteria for selection. In Australia, for example, to qualify for resettlement under the Women at Risk Program, a woman must be living without the protection of a male relative and be in danger of victimization, harassment or serious abuse because of her sex, and she must be able to pass medical and character checking procedures (Manderson et al. 1998). Similarly, Canadian criteria for the selection of refugees for resettlement insist that the person must have been recognized as a refugee by UNHCR, and that in addition they must meet the standard of admissibility, which generally means that they should demonstrate the potential for successful integration and settlement in Canada. But as Boyd (1993) argues, the characteristics used to evaluate such potential are largely of a socioeconomic nature such as education, job skills or knowledge of English or French. And since gender inequalities in many countries mean that women have fewer educational opportunities and less job skills, these criteria may discriminate against them (ibid.). This critique of the Women at Risk Program also highlights a more general problem with resettlement programs in general, namely, that the refugees who are chosen for resettlement are often those who are most desirable in terms of a set of criteria set out by the host country, and these criteria can discriminate against women who have had fewer educational or employment opportunities in their countries of origin. This perception of discrimination in selection for resettlement is widespread in countries with large refugee populations. A Tanzanian official in the Ministry for Home Affairs thus explained to an Oxfam researcher that Western states only want to resettle the 'healthy, brainy refugees who are more likely to integrate easily' (Oxfam 2005: 51).

In fact, the total number of women who have been resettled under the Women at Risk Program has remained minimal for the reasons explained earlier. Canada, for example, accepted a total of 586 women and children through the Women at Risk Program between 1988 and 1993, which comprised only 0.8 percent of the total number of refugees accepted into the country. 'In other words, the Women at Risk Programme, laudable in its conception, has in practice scarcely touched the numbers and proportion of women refugees resettled in Canada' (Macklin 1995: 220). Figures for

2005 show that a total of 2,777 women were resettled worldwide. The main countries of destination for these women were Australia (921), the US (918), Canada (360) and Sweden (168) (UNHCR 2006). Again these numbers represent a tiny percentage of those women who are living in refugee camps in Africa, Asia or the Middle East, and more importantly of those women who continue to run daily risks of sexual attacks or other violence. Moreover, evidence from Australia shows that the women who are most likely to be resettled originate in Europe or the Middle East rather than from Africa, and that as a consequence 'the Women at Risk programme seems to have barely touched the problem of the high proportion of immobile refugee women, mainly in camp situations in countries of first asylum or refuge' (Kneebone 2005: 12).

In addition to this confusion about which women are 'at risk' and the limited numbers actually chosen for resettlement, it can also be argued that the program is weakened by its failure to address the wider issues of protection of women by focusing only on resettlement of these women to third countries. Finally, it can be argued that resettling women to a Western country is not sufficient to achieve effective protection. As Pittaway and Bartolomei (2006: 91) argue: 'The response to the special needs of women at risk in receiving countries . . . is often sadly lacking. Many countries do not understand, nor are equipped to deal with the high levels of trauma which can be the result of protracted refugee situations, endemic sexual and gender based violence, and torture.' The fact that once they have been accepted for resettlement and have received legal status in their host country, these women cease to receive any special support or help can thus be a barrier to their integration into a host society or to the fulfillment of their continuing needs for protection and assistance. Single women with children, as those resettled under the program usually are, may have particular needs and continuing vulnerabilities when they arrive in the host country that may thus remain unmet, and so the value of assisting women in resettlement can be limited 'if the conditions which led to their classification as "at risk" during the assessment period cease to be recognised during the period of resettlement' (Manderson et al. 1998: 282).

REPRESENTATIONS OF THE REFUGEE

In seeking to understand obstacles to the achievement of gender equality in refugee protection it is also necessary to examine critically the global norms that have been created, and the frames that are used to represent women refugees and asylum seekers. It might be argued that one of the reasons for the uneven impact of global norms in this area is that they are based on frames that represent women refugees principally as vulnerable victims, thus essentializing a particular set of gendered roles and failing to take into account the underlying gendered relations of power. Representations of refugee women as helpless victims also act to depoliticize these women's experiences and activities (Baines 2004). Rajaram (2002) points to the way in which humanitarian responses to refugees amount to a generalizing and depoliticized depiction of these refugees as helpless victims. Refugees are thus rendered speechless and without agency, and as Malkki (1996) argues, they are identified not in terms of their individual humanity but as a group whose boundaries and constituents are removed from their historical context and reduced to norms relevant to a state-centric perspective of international relations (IR). This depoliticization can be argued to be particularly acute with regard to women refugees and asylum seekers, as women tend to embody as particular kind of 'powerlessness' in the Western imagination (Malkki 1995), and are thus idealized as 'victims' without agency.

This use of strategic frames of women as vulnerable victims in need of protection is prevalent amongst practitioners in the international policy community (Carpenter 2005), and it can be argued that the symbols and signifiers of women as vulnerable victims form a valuable part of the 'cultural tool kit' (Swidler 1986) of these practitioners. Images of women and children in refugee camps have become common in fundraising campaigns by UNHCR and NGOs. In some contexts these images have been shown to be highly effective in raising public awareness of refugee issues and of attracting donor support for particular humanitarian crises, or in drawing the attention of political leaders. In Somalia, for example, Loescher comments on the way that 'widespread media coverage of starving women and children finally turned policy makers' attention to the disaster' (Loescher 2001: 303).

However, although such framings might be assumed to be beneficial to women as they are supposed to be used to mobilize support for specific protection measures for women, these frames are in fact essentializing of gender difference and ignore women's agency and voice. A different way to approach this problem of the essentializing nature of the frames used to describe women asylum seekers and refugees, and of the framing of particular issues of persecution in terms of preexisting and essentializing norms, is to relate these problems to the question of how gender issues become (or do not become) securitized and the fact that asylum-seeking women themselves are often excluded from the process of framing their own claims because they lack a voice. In a critique of the Copenhagen School, Hansen uses the example of honor killings in Pakistan to argue that those who are constrained in their ability to speak about their security/insecurity are prevented from becoming 'subjects worthy of consideration and protection' (2000: 285). She concludes that: 'Silence is a powerful political strategy that internalises and individualises threats thereby making resistance and political mobilisation difficult' (306). This critique might serve as the basis of a wider criticism of the ways in which the voice of women asylum seekers and refugees is ignored in the framing of issues relating to gender-specific persecution. The discursive opportunities that exist are not open to these women for reasons of political, social and economic marginalization and exclusion. The NGOs and associations that make claims for gender-specific policies and legislation do so on behalf of refugee and asylum-seeking women, these women themselves have little or no voice in the process. Speaking for women asylum seekers and refugees leads to representations and framings of them that rely heavily on preexisting cultural norms, as argued earlier, and that contain these women in their role of victims. Real understanding of the gendered causes of forced migration would take into account the voices and perspectives of those women who flee, and would adapt solutions for protection to specific experiences and to particular national and local contexts.

CONCLUSION

A goal of feminist constructivist analysis must be to give a voice to those considered marginal in international politics (Locher and Prügl 2001). As Steans and Ahmadi conclude: 'Agreements on principles or statements of good intent are of little use if they are not followed up with implementation and enforcement measures or if they are undermined, subsumed or spoken for only by elites. Impediments to women's participation in decision making processes remain, while practices of inclusion and exclusion in relation to NGOs . . . also silence women's voices' (2005: 244). If the interests of women fleeing armed conflict and gendered violence and seeking protection as refugees are truly to be guaranteed, then the voice of these women needs to be heard. It is important to listen to the voices of women seeking asylum and refugees if the trap of essentializing their experience and treating them as passive victims is to be avoided. Women do need protection and are vulnerable in some circumstances, but this should not be generalized to assume that they are all just 'vulnerable victims.' Cockburn argues that women should only be treated as mothers, as dependents or as vulnerable when they themselves ask for this special treatment. 'When, on the contrary, should they be disinterred from "the family", from "womenandchildren", and seen as themselves, women—people, even? Ask the women in question. They will know' (Cockburn 2004: 29).

NOTES

1. Interviews with author 2005, 2006 and 2007.
2. Interviews with the author.
3. Cynthia Enloe has explained eloquently the ways in which the utilization of the category 'womenandchildren' acts to identify man as the norm against

which all others can be grouped together into a single leftover category, reiterating the notion that women are family members above all, and allowing the state and international institutions to play a paternalistic role in protecting these vulnerable women and children (Enloe 1993).
4. By the mid-1990s UNHCR employed over 5,000 staff worldwide.
5. Interviews with the author at UNHCR headquarters and in national bureaus in Europe, 2005, 2006 and 2007.

10 Experiences, Reflections and Learning
Feminist Organizations, Security Discourse and SCR 1325[1]

Laura McLeod

Resolution 1325 was passed by the Security Council on 31 October 2000, urging for a gender perspective within UN peacekeeping and post-conflict processes. The resolution is designed to affect the organizational arrangement of the UN system (Rehn and Sirleaf 2002: 3), urging for increased representation of women in the prevention, management and resolution of conflict, including UN peacekeeping and field operations. Additionally, SCR 1325 encourages training about, and consideration of, gender impacts in relation to conflict and post-conflict management and forms part of a 'new' security environment within the UN expressing a concern for women, peace and security: a concern reaffirmed with Security Council Resolutions 1820 (June 2008), 1888 (September 2009) and 1889 (October 2009).

The success of SCR 1325 as a gender mainstreaming tool is debated by feminist scholars. Some view the resolution as a radical document with the potential to have a significant impact upon the UN system and conceptualizations of security (Cohn 2004, 2008; Cohn et al. 2004; Florea Hudson 2009; Sylvester 2009). Others suggest that SCR 1325 is problematic in terms of how to apply gender mainstreaming (Barrow 2009), or that understandings of (gender) violence and (international) security restrain the possibilities of SCR 1325 (L. Shepherd 2008). While SCR 1325 is a document primarily concerned with UN processes, feminist organizations have seized upon opportunities offered by it (Cohn 2004, 2008; Porter 2007). This is unsurprising given that actors within the transnational feminist movement during 1998–2000 pushed the Security Council to pass a resolution considering gender (Hill et al. 2003; Cockburn 2007: 138–143). That is: the impetus for SCR 1325 came from actors involved in transnational feminism. Since the resolution was passed, many grassroots women's NGOs in post-conflict zones have invoked the resolution to ensure leverage within UN-related peace-building processes (Porter 2007; Cohn 2004, 2008; Cohn et al. 2004).

This chapter explores some of the ways grassroots feminist NGOs have responded to SCR 1325, in particular how interpretation(s) of the resolution has affected the security discourse of feminist-pacifist activists. The prominence given to activist conceptualizations of security exposes the extent to which SCR 1325 is a 'venue for the traveling of feminist thinking and women's organizing' (Svedberg and Kronsell, this volume). The focus upon how gender concerns has traveled from an institutional to NGO context contrasts with the previous chapter, which examined how concepts about gender has traveled through UNHCR (Freedman, this volume). I argue that for 'gender security' and SCR 1325 to really travel, they need to have a direct relevance to the local context. This chapter reveals how the processes of self-reflection and learning enable activists to adapt and transform understandings of gender security and SCR 1325, so that the resolution becomes relevant for the values and ambitions of the group, acting within a specific tempo-spatial environment.

The focus is upon one Serbian feminist NGO, Women in Black (WiB), and the ways in which activists within the NGO have conceived of security simultaneously *in relation to* and *through* SCR 1325. WiB forms part of an international peace network connected by ideas of feminism, antimilitarism, peace and peaceful protest (Cockburn 2007: 51–53). WiB's criticisms of the institutions and practices of militarism play an important role in the group's explicit signification of an alternative vision of security, and how this vision can be embodied within SCR 1325. As a document produced by the UN Security Council, and frequently known as the resolution on 'Women, Peace and Security,' particular notions about 'security' are performed within the resolution.

Laura Shepherd suggests that embedded within SCR 1325 is a configuration of security emphasizing a particular set of discursive logics '(re)produc[ing] the international as a cooperative and influential domain' of peace (2008: 165). Acknowledging that SCR 1325 emphasizes specific visions of the international, sovereignty and peace within its conceptualizations of security, how do feminist-pacifist activists intervene into, and modify, the (re)production of security discourse performed in relation to SCR 1325, to make the document relevant to their local context and long-held political values and ambitions? To expose some of the processes behind the traveling of 'security' from its performance in SCR 1325, to how WiB conceive of the document, an analytical strategy focusing upon security discourse is utilized.

A discourse is made up of a series of (dis)connected meanings (significations), which can then be articulated and represented. This also works in reverse: the process and practice of articulation and representation can also shape significations. In the first section of this chapter, WiB's feminist-pacifist stance will be delineated, showing how their *articulation* of security discourse is connected to their feminist-pacifist values. The middle section of this chapter will analyze the process of self-reflection and learning through which activists deliberately *(re)signified* a meaning of security relevant to, and shaped by, their own circumstances and values. Through this space for reflection upon security, activists also learn about SCR 1325, and consider ways it could be used strategically in a security discourse to support the existing objectives of the group. The final section of this chapter focuses upon a reading of the discursive logics within the localized draft resolution produced by WiB, a document inspired by SCR 1325, which *represents* (some parts of) the group's security discourse.

Through an examination of the discursive logics surrounding WiB's significations, articulations and representations of security, this chapter identifies some processes by which the resolution has traveled out of its institutional context within the UN system and is (re)shaped to support specific and localized criticism of the institutions and practices of militarism.

FEMINIST-PACIFISM AND SECURITY

WiB is an international feminist-pacifist network with local groups pursing their own visions, shaped through the historical context of the area and perceptions of contemporary political, social and economic realities faced by activists. The WiB network originated in Israel in 1988, when Israeli Jewish women held vigils to protest against the Israeli occupation of the Gaza Strip (WiB 2005b). Looking to Southeastern Europe, WiB is the strongest feminist-pacifist voice in Serbia. The nucleus of the Serbian WiB network is based in the capital, Belgrade. Belgrade WiB was founded on 9 October 1991, shortly after hostilities in Croatia had escalated (WiB 1994a).

The group's formation during the midst of a nationalist civil war, a war that saw the disintegration of Yugoslavia, meant that activists sought to express their understandings of the gendered mechanisms behind war and nationalism. These understandings subsequently shaped the group's aims and activities. Since the late 1990s, there has been rapid expansion in the feminist-pacifist movement in Serbia. Many of these new activists maintain a connection with WiB in Belgrade, either as individuals or groups, and participate in the WiB (Serbia) network. When WiB is mentioned in this chapter, it generally refers to the groups and activists that form the WiB network in Serbia.[2]

Staša Zajović, one of the founding coordinators of Belgrade WiB, made the 'firm decision' that a feminist-pacifist group was needed after experiencing the patriarchal structures and attitudes of other antiwar actions in Belgrade in 1991 (WiB 1994d: 121). The rejection of patriarchy is embedded in all actions taken by WiB, from the decision to become an activist, to the way the office is run, to ways that ideas and values are expressed. For the majority of WiB activists, becoming a pacifist is a political and ideological decision that they have made as active agents rejecting nationalism and militarism (Zajović 2007a). Activists, who are 'always disobedient,' protest through nonviolent means to oppose war and war politics, believing that there is a need for the state to accept political responsibility for the war crimes committed in the name of "Serbia" (ibid.). The core values of WiB can be best summarized as feminist antimilitarism and an insistence upon political responsibility.

The issue of political responsibility remains a sensitive and controversial social and political topic in Serbia. Expressed by WiB activists through the slogan 'not in our name,' political responsibility refers to the perspective that Serbian institutions and society needs to confront, account for, and deal with the consequences of war crimes committed in the 1990s, as well as militarized violence that remains embedded in society (Zajović 2007a: 31–38; 2007b). Critiques of 'the criminal politics of the regime' emerged during the wars, when activists held silent vigils, wearing black, every Wednesday afternoon in Belgrade's main square (quotation from Zajović 2007a: 31; see also www.zeneucrnom.org). Activists cited intense nationalism as the motivating force behind the wars, connecting war and its consequences to the policies of Serbian government (Hughes 1999).

After the wars in Croatia and Bosnia-Herzegovina officially ended in 1995, WiB continued to criticize the politics of the Milošević regime, and in particular increasing political violence in Kosovo from the late 1990s. The group protested against ethnic cleansing and increasing regime oppression that accompanied the political tensions in Kosovo (WiB 2006). Since the fall of Milošević in October 2000; protests have continued to demand social justice and human rights, emphasizing opposition to nationalism, war and the consequences of war, connecting these ideas to demands for the Serbian state to take responsibility for its role in the war crimes committed in the 1990s.

Although the WiB network incorporates a variety of perspectives upon feminism and pacifism, a generalized understanding of the group's feminist-pacifist outlook is possible through publicized material. For WiB, supporting peace is not a passive action: Women and men[3] are active agents making a political choice to stand for a conceptualization of peace linked with the desire to eliminate patriarchy. Unlike Elshtain's Beautiful Souls (1995), or Ruddick's socially constructed carers (1989), the position of WiB highlights that activists make a decision based upon political and ideological choices to *become* pacifists, rebuffing the traditional 'social role of women as martyrs and victims' (WiB 1994c: 17). Through rejecting the biological oppression limiting both sexes, WiB activists wish to restructure and reconceptualize existing social foundations. By stressing their politicized activism, WiB move away from conceptualizations of women as 'passivematernalpeacelovers,'[4] and draw attention to a feminist-pacifist position that aims to unsettle the patriarchal foundations of society.

WiB espouse a set of feminist-pacifist values emphasizing the agency of activists as well as underscoring the importance of political responsibility. These values, embedded with hopes for the future, form an aspect of the past interacting with the present, as these values form the knowledge framework which shapes contemporary articulations of security. Documentary analysis suggests that 'security' was not explicitly articulated as a key value of WiB until 2005; which is around the same time that SCR 1325 became one of the strategies deployed by the group to achieve their objectives.

Although the fundamental values of WiB have not changed, 'security' has gained conceptual popularity, and as a consequence, the concept has started to become more explicitly mentioned. This is a point acknowledged by Zajović (2007a: 49), who states:

> Although only in recent years had the issue of security received our special attention, our feminist-antimilitarist actions have always challenged the traditional militarized understanding of security.

A particular conceptualization of security which enhances WiB's preexisting feminist-pacifist beliefs has been articulated by activists. Although the *explicit* and *politicized* articulation of security was a new development in 2005, the precise configuration of security discourse has connections to the group's long-held values of active, feminist-antimilitarism.

WiB's articulations of security reject traditional notions of militarized and armed state security and argue for a shift to human security where women are visible (Zajović 2007c: 179–180). The group's understanding of human security is a conceptualization that mirrors the academic Critical Security studies agenda that challenges the neoliberal foundations of state sovereignty, urging for a vision of individual security based upon morality and emancipation (Booth 2005). Pacifism is strongly grounded in the group's interpretation of security, which:

> is not about borders; [and is not] achieved with weapons. Just and lasting peace is the basis of security and it can only be achieved through creating a society in which all causes of war—including nationalism, patriarchy and exploitive economic systems—are eliminated. (Vuković 2007: 183)

Indeed, peace and human security can share similar discursive logics, and are sometimes conceptually connected in the academic literature: for example, Betty Reardon argues that women 'see peace as the route to security rather than the other way round' (1993: 21). Since human security and some versions of peace, especially broader visions of peace which account for additional structural violences, share similar discursive logics, it is possible for WiB to incorporate security into their feminist-pacifist values.

However, conceptual acceptance of a gender-sensitive security discourse does not translate into immediate acquiescence of SCR 1325. The provisions within SCR 1325 urging for the gender mainstreaming of peacekeeping operations highlight interesting questions for feminist antimilitarists. WiB state that 'the participation of women [in the armed forces] does not decrease the militarist and oppressive character of the army. It only signifies "equality" in killing and violence' (Zajović 2007c: 179). These concerns are also echoed on the international stage. In the process of crafting SCR 1325, pacifist organizations in the NGO working group made compromises to ensure its passage through the UN system (Cohn 2008: 194–200; Cockburn 2007: 147–148). One group—Women's International League for Peace and Freedom—muted its discourse about the connections between militarism and gender (Cockburn 2007: 148). For many feminist-pacifists (including WiB), SCR 1325 is problematic as the discursive foundations of the resolution fail to present a significant challenge to questions about militarism and gender within institutions of war and peace.

These concerns about the need to interrogate the structures believed to link militarism and gender were voiced by WiB during discussions to create a draft National Action Plan (NAP) for the implementation of SCR 1325 in Serbia. In March 2010, the Belgrade Fund for Political Excellence (BFPE) and the Ministry of Defense published recommendations towards a NAP to implement SCR 1325 in Serbia.[5] While the recommendations recognize the harassment faced by activists of the peace movement, 'especially those prominent in public as fighters for the truth about wars in former Yugoslavia' (BFPE 2010: 48, 50), the emphasis of discussions have been influenced by different security and gender logics. The recommendation for the NAP highlights the role of women in decision-making processes relating to defense and security, legal protection of women during conflicts, gender mainstreaming of the Serbian armed forces and integrating gender in security sector reform policy (BFPE 2010).

The *security logics* within this initiative are based around a discourse of human security, and perceive Serbia to be both a post-conflict zone and a future player in external military-based peacekeeping operations.[6] The *gender logics* that underpin these ideas equate gender with women, and equate gender mainstreaming to bringing more women into operation. WiB are no longer participating in these discussions as they feel that SCR 1325 is being 'reduced to a rhetorical level, to a formal level and without any link to the realities [we face] in this country.'[7] In other words, WiB activists take issue with how human security and SCR 1325 is conceived by some of the institutions working on the draft NAP, as well as the avoidance of topics that activists believe are important to achieving security in Serbia.

The interpretation of SCR 1325 partially depends upon how gender and security are discursively constituted. That is, the intersection between WiB's gender politics of feminist-antimilitarism and their security discourse has shaped the response to SCR 1325. While the ways in which 'security' is conceived affects the (re)production of SCR 1325, concurrently, SCR 1325 has been productive of how security can be conceptualized. The reminder of this chapter looks at how WiB formulated their security discourse in the context of their gender politics, demonstrating how the group's use of SCR 1325 has been product/productive of their feminist-pacifist security discourse. That is, SCR 1325 has been (partly) productive of WiB's security discourse, as the resolution has acted as a venue through which activists reflect and consider their own significations of security. Furthermore, WiB has created a localized resolution, inspired by SCR 1325, which acts as an articulation and representation of the group's security discourse.

A SPACE OF ONE'S OWN

For many members of WiB, significations of security echo the discursive logics of their long-held feminist-antimilitarist principles, so although WiB only started to emphasize security from 2005, their ideational values did not alter. Through tracing the formation of an *explicit* security discourse, the productive nature of long-held values in the interpretation of SCR 1325 become apparent, highlighting how the resolution has been, and is, product/productive of ways that WiB activists conceptualize security. The discursive terrain of SCR 1325 interacts with WiB's feminist-pacifist values to form significations, articulations and representations of security. To make it possible for SCR 1325 and the discourse of security to be utilized, activists first need a space to reflect, consider and learn about both 'security' and 'UNSCR 1325.' This section explores the notion of 'a space of one's own' as a means of (re)producing significations of security through reflection upon personal experiences and collective values.

Before NGOs can use SCR 1325—that is, to explicitly refer to the resolution in their campaigns—steps need to be taken so that activists can learn about the resolution and interpret the concepts involved. Individual activists and groups need the space to reflect upon and learn about the concept of security, which is embedded within SCR 1325. The ways in which particular concepts are framed and thought about impacts upon our actions and responses: (re)assessing the constitution of these concepts could have a significant impact upon the application of SCR 1325 (L. Shepherd 2008). Many civil society leaders, including Aida Ćorović, a Woman in Black activist in Novi Pazar, southwest Serbia, point to the need to learn about and localize complex topics and concepts before it can be meaningful.[8]

Physical and mental space to reflect upon the meanings and possibilities embedded within security discourse and SCR 1325 is crucial, and much of the space required was provided through a yearlong educational project held in 2005 on Women, Peace and Democracy, supported by UN Trust Fund money[9] (Vuković 2007: 185). The project included a series of workshops and seminars where activists considered ways that security could be (re)signified in light of their experiences and beliefs. Feminist commentators have long recognized the importance of 'a room of one's own' to learn, write, form ideas or to make changes (Woolf 1993; Tickner 2006b). During 2005, regional seminars connected to the Women, Peace and Democracy project were held to enable activists around Serbia to explore feminist-antimilitarist ways of conceiving of security (Duhaček 2005).

During the workshops, sessions 'advocated for the promotion and implementation of UN Security Council Resolution 1325.' The coordinators of the seminars emphasized 'establishing a clear connection between these [theoretical ideas about security] and the everyday life of our workshop participants' (Duhaček 2005). My own field interviews with 34 WiB activists between February and August 2008 indicated that, for many, these workshops were the first time that activists had seriously considered and (re)thought various meanings surrounding security. The majority of activists in interviews talked easily and comfortably about their visions regarding security: a strong indicator of having had a 'space of one's own' to consider the issues at stake.[10] Research findings indicated that the overwhelming signification of security amongst activists drew upon concerns with freedom from fears that impede upon everyday life: equality; freedom of speech and movement; economic, social and political stability; and human rights.

Nadja Duhaček, an activist who led some workshop sessions, felt that most women connected (in)security primarily with economic factors first, such as unemployment, lack of income and an inability to make concrete plans for the future due to economic instability.[11] This was something unexpected: Zajović was 'sure that women would link security with repressive apparatus and the police,' but activists emphasized a human security approach, based upon their experiences.[12] As Christine Sylvester argues, security is a 'sense,' and 'we might start where security hurts or annoys us as individuals. We might think, that is, about what security feels like and does not feel like' (2010c: 24–26).

During field interviews, when participants were asked about how they defined security, the immediate response focused upon highly personal 'senses' of *in*security before relating these to broader notions of human security. It appears then, that activists constructed a notion of security through its opposite: insecurity. Personal experiences are crucial to shaping (re)significations of security: In recalling particular experiences and memories, the sense of contemporary realities and future hopes mediate to perform a particular (critical) signification of security where the location of the referent subject is the individual.

Nada Dabić coordinates Esperanca, a feminist-pacifist organization connected to the WiB network, and based in Novi Sad, the largest city in Vojvodina, an autonomous province in the north of Serbia. She stresses that by security, she means:

> [not] only my physical security, I need my psychological security. If we do not have a mutual language, if we have different opinions, that doesn't give me the right to come and harass your family, or for you to harass mine. That doesn't give me the right to fire you. That doesn't give me the right to psychologically rape you each day through the media.[13]

Nada's response has been shaped by her experiences. An hour or so earlier in the interview, she jokingly describes herself as the 'third victim of Slobodan Milošević' partly because she was fired from her job in January 1988 for publicly criticizing Milošević's policies: her description of what security means includes a reference to job security. Her mention of the need to accept multiple languages may have been shaped by her experience of living in Novi Sad, a city in Vojvodina, a province with 27 recognized nationalities and six official languages. The remark that the media should not 'psychologically rape you each day' may refer to the way certain sections of the Serbian media have, and continue to, utilize(d) rhetoric of nationalist hatred and reproduce violent constructions, causing insecurity for individuals, especially human rights defenders (Zajović et al. 2007: 208–220). Nada's views of what makes her, and people around her, insecure shapes her definition of what security means to her; a way of thinking strongly connected to the feminist principle that the personal is political.

The 'senses' of (in)security expressed by Nada have been framed within the public discourse of WiB as a critique about militarized structures in Serbian society. Implicit within Nada's concerns about (in)security is a belief in the structural impacts that war and nationalism have had in the creation of these senses of insecurity. The signification of security articulated by WiB activists rests upon discursive logics that criticize militarism and its (perceived) consequences: war and nationalism. Based upon notions of human security, together with feminist-pacifist values, activists have (re)articulated their own significations of security, represented in relation to SCR 1325.

This critical security approach is clear from the publications produced by the NGO, including the 96-page booklet *From the Traditional to the Feminist Concept of Security: Resolution 1325* published at the end of 2007 (Zajović 2007b). The security discourse underpinning this publication is a highly critical vision, constructed in opposition to a traditional (state-centric) vision of security, and has a strong ontological focus upon the gendered individual. The document embodies a vision of security concerned with expanding ways in which security is conceived, placing emphasis upon criticizing the state and highlights ways in which SCR 1325 supports their activities (Zajović 2007b: 26–35).

During 2005 security discourse and SCR 1325 began to be deployed explicitly in relation to each other as part of WiB's articulations of their political agendas.[14] The Women, Peace, and Democracy seminars during 2005 was the first time activists began to seriously consider alternative significations of security, but there was no ideational alteration, shift, modification or change. Rather, the group's feminist-pacifist values began to be connected to different institutional terrains/concepts, including SCR 1325 and a (critical) concept of security. Critical feminist approaches argue that genuine peace and security are dependent upon social justice, domestic reform, women's rights, coexistence, tolerance, participatory democracy, transparency and nonviolent dialogue: In other words, meaningful peace requires security (Porter 2007: 118).

These critical conceptualizations of security share similar discursive logics to WiB's pacifist position. The conceptualization(s) of security that WiB activists have influence the utilization of SCR 1325, and concurrently, SCR 1325 has some bearing upon how security is thought about. Having considered the concept of security, WiB started to talk about SCR 1325, and have used, and continue to use, the resolution and its discursive terrain as an advocacy tool in several ways. SCR 1325 can become a tool for feminist organizations only when activists have had the space to learn about the resolution, the concepts attached to it—including security—and the implications for their existing activities.

Activists, through learning about the possibilities of SCR 1325 during the 2005 workshops, considered the extent to which the resolution could enhance existing aims and objectives. Staša Zajović insists that:

> Resolution 1325 is *one* of our subjects, one in many. It was simply a continuation of what we have been doing since we set up WiB. We have been dealing with security from the aspect of nonmilitarization since 1991.[15]

Staša makes the point concisely that UNSCR 1325 fits in with long-held values within WiB, and it was a perpetuation of their previous activities.

Through a 'space of one's own,' activists were able to learn about SCR 1325 and reflect upon their experiences to relate the group's security discourse to their existing gender politics. SCR 1325 is part of a far wider remit held by WiB. The resolution is simply an advocacy tool that can be deployed in order to achieve some of WiB's aims, particularly their nonmilitarized perception of security. The final section of this chapter unpacks the discursive construction of WiB's Draft Resolution on Women, Peace and Security to expose ways in which the performance of security is connected to the group's long-held feminist-pacifist stances.

THE DRAFT RESOLUTION AND LOCALIZING WOMEN, PEACE AND SECURITY

SCR 1325 stresses the importance of 'local women's peace initiatives and indigenous processes for conflict resolution' (Article 8b). Indeed, women's organizations worldwide have responded by localizing the resolution and highlighting ways that SCR 1325 can be initiated in particular contexts (see examples in Cohn 2004, 2008). In a similar manner, in October 2005, WiB issued a Draft Resolution on Women, Peace and Security, inspired by UNSCR 1325 (WiB 2007). The document contains a series of localized recommendations based upon their discursive logics about feminist-pacifism and security: localized because elements of SCR 1325 have been adapted to WiB's critique of Serbian politics.[16]

The final section of this chapter fuses the earlier discussion of how security discourse is located in relation to WiB's gender politics, with the ways in which SCR 1325 was a venue enabling activists to reflect upon their experiences and preexisting values to consider personal significations of security. Through a reading of the discursive logics embedded within the draft resolution, it is apparent that WiB's articulation and representation of security discourse in the draft resolution is product/productive of UNSCR 1325 *and* the group's gender politics.

SCR 1325 has faced criticism for its 'conceptual gaps, for the lack of guidelines in practical application and for the failure in implementation' (Porter 2007: 3). However, these failures are also the document's strength. UNSCR 1325 is a flexible document that can be implemented in different ways, as interpreted by local initiatives. Additionally, the perceived weakness of the resolution, in terms of the lack of clear guidelines, has been an empowering tool for local women's NGOs, including WiB. Staša Zajović has recognized that UNSCR 1325 has 'many ambiguities' and lacks mechanisms for implementation (2007c: 178). While 'it is very important that the resolution allows free space for creativity,' Staša feels that the looseness of the resolution is one of its potential problems.[17] However, the looseness of UNSCR 1325 has enabled the resolution to be interpreted and applied to the *specific* issues faced by a *particular* state, and to be used in a strategic way to enhance the preexisting aims of activists.

WiB have localized SCR 1325 'very seriously,' to ensure that it 'was not just a global resolution,' but a resolution with clear, tangible and plausible *local* possibilities.[18] The Draft Resolution is an important articulation of WiB's position because it demonstrates ways in which SCR 1325 has relevance to their existing political objectives. Each 31 October since 2005, activists from WiB have presented to the National Assembly of Serbia a 'Draft Resolution' with their recommendations for how SCR 1325 could be implemented in Serbia (WiB 2007). The document is inspired by principles embodied in SCR 1325 *and* WiB's long established feminist antimilitarist perspectives, with requests specific to the political circumstances with which WiB activists are concerned (Zajović 2007a: 49). The Draft Resolution can be read as an intersection of WiB's gender politics *and* security discourse.

Recommendations within the Draft Resolution demand:

- the full and equal participation of women in decision-making
- that the state 'support and prompt' conflict resolution without the use of force or violence
- protection and respect for women's human rights and human rights defenders
- criminalization of the denial of war crimes and genocide, including the genocide in Srebrenica

- adequate compensation and support to families of victims of war and war crimes
- uprooting the culture of war that legitimizes violence against women (WiB 2007).

These specific ways that WiB believe that SCR 1325 could be implemented in Serbia are very clearly rooted in the contemporary political, social and economic environment that the activists are concerned about, underscoring their hopes for the future. Despite a strong location in the present, these policies have a discursive link and heritage to the preexisting values of the group. Security discourse is connected to each of the recommendations; as for WiB activists, security means peace, achieved through challenging the structural foundations of militarism and achieving transitional justice, including political responsibility.

The Draft Resolution is based around the insistence that women's interest and participation in the peace building process are crucial to 'establishing lasting and stable peace and security' (WiB 2007: 187). This not only highlights the critical conceptualization that security is important for meaningful peace, but also emphasizes that women have a contribution to make within the peace building process: women have a role as agents in postwar reconstruction. This perspective echoes the group's rejection of images of women as 'passivematernalpeacelovers,' an image which Staša Zajović feels is an important opportunity offered by SCR 1325, because of the key role Serbian feminists have played in the region in terms of their 'constant demands [for] responsibility for the war crimes.'[19] The insistence that women are agents for positive social change connects to the group's feminist discourse concerned with uprooting the patriarchal structures of society.

The explicit connection made between gender violence, which is articulated as violence against women in the Draft Resolution, and the 'culture of war' highlights a reasoning connecting militarization processes with violence in society. These structural logics have long been articulated by WiB: a 1992 leaflet argues that 'we know that militarism and domestic violence are interconnected . . . when the violence against women ceases—the wars will stop' (1994c: 18). These discursive links made by activists between violence against women and the culture and institutions of war highlight the belief that through pushing for an alternative, it is possible to transform and uproot the structures of patriarchal violence. The Draft Resolution echoes these anti-foundationalist ontological perspectives, locating them within an alternative vision of security discourse.

Demands insisting that contemporary Serbian society and its government bear political responsibility for war crimes committed during the 1990s form a central kernel of the Draft Resolution. The document includes demands for the application of lustration laws, stressing the importance of achieving social justice through punishing those who committed war crimes, and a stipulation that the Law on Assistance to the Hague Indictees and their families to be revoked (WiB 2007). Additionally, there is an insistence that the state should criminalize the denial that Serbia had a role to play in the war crimes and genocides committed during the Balkan wars of the 1990s. These demands resonate with activist refusal to support the war politics of the Milošević regime during the early 1990s (WiB 1994c: 17). These preexisting discourses have been (re)articulated through contemporary realities: in particular, concerns for women's human rights defenders.

Activists insisting upon the need for political responsibility are particularly endangered in Serbia. WiB and other individuals associated with the political responsibility agenda frequently experience media abuse, social violence and institutional attacks (Zajović et al. 2007: 208–220). The experiences of insecurity faced by activists urging political responsibility has shaped this particular discourse of human security, placing emphasis upon freedom of speech and expression. A concern with exercising human rights, especially freedom of political expression—that is, to feel safe and secure in insisting upon political responsibility—was the predominant (in)security concern voiced by WiB activists during field interviews. By highlighting the insecurity of human rights defenders through the Draft Resolution, WiB are emphasizing the elements of SCR 1325 (articles 8b and 11[20]) that, framed in a particular way, activists feel are especially relevant to their experiences.

A discursive reading of the demands within the Draft Resolution reveals that WiB have interpreted SCR 1325 in a way that makes their gender politics clear. The Draft Resolution has a strong connection to the group's existing ideational values about feminist-pacifism and political responsibility, deliberately positing an alternative politics focused upon the individual. In many respects, UNSCR 1325 was a venue that enabled activists to reflect upon their experiences and preexisting values to consider personal significations of security, which were then articulated and represented in the Draft Resolution.

CONCLUSIONS

SCR 1325 embodies a particular arrangement of gender (violence) and (international) security (Shepherd 2008). The resolution is sedimented within evaluative frameworks and discursive terrains of institutions claiming authority over SCR 1325 (Shepherd 2008: 160). UNSCR 1325 is simultaneously an empowering and problematic document: Careful consideration of meanings surrounding 'gender' and 'security' is critical to exploring ways of implementing the resolution. My analysis of WiB's actions demonstrates some processes towards formulating alternative configurations of 'gender security.' Critically, this analysis demonstrates ways that 'feminist thinking from one place goes through transitions and adjustments on its way to make sense and become valuable tools for feminist analyses in new sites and settings' (Svedberg and Kronsell, this volume). The notion of a 'traveling concept' is insightful and can be expanded: The genesis for SCR 1325 originated within international (feminist) NGOs before formal acceptance by the Security Council in October 2000 (Hill et al. 2003). Since, the resolution has been a tool for grassroots (feminist) NGOs—as long as NGOs have had the opportunity to adapt the security discourse embedded within UNSCR 1325 so that the resolution has direct relevance to the local context.

By exposing ways in which grassroots NGOs learn about international documents, institutions and concepts in order to localize the potential impacts of these international concerns, the ideational process and environment needed for reflection and learning about/upon experiences is reveled. International documents, institutions and concepts can support preexisting (localized) values, aims and objectives of a local NGO *if* activists have a space to learn and reflect upon how their experiences and gender politics relates to wider international agendas. More significantly, a room of one's own allows for conceptual traveling, enabling strategic political framing and action. WiB have adapted SCR 1325 within their Draft Resolution, so their preexisting gender politics concerned with feminist-antimilitarism and political responsibility is reflected. This is indicative of some of SCR 1325's potential: as an international document giving some support and clout to alternative visions of gender security.

It is clear that gender politics shapes how security—embedded within the discursive terrain of SCR 1325—is conceived, as well as perspectives about how SCR 1325 could be implemented. Since WiB's gender politics focuses upon political responsibility and feminist-antimilitarism, these issues are in their view critical for successful implementation of SCR 1325 in Serbia. In contrast, actors working towards the draft NAP for the implementation of SCR 1325 in Serbia do not necessarily see political responsibility issues as relevant or important for successful execution of the resolution. More broadly, it is apparent that implementation of SCR 1325 will not be a simple task of deploying a gendered notion of security, because the ways in which security is constituted are not only affected by interpretation of gender, but also political positions' relation to war, conflict and peace building.

These competing views about how best to achieve 'gender security' suggest that securing security verges on the impossible (Edkins 2002). This analysis reveals the complexity of gender security. On the one hand, SCR 1325 embodies a specific configuration of gender (violence) and (international) security (L. Shepherd 2008), but there are alternative ways of achieving gender security *within* the limitations and possibilities of the document. These alternative visions arise out of a space of one's own to reflect upon preexisting values and to learn about new ideas and concepts in relation to one's own experiences, to enable a concept and/or document to really travel into a specific local context.

NOTES

1. The research for this chapter derives from my PhD thesis 'Gender Politics and Security Discourse: Feminist and Women's Organising in "Postconflict" Serbia,' made possible by ESRC funding (PTA-031-2005-00220). I am grateful

Experiences, Reflections and Learning   149

to Adam, Aleksander and Gordana for their transcription work. I am also thankful to Georgina Waylen, Maud Eduards and the editors for their perceptive comments upon my drafts. Finally, I am indebted to those who I interviewed in Serbia during the course of 2008 and 2009: I can only hope that this does your work some justice. Any mistakes are mine.
2. This is the case even where groups are not named *Žene u Crnom* (WiB). There exists a diverse range of possible involvement with WiB-Serbia. Some groups are explicitly part of the WiB network, and are overt about their feminist-pacifist stances. Other groups have several activists who support WiB, but the organization itself is not explicitly connected to WiB.
3. Pacifism is a political choice, and so men are also freed from gendered restraints, and are able to join a feminist organization rejecting militarism. See the workshop report in WiB (1994b) and the discussion by Cockburn (2007: 220–221).
4. Inspired by Cynthia Enloe's 'lootpillageandrape' (2000: 1, 132), a way of highlighting frequent gendered constructions.
5. Email correspondence, program coordinator, Belgrade Fund for Political Excellence (BFPE), 22 March 2010. BFPE is a nonprofit, nonpartisan organization supporting democratization and European integration processes in Serbia.
6. Interview, program coordinator, BFPE, Belgrade, September 2009.
7. Interview, Staša Zajović, coordinator of WiB-Serbia, Belgrade, September 2009.
8. Interview, Aida Ćorović, coordinator of Sandzak Women's Forum, Novi Pazar, July 2008. Aida has been involved in WiB since 1991.
9. United Nations Trust Fund to End Violence against Women is a fund administrated by UNIFEM to give grants to innovative initiatives aiming to eliminate gender based violence. Zajović (2007a: 51–53) outlines all the seminars and topics covered by WiB.
10. Of course, the very act of being interviewed can also provide a space for reflection.
11. Interview, Nadja Duhaček, WiB activist, Belgrade, April 2008.
12. See note 7.
13. Interview, Nada Dabić, Coordinator of Esperanca, a feminist-pacifist group part of the WiB-Serbia network, Novi Sad, May 2008.
14. WiB have carried out other activities with reference to SCR 1325, including campaigns in collaboration with the Kosovo Women's Network and campaigns highlighting the insecurity of Women's Human Rights defenders.
15. Interview, Staša Zajović, coordinator of WiB-Serbia, Belgrade, June 2008.
16. This is a very different initiative to translating SCR 1325. A Serbian translation of the resolution was made through the peacewomen project. See http://www.peacewomen.org/1325inTranslation/index.html (accessed 17 October 2009).
17. See note 15.
18. Interview, Slavica Stojanović, director of Reconstruction Women's Fund, Belgrade, March 2008. WiB activist since 1991.
19. See note 15.
20. SCR 1325 Article 8b urges for 'measures that support local women peace initiatives' and article 11 'emphasise[s] the responsibility of all States to put an end to impunity and to prosecute those responsible for genocide, crimes against humanity, and war crimes.'

Theme IV
Gender Subjectivity in the Organization of Violence

11 Nordic Women and International Crisis Management
A Politics of Hope?

Elina Penttinen

> 'It is these little things. I brought the kids in school in Sri Lanka a telescope made in Finland. I figured that maybe, when these kids will look at the night sky and see the moon, then maybe they will realize that war is in fact a really stupid thing.'[1]

Violence against women in recent conflicts and the visibility of this violence have led to a demand for more female personnel in peacekeeping and civilian crisis management (CCM) missions. Following the lead of Norway and Sweden, Finland published a National Action Plan (NAP) in 2008, so as to implement SCR 1325 (see McLeod, this volume). In practice, the plan should result in increasing the number of women on peacekeeping and CCM missions, and add a gender element to all projects conducted. The demand for more women in international missions as articulated in the resolution and in the NAP is the starting point for the case study that this chapter presents: What is it that women are expected to contribute? What kind of competence is in demand? The chapter investigates the meanings of gendered and ethnified subjectivity in security politics in which Nordic women are seen as the solution for better crisis management and a key element in reaching operational efficiency. The study draws from in-depth interviews with Finnish female police officers and their narratives on providing security.

In spring 2007, we were gathered in the Ministry for Foreign Affairs in Helsinki, in order to begin drafting the first Finnish NAP to implement SCR 1325.[2] The task at hand was to make history and create the first Finnish NAP to be published in 2008. The group consisted of the representatives of key ministries, NGOs and academics from different universities in Finland. My position was to represent Tampere Peace Research Institute, Tapri, and as such embody a critical point of view towards the possible essentialization and the universalization of the category of women that might trickle into the text. In other words, my position was to be vigilant about how so many times women are represented as victims of war and their position of agency and subjectivity is dismissed, and how the violence against civilian and vulnerable groups of men is forgotten (Carpenter 2006; Väyrynen 2004).

Little did I know that I would encounter the revival and reinvention of the feminist international relations (IR) 1980s all over again, only to be represented as a brand-new approach for better peacekeeping and crisis management. In other words, the solution for overcoming the numerous problems in peacekeeping and crisis management was to increase the number of women. To me it sounded an awful lot like the add-women-and-stir approach (Murphy 1996) from a feminist IR past.

The faith and hope placed in women was fascinating and surprising since recent feminist IR literature had already so profoundly debunked the myth of women as always more peaceful and more empathic than men[3] (see Parashar, this volume; Sjoberg and Gentry 2007; Zarkov 2007) and shown how women are just as capable of perpetrating violence in wars (Jones 2006) and misconduct in peacekeeping and military operations (Masters 2009). It was surprising in respect to the abundance of postcolonial feminist literature on the contradictions in rescuing women through the means of Western military operations (Khan 2008; Narayan and Harding 2000), which render third world woman without voice, and which indeed could be more about the maintaining of coherence of Western subjectivity than enabling women in post-conflict situations (Penttinen 2004, 2006).

Also Eisenstein (2007) has warned against the use of sexual decoys, opening ways to look at gendered agency and subjectivity beyond gender appearances. She has argued that women's rights are manipulated and mobilized for what she sees as imperialist ends. What she offers is a way of looking beyond the appearances of gender or women's rights by becoming aware of the unquestioned dualist way of thinking about gender and politics. Feminisms are at risk of falling into the lure of sexual decoys as the attention is placed on either women active in peacekeeping and the military, or women to be protected and saved in the conflict zones and war. In other words, there is a need to create women as a category, in order to strive for women's rights or have a politics of increasing them. Following Eisenstein's emphasis on pluralism, one could say that it is not always individuals gendered as women who need women's rights or represent who women are or are the women to be saved.

The fact that women indeed form a minority in both military operations and CCM missions leads almost too easily to the conclusion that by gender balance the operations will be in balance. Yet, in the NAP drafting meetings it seemed that there was a feeling of something more than just increasing women in order to reach gender equality. There was a sense of women bringing added value to the operations.

The answer to what that something more is can be characterized by three main themes of underlying, unquestioned assumptions. First there is the assumption, that women are more empathic and sensitive to the needs of women and children in post-conflict situations. Therefore, hiring female personnel will result in better recognition of the women's needs in the host country. Women will be sensitive to other women's situations and needs, because both have similar gendered experiences. Second, female staff is easier to approach and report crimes to by the local population. Therefore operational efficiency will be increased as women (and also men) in the host country will more likely report crimes and seek help. Men in uniform can appear suspicious to local population, because of the atrocities perpetrated by other men during the war, but a woman in uniform will not have the same effect. And last but definitely not least, male colleagues in peacekeeping and crisis management will be less likely to engage in misconduct when women colleagues are present. In other words, men will behave better when women are around. This will ameliorate the overall image and impact of the operation and ease the trust and cooperation of the local community in the host country.

This chapter stems from curiosity toward the role assigned to women in crisis management, leading to interview research with female police officers who had been on police, monitoring or peacekeeping missions. In these interviews, the police officers were asked to reflect on the relevance of the politics of increasing women, so as to consider how the underlying assumptions related to their everyday work. The goal was to find out how the women, who were seen as the solution, saw themselves. In other words, to hear the female police officers' own opinions on whether the increased amount of women would result in operational efficiency and improved relations with the local population. Next I will discuss how the recognition of changing security environments has contributed to the politics of increasing the number of women in peacekeeping and crisis management as this is also how the female police officers contextualized their own relevance as Nordic women in crisis management.

A HOLISTIC APPROACH TO HUMAN SECURITY

The debate on the increasing number of women takes place in the context of recognition of a changing global security environment, in which civilian populations have become the targets of violence (Appadurai 2006; Kaldor 2006). In this context there is also a need to develop civilian and military peacekeeping toward crisis prevention instead of reactive operations. In other words, with the recent unfolding of violence, which targets the civilian population in extreme ways, the subject to be secured through crisis management is human well-being, instead of security of institutions and the state (Toiskallio 2004). Therefore, there is a shift toward prioritizing human security (Kaldor 2004).

The shift from reactive to preventive crisis management changes the demands on peacekeepers and civilian experts. The concept of comprehensive security grasps the effects of the changing of security environments for military and civilian security agents. It emerged from the difficulties in the war in Kosovo in which NATO took on a number of humanitarian responsibilities without being adequately equipped for them (Micewski 2004). Also the shortcoming of UN peacekeepers to prevent the Srebrenica massacre in 1995, in Bosnia, raised the need to question how peacekeepers in the future will be able to prevent such atrocities and indeed be able to respond immediately in the right way as human lives are at stake. In this setting Toiskallio (2004: 109–110) introduces the action competence approach, which relies on a holistic understanding of human being through four modes of existence, which are the physical, mental, social and ethical existence. In other words, the new soldier or crisis management expert is an embodied agent engaged with the world as a human being. From the being in the world arises right action. This model therefore moves beyond the mind–body dualism and its gendered dichotomies.

In an actual crisis situation ethical action may mean exceeding one's mandate if the situation so demands. Therefore, ethical competence, as Toiskallio explains, is an individual capacity, instead of a capacity of an institution or operation, introducing the idea that military or crisis management actions are 'fundamentally human acts' (2004: 108).

In this setting the assumptions behind the politics of increasing women in order to increase operational efficiency coincide with the idea of a new security agent who embodies action competence, in a security environment facing new anxieties, complexities and insecurities (Toiskallio 2004). As action competence is an approach that is based on a holistic concept of a human being it may be mistaken as a feminine quality, although it is not. It surpasses the binary logic by emphasizing the human being as a living body-mind-spirit being always connected to the world, instead of as a separate entity, or as a rational mind trapped in a physical body. Use of intuition (body–mind knowledge), ethical and empathic action that follows from being in the world look like feminine qualities only as long as the dualist concept of a human being is unquestioned. In other words, as long as individual subjectivity in crisis management is understood through separation of the security agent from the secured, agency which arises from the connection with the world as mode of being, may seem like a feminine way of doing things. As women are associated with empathy and care, doing security from the position of being may be mistaken as a feminine expertise, whereas instead it questions the fragmented worldview (Bohm 2008; Kallio-Tamminen 2008) and the entailing understanding of human beings as separate from the natural world that they observe (Bohm 2008; Kabat-Zinn 2005).

In a sense the illusion of reducing action competence to female gender is understandable, since women form a minority in crisis management operations and as they have been able to perform in ways that go beyond the mandate or professional expertise the conclusion may be that it is indeed women who are in demand instead of human beings who embody and master the action competence as new security agents.

Being able to act in a right way in the now is what separates a master from an expert, explains Klemola (2004). At the level of a master, one no longer needs to think and calculate one's actions; instead they rise from intuition and mastery of the skill (body-mind-spirit-social knowledge). At the level of an expert one still needs to reflect analytically on the right action one is able to perform skillfully. In other words, the actions of a master are in the flow and in balance with the present moment. On the basis of my research I want to argue that the female police officers interviewed for this research have become masters of police work in crisis management. It is their capacity for the right action at the right time that turns into an understanding of the added value of gender as women. And because of the unquestioned binary logic, the feminine care, empathy and high integrity performed by their male colleagues goes unnoticed. One could also say that it is because of this same binary logic that focus on men in the context of militarism turns to misconduct, aggressiveness or hypermasculinity. Is it even possible to discuss empathy, care and nurturing in the context of militarized masculinities? Yet, let us now turn to the female police officers and on how they see the meaning of their gender in providing security in the changing security environment.

WOMEN ON A MISSION

Despite the recent discussion on increasing the number of women in crisis management, the fact is that women still form a minority and some countries do not second any women at all. This is also true about the European Union Rule of Law mission in Kosovo (EULEX), which began during the time of emphasis placed on gender mainstreaming and especially on gender equality. However, in the EULEX mission, for example, at the first category level there are no senior staff positions held by women in either office head of mission, justice, administration, police or customs. Some European countries do not include any women at all among their staff seconded for ESDP crisis management missions.

In this sense, there is a feeling of exceptionality concerning the female police officers in crisis management. This exceptionality, according to the women I interviewed, might represent itself in a sense that they were put on a pedestal, or treated with complete nonchalance. As one of the interviewed officers mentioned: 'I have noticed that as for both to colleagues from the local police and local women and the like, as a woman, I am extraordinary, that as a woman I am so much more, easier to approach, to talk to.'[4] In this sense, the role expected of women on the basis of their gender is put into practice. Being a female may serve as an element of surprise in the interaction with the locals, which can work for the benefit of the police officers on the mission. Yet, the gender element might have mattered even more in relation to their international colleagues. Due to national balance in UN missions some of the CCM staff were not fully qualified for the task at hand. For the Finnish female police officers such things as being afraid of driving or being afraid of the dark were incomprehensible, or being unwilling to do work in uncomfortable situations. The following story of the first day on the mission of one female police officer explains this point:

> It was actually my first day on the job, and although it was late March it was surprisingly cold and it was snowing, not much, but snowing anyway. We were one Indonesian and Jordanian, one interpreter and one Serb and Croat from local police. It was about eight in the morning so we went out from the police station and the interpreter says: 'Okay, so we will meet back here at 1 p.m.' The internationals used to go back home when it was cold! And I said, 'What, we came here to work and we are going to patrol. And no one is going home.' I was the only female there, and still at that time the same rank as them. They would not believe me and insisted that it was too cold and that they always stayed at home when the weather was like that and said, 'Why don't we vote on it?' I said, 'That's fine, let's vote, but one woman's vote equals a thousand and today we are going to walk!' The boys were quite sour the whole day, but in the end I earned their respect.[5]

Many felt that as women they have to prove themselves by working twice as hard, but that it was okay since it was not any different back home in Finland. Often the conversation would turn to discussion about the difficulties, lack of respect, belittling and harassment they had experienced as young policewomen when they had joined the police.

In the international missions their experience, work ethic and nationality would, on the other hand, yield positive results. The women felt that Finnish police were given more responsibilities and higher positions in the organization due to their professionalism and dedication. Finnish nationality itself was an asset because of the political history of Finland gaining independence from Russia and not having a past as a colonizer. Gender and nationality combined with expertise was something that the women did find working for them in their actual everyday work on the missions. 'None of my Nordic colleagues would use their gender for their advantage, but they would use their professionalism along with their gender to get things done properly.' On the other hand, the Finnish women differentiated themselves from unqualified women, who had been seconded for the job on the basis of national balance, but in practice did not rise to the task. Some might have even resorted to flirting in order to get the male colleagues do the job for them.[6]

The reasons to get involved in international missions was described with the sense of empathy, care and setting an example for others what 'a woman' can do. A sense of purpose and personal fulfillment was gained in the possibility to assist post-conflict countries in establishing rule of law, or bring stability, even if it would be only for a little while. The important aspect was to give one's contribution and in the everyday life of the crisis management mission do everything one could in one's job and help, even if it would mean only one person at one time. Instead of seeing the host country as full of problems, local people as helpless victims and themselves as better than others, the approach was to face every day as full of opportunities and potential to make a difference. 'The way I see it, is that those areas that we go to, Kosovo or Darfur, are so full of possibilities. One just needs to see them and go for them. There is so much that we can do, than just the job we are sent out to do.'

Action competence is not only about knowing what right action is, but indeed recognizing what is appropriate and acting upon that recognition in the particular moment in time, even if it would exceed the mandate. It is one thing to know what to do, and another to have the courage, the intuition, the mastery to do it, as the events and circumstances unfold in a specific moment in time. In this sense the women interviewed relied on their professionalism and expertise. Often this meant action in a situation, or in an event, that could not have been planned ahead. In one example a police officer was able to retrieve a kidnapped girl from a Tamil Tiger training camp by literally going to the camp with her interpreter and demanding the return of the girl, whom she had seen being kidnapped.

> We just happened to be there, and it was because I saw it myself that I went after her and I just marched into this center. I knew that the girl was there, since I knew where they took them, before moving the kidnapped children in the training camps that are out there in the country and not within our area. So, it is important to get to them before they are transferred. The guard at the gate of course denied everything and told us 'There is no girl here! No child has been brought here!' But there was absolutely no use for this since I had seen them take her and I was not leaving without the girl. We get into an argument and the guard, a short fellow, starts yelling at me: 'If you go any further I will shoot you!' At this point my interpreter starts intervening and telling me that this may not be a good idea, that I should listen to the guard and that we really should go, it is not safe. But I tell him to just tell the guard to 'Go ahead! Shoot me! Let it all out! I have diplomatic immunity and if he shoots me there will be a big case about it.' Well, it was not exactly true, we did not have access inside the camps, but it was a good argument to use since that camp was in our area. His superior came and at that point and we really got into it, not in a physical fight but close. They did not shoot me then, but later my interpreter said that he would not have been so trusting.

This story is obviously about having the courage to act beyond one's mandate, but also being able to act in the moment in the right way. It does not arise from technical expertise, but body–mind knowledge, which is the ground for the confidence of the police officer in carrying out the rescue. The connection with the interpreter is also crucial. The motivating factor for this police officer was that as a mother she could empathize with pain of losing a child. She goes out of her way to rescue a girl, as she knows she can do it and because she sees herself not separate from the people in Sri Lanka but connected by the same human experience. It is this emotional involvement that turns into intuitive action and determination in the present moment, exceeding the limits of the mandate. This kind of competence will have concrete consequences, at least for that one girl and her family.

The concept of flow (Seligman and Csikszentmihalyi 2000) is also useful in explaining the ways the female police officers described their work. Police work was characterized as being in alignment with passion and sense of self, mastering the skill of crisis management and incorporating the four modes of action competence. One has to understand that the conditions and situations in which the crisis management staff work are not easy and are far from luxurious. Workdays are long; on UN missions the work is done in one-month stretches, including weekends. On the ESDP missions people are potentially always on call, even after official working hours. On the international missions one needs to be ready to work more hours, and in difficult and changing situations, without the safety and balance of work and personal life that can be maintained back home. Therefore, the police officers who work in international crisis management need to be in balance and have strong self-confidence.

Obviously not everyone is motivated to do their work with a sense of passion and action competence; some seek to go on the mission for the financial benefits and excitement or because mission life itself has become the routine, not the exception. In general the personnel from Nordic countries, according to the police officers, bring their work ethic with them, but more importantly their determination and expertise. The competence to act in the present moment and carry individual responsibility for one's actions is at the core of the term action competence. Instead of representing an institution such as the EU or the UN, they saw themselves as the resource, as the expertise, they wanted to share with the local police or people in the host country.

In this respect it is important to say a few words about the personal motivation of these female police officers in respect to international missions, regardless of the difficulties such work places on their personal lives. The motivation to go was genuinely about the willingness to be involved and assist in the process of transformation for a more secure environment. 'The reason for me to go was to be there for them, to be present and share my expertise. Our job was to unite the local police and who would be better for the job than a Finnish policewoman.'

Huhtinen (2004: 98) argues that '[s]ecurity is a feeling, not a fact.' In this respect the female police officers saw their work providing a sense of security for the local population by mentoring the local police. Similarly, gaining and learning from international colleagues and forming friendships with the local population were things gained from the mission and considered invaluable. Listening to the stories of these women gave the impression that they followed their own intuition and were truly ready to take chances in order to carry out their work in the mission area. They represented the courage and strength that follow from professional experience, self-confidence and the capacity to work in cooperation with other international colleagues as well as the colleagues from the host country. The stories of how they got to be in particular missions and the events that followed seem to be filled with incredible coincidences, surprising events and situations that come up and play out in unanticipated ways.

Although feminist literature is about change, the recent literature on war, peacekeeping or security has said very little on what is working well in crisis management and placed very little attention on those exceptional spaces where something positive can be created by the dialogue with security agents and population in the host country. In feminist security studies, the aspect of healing, recovery and empowerment are rarely addressed, but instead it is common to focus on inequality, gender subordination and violence. In regard to peacekeeping there is a tendency to look for misconduct, of both male and female staff, and a lack of discussion about how security agents are able to exceed the limits of the possible, resulting in saving just one girl at one time from the hands of the militia, creating a connection with an Albanian grandmother at one in the morning during a house search or organizing a collection of used footballs from Finnish sports teams for kids in Kosovo.

But to achieve this flow, the police officers explained, one has to give up all prejudices about the other and not demand them to change, whether it was the culturally different colleagues at work with their quirky habits (in respect of Nordic habits), or the locals with different culture and habits than any of the internationals. In other words, right action stems from a sense of acceptance of the present moment as it is and deep understanding of the connectedness of oneself with others in the world.

'Some say that we are so different, but the way I see it, is that we are very much the same.'[7]

RESPONSIBILITY TO PROTECT (WHOM AND WHAT)?

As noted earlier, the rationale of increasing the number of women in peacekeeping and civilian missions is that they will be better received by local populations, which in turn will increase operational efficiency. Yet, when the meaning of gender was addressed in the interviews, discussion would most often turn to the ways that male colleagues related to the female police officers on the same mission. What was shared by the women was that a female colleague represented a person with whom one can share one's worries and hardships on the mission or at home. It was easier for the policemen to discuss difficulties in personal life with their female colleagues, indeed, because femininity is associated with empathy and care.

The stressful atmosphere of mission life and being far from home added to the personal and professional pressure. This pressure might unfold as suggestions and passes and outright sexual harassment in the setting in which women form a minority in an overall masculinist institution (see Haaland, this volume). Some of the female police officers had also been on military peacekeeping operations and had experience from such intense situations, which differ from the civilian missions. On the civilian missions these women felt they were subject to fewer sexual advances and less pressure as it was easier for the internationals to form relationships with locals, which often did happen, for example, with interpreters.

Generally, heavy drinking and partying were activities that their male colleagues would engage in during weekends and days off. The women interviewed were not so keen on such activities, and some saw it rather as a threat to the security of the mission. 'I always worried about what the guys would blurt out while drunk. If you drink on the mission, you better not do it with the locals.'[8]

In the stories on what the life on the mission is like, partying and drinking and bragging about partying and drinking were things that seemed to color the everyday of mission life for the male colleagues, from whom the female police officers wanted to differentiate themselves. Certainly this did not involve all the men on the missions, nor is true that women would never be involved in such activities, yet it portrays the kind of culture or life of the male internationals in a foreign country.

The mission itself was referred to as a different world or even as an isolated island in which different rules apply. This referred to culture of a place that the internationals form in opposition to the host country and the place that is 'home.' It seemed that things that cannot be done at home are allowed and accepted as normality in this separate and isolated world of the mission (place upon a place). Therefore, drinking, promiscuity and sexual affairs were accepted as part of normal mission life. Yet, the place is an aquarium, for although contained, the actions of the crisis management experts cannot remain hidden as conduct and misconduct are also known by the locals in the host country. The resentment for this masculinist culture creates a demand for change and it is indeed perceived that female police and military will break this culture of hegemonic masculinity.

Female police officers were perceived as less likely to share the masculinist and imperialist culture of drinking and sexual exploitation. However, increasing the number of women on the mission to take care and look after their partying colleagues might be a heavy burden to bear. The expectation that the women would take a position of empathy and care was something that all the female police officers at some point had to deal with. In these moments, situations and events, gendered identities concretize and expectations are negotiated, although the female police officers had not set out to go on the mission in order to offer care for male colleagues as their main goal.

In this respect it does seem that politically it would be a wise move to send individuals from Nordic countries that are gendered as women, for they are on the basis of their female body and Nordic cultural background given a better chance, as physically they do not represent the male majority and are less likely to engage in imperialist mission culture or exploitation. Yet, equating female police officers with competence for right action, empathy, care and high integrity in turn creates the position of the male police officer as the binary opposite prone to misconduct and irresponsibility. Certainly this cannot be the intention of the range of Nordic 1325 NAPs. However, as the image of the ESDP missions is also important and the demands for loyalty are strong, the purpose of sending female staff to keep their male colleagues in line seems to be about protecting the image of the CCM mission, in addition to taking care of the male colleagues.

CONCLUSIONS

So, to answer the question: What exactly is the purpose of increasing the number of women in crisis management? I would like to answer by saying that what indeed is in demand is an internal gender balance of an ethically competent security agent. In other words, what is sought after is the capacity to manage oneself before going to manage others. It is indeed about the four modes of physical, mental, social and spiritual competence and moreover personal responsibility over one's being and actions. Action competence can be likened to emotional intelligence (Goleman 1997) or body–mind intuitive form of knowledge characterized as flow, which emerges from the mastery of a skill. In terms of crisis management it is a matter of being able to act in the right way, in the present moment, in alignment with body-mind-spirit, even though it might mean exceeding the mandate and institutional limitations.

As such the politics of increasing the number of women is a politics of hope. For it is hoped that (Nordic) female police officers are more likely to embody this subjective gender and body–mind balance and operate from the position of action competence. Hoping as a form of politics is not a strong form of politics. Hoping is without agency, and as such, it is weak. When one hopes that a desired outcome will happen, one gives up one's own power to influence the outcome. Hoping is passive and leaves outcomes to be determined by circumstances that are also seen as without agency. One simply hopes that the people sent on the missions will act the way they are supposed to and fulfill the demands expected of them and the power that is required to keep power relations in place remains invisible (Enloe 1996). The politics of SCR 1325 aim to be stronger than that and replace hope with a demand for right action.

Certainly, the politics of hope is not without any grounds at all. Indeed, this hoping is based on the experience of the past, which shows that dedicated, professional and hardworking female police officers seek to go on missions and are willing to put themselves on the line. Yet, the weakness relies on the fact that responsibility, dedication, empathy and care cannot be reduced to gendered subjectivity, and in this case to female police officers.

However, as women are a minority in the police and military and as such an exception, women are also under closer scrutiny of their behavior. Women in the police or in the military cannot use the phrase 'boys will be boys' to legitimate heavy drinking or use of commercial sexual services. Yet, a woman may choose to adopt also this same attitude and same behavior and be one of the guys (Jukarainen, this volume). Her female body does not prevent her from such activities.

It seems that the increase of women is a corrective measure to the misconduct and problems that have arisen from the so-called mission life. Hoping that men behave better when women are around puts an enormous task on the women on the missions, especially as there are so few of them. Despite the politics of increasing the number of women in crisis management and regardless of the number of countries that have published SCR 1325 action plans, the number of women selected to crisis management is still very low as some countries do not second women at all. Also in this regard, the politics of hope is not very effective.

Indeed, one could argue that the politics of SCR 1325 action plans is not add-women-and-stir, but add-women-and-hope. Instead of politics of hope, I argue for the balance of masculine and feminine subjectivity, self-reflexivity and responsibility and call for recognition of the capacity to manage oneself before attempting to manage others.

Moreover, it must be recognized that the capacity and competence for empathy, feminine care and emotional intelligence need not be a position embodied only by Nordic female CCM personnel. These qualities may be embodied by individuals gendered as men, or as the others, local women and men. What is required is a transformation of the possibilities of gendered and ethnicized subjectivities, so that there are other ways to recognize and assert masculine subjectivity of the international than the disrespectful, exploitative form now so familiar from the peacekeeping operations as well as from civilian missions. This is necessary if indeed there is a desire to increase the number of women, for otherwise the task of empathy and care may just be too much for the actual women on the missions whose mastery of skills in crisis management go to protecting the image of the mission instead of assisting the host population to establish human security.

NOTES

1. Quote from interview with a female police officer November 2007.
2. In this same volume, McLeod shows how SCR 1325 can be given new meaning in terms of building hope for a more secure society in Serbia. In other words, the resolution had been adopted for different purposes and politics that perhaps were also something that the Finnish working group was hoping to achieve elsewhere, by focusing on the idea of increasing the number of women. Moreover, the process of establishing NAPs seemed to quickly become a competition of who could put together the best SCR 1325 of the Nordic countries (involving Finland, Norway and Sweden).
3. Parashar discusses this same literature in a different light and shows the complexity on how women experience war that defies the binary logic between passive victims or violent women as deviant.
4. Interviews in November 2007.
5. Interview January 2008.
6. This comment also represents the attitude in general of Finnish police officers, both male and female. They are proud that they are there to do their work as well as possible, not to party, socialize or flirt with colleagues. One female police officer commented that Finnish officers are even seen as being too serious about their work.
7. Interview November 2007.
8. Interview January 2008.

12 Women in Militant Movements
(Un)Comfortable Silences and
Discursive Strategies

Swati Parashar

INTRODUCTION

'But I thought feminism is all about being antiwar. Why are we debating the "war" question in feminism? Should we not be talking about antiwar strategies?'[1]

This anxiety expressed by a senior feminist academic at a workshop on the 'war question in feminism' in Sweden, which I also attended in September 2008, sums up the angst within feminist (particularly international relations [IR]) scholarship, which has yet to come to terms with the multiple roles of women in war situations. One would think that feminist scholarship has moved beyond reductionist analyses of women as 'victims' of war, as civilian casualties, collateral damage and as antiwar/peace activists (Sylvester and Parashar 2009). However, the (un)comfortable silences or excessive curiosities I have often encountered in conferences and workshops where others or I have raised the issue of violent/militant women suggests that gender essentialization and/or exceptionality continue to be the discursive frameworks that inform analyses of women's violence and thereby perpetuate war myths (Sjoberg and Gentry 2007; Parashar 2009; MacKenzie 2010). The question asked of women's violence and their participation in wars is always about motivations and subjectivity. The assumption here is that there is always a personal (is not political?) motive involved and women's political violence is often the consequence of patriarchal manipulations. Feminism itself has remained camped within peace and antiwar discourses and has situated war outside the 'everyday' experiences of women (Sylvester 2010b).

Judith Butler reminds us that 'gender is a performance with clearly punitive consequences' (1988: 522). What, then, are the implications of this performance in wars and conflicts? How does Butler's gender, a historical situation (not an embodied fact) interact with war as another historical situation? Contemporary wars are enactments of identity politics (Kaldor 2006) and gender plays an important role in how these wars are legitimized and exceptionalized. Participation of women on the one hand legitimizes the war and on the other also allows for the war and women fighters to be presented as 'exceptional.' Gender codes are written into the performances of major actors (men, women, states and nonstate militias) in these wars. Such wartime gender codes have a dual capability, of either subverting social and political norms or perpetuating war myths. My particular research interest is the gendered performances of women militants (as part of nonstate militias) and their impact on the feminist assertion that the 'personal is political and, therefore, the international.' How do we understand 'militarized femininities'? If wars are not exceptions and neither are women's roles in them (MacKenzie 2010), why must feminist scholarship exceptionalize women's violence and cage them in the binary discourse of agency and victimhood, thereby denying possibilities of any empowerment, joy, fear, vengeance or any other kind of politics?

Wars are rendered exceptional (MacKenzie 2010) and nonstate actors who wage wars against states and peoples are the deviant 'other.' While women in the state armed forces have generated a degree of gendered analyses, it is the absence of the study of these 'other' women in nonstate militant projects (Roy 2009) that I am interested in. Post-9/11 policy and academic fields witnessed a flurry of writings emerging on nonstate actors as the 'enemy other.' 'Terrorists' (like Osama bin Laden, Vellupillai Prabhakaran)[2] and 'terrorist groups' like Al Qaeda and the Liberation Tigers of Tamil Elam (LTTE) have been represented as the evil and irrational nonstate actors challenging the might of rational and benevolent states. In these wars between good and evil (Bush versus Bin Laden) women are either invisible or rendered voiceless victims whom men on both sides claim to be protecting (Sylvester and Parashar 2009). There has been lack of sustained and critical engagement with women who perform multiple roles in these wars and especially as perpetrators, planners and patrons of militant activities.[3]

In the next three sections of this chapter, I discuss the nature of contemporary wars as postmodern with blurred boundaries and shifting identities and, using examples from Kashmir and Sri Lanka, explain how these 'new wars' might affect gender performances especially of women as combatants and as support bases of violent political projects. I further discuss the exclusions of these women militants from academic and policy discourses and national narratives and highlight how they present a theoretical conundrum for IR feminists. I conclude with a discussion of the politics of silence around the lives and choices of these women and the discursive spaces available to IR feminists to analyze war stories that challenge these exclusions and silences.

NEW WARS AND IDENTITY POLITICS

The post–Cold War period is marked by the politics of 'new wars' where the 'claim to power is on the basis of seemingly traditional identities-nation, tribe, religion' (Kaldor 2006: 72) and other such particularistic identities. Globalization and declining state power are two main reasons cited by Kaldor in her discussion of new wars and identity politics. These new wars are mostly protracted wars where the frontiers are blurred, where identities are constantly shifting and where civilians are bombed and killed indiscriminately. Miriam Cooke has described these new wars as postmodern wars, which:

> fall into post–World War II nuclear period and maybe individually situated in a post colonial context.... Such wars provide multiple discursive spaces in which individuals can find, retain and interpret agency.... Postmodern wars highlight and then parody those very binaries—war/peace, good/evil, front/home front, combatant/non combatant, friend/foe, victory/defeat, patriotism/pacifism—which war had originally inspired. (Cooke and Woollacott 1993: 179–180)

An important aspect of these new wars is the presence of a large number of actors (men, women, militant groups, states), identity politics and divergence of strategies and objectives. Politics is no longer confined to the high levels and acquires an 'everyday' character as violence and the struggle for power enters 'home' and the 'private' (Roy 2007; Das 2007). Violence of these new wars is pervasive and is not only shaped by the identity politics[4] but also has an impact on the political project that deploys it. 'Violence is not necessarily the exclusive character of the "other", but rather, and perhaps even above all, a means through which the "self", whether individual or collective, is constituted and maintained' (de Vries and Weber 1997: 2). Women cannot be kept out of such wars and violence as it enters their traditional domain of the private home. Women, thus, participate in these postmodern wars and in the identity politics, where anarchy and order, voice and silence are not just paradoxes but can be simultaneously present in the blurring of boundaries and the production of the 'self' and the 'other.'

I extend this understanding of new identity wars to the two political conflicts in South Asia, Kashmir and Sri Lanka, which are based on different ideologies but with relatively similar objectives and identity politics. Both these conflicts are products of colonial and postcolonial politics and sociocultural interactions (between majority and minority communities) and have a long history of organized militancy and guerrilla warfare targeted against the state, its security agencies and unarmed civilians as the 'other.' The secessionist (antistate) politics in these two conflicts derive their moral and ethical legitimacy from constructions of victimhood at the hands of an oppressive militarized state and of the 'other' as the decadent enemy.[5] Transnational networks have provided moral and material support to these movements and internecine rivalries have had severe impacts on their politics. These two antistate secessionist movements have also gone through periods of ceasefire and political engagement that have not paved way for a long-term resolution of the conflicts (Parashar 2009, 2011). The 'everyday-ness' of violence has affected the lives of people, the economy and the infrastructure in both Kashmir and Sri Lanka.[6]

However, despite these similarities, these conflicts differ significantly in their methodology, propaganda, network and ideology. In Sri Lanka, the conflict is between two major ethnic groups (Sinhalas and the Tamils) and the antistate resistance by the Tamils has a distinct ethno-nationalist origin. The resistance itself has gone through several stages of political and violent engagements and the actors have transformed over the years. Pockets of resistance organized around several militant groups gradually got crystallized around the LTTE, led by the charismatic Vellupillai Prabhakaran. One ethnic community (Tamils), represented by one resistance group (LTTE) organized around the cult of its leader, Prabhakaran, and engaged in long, drawn-out guerrilla warfare, including terror tactics like suicide bombings and political assassinations against the Sinhalese state and civilians. This sums up the situation in Sri Lanka until May 2009.[7]

Kashmir offers a much more complex conflict scenario, involving many actors and claimants to nationalism and representation. The external factor is a strong determinant as the militant groups are based in the territory of a neighboring state (Pakistan), and apart from the local indigenous population also have within their cadres mercenaries from Afghanistan and Pakistan. The antistate militancy is targeted against the Indian security forces and Indian citizens (Hindus, Muslims and Sikhs) seen as the 'other' who are soft targets in Kashmir as well as in other parts of India. Religious identity plays an important role in the nationalist project and the secessionist demands in Kashmir. I, therefore, categorize the Kashmir conflict as a religio-political movement that relies heavily on religious symbols (Parashar 2011).

Women have been victims of the terror campaign unleashed by militant groups both in Kashmir and Sri Lanka and much has been written and documented about women's sufferings and their survival strategies that have challenged normative gender roles in these conservative and traditionally patriarchal societies. However, the lack of scholarly engagement with women's involvement in the militancy and how they negotiate their roles as cultural bearers of national identities show that mainstream discourses continue to be gender blind, excluding women from the local and international arena and most importantly denying them their politics and what I call political labor. These two cases of militancy in Kashmir and Sri Lanka have used a range of tactics and women have been engaged at the logistical, ideological and even at the combatant levels. Women have facilitated and participated in violent activities that include guerrilla warfare, conventional combat and suicide bombings, and have acted as couriers of bombs, weapons, money and messages. What is intriguing is the absence of women in the national narratives of these political projects, or their stereotypical portrayal as 'victims' of militarized masculine projects that I address in the section ahead.

WAR STORIES AND THE POLITICS OF SILENCE/S

Despite some scholarly and policy interest in women's roles in Islamic insurgent movements in Palestine, Chechnya and even Iraq, Kashmir stands out as a case where women's silence in the dominant accounts has rendered women invisible. Men have claimed heroism and sacrifice in the Kashmiri militant movement. Some of the dreaded militants' stories have become part of popular folklore[8] whereas women's support to and participation in the popular militancy has almost been a taboo subject. 'Women have been the worst sufferers in the conflict,' I was often told during the interviews.[9] The only stories that are ever privileged are stories of pain, mourning and suffering. Unlike any other national project, Kashmir has only absented women from its politics. The silence of women is almost deafening. The message is often clear, women do not do politics or militancy, but their grief and mourning serve many political projects. It testifies to the state oppression and establishes the direct assault of the state on public morality and religious traditions. This is the gendered story of Kashmir. Individual silencing (on women's roles in the militancy) has created a collective silencing in the case of Kashmir. This politics of silence itself is not always imposed and may even be a negotiated survival strategy for women in a highly patriarchal society and polity (D' Costa 2006: 144).[10] I argue that silence can be, among several things, a gendered response within a patriarchal project that marginalizes women from politics and from public discourses.

Actual Kashmiri women serving in different militant groups as combatants have been very few in number, but without their support militancy against the Indian state would not have acquired enormous popular legitimacy in the 1990s.[11] As several men confided, their armed resistance would not have survived without the active support of the women members of their families. Motherhood is especially venerated as Kashmiri mothers have in the past encouraged their sons to take up arms against their oppressors. A former militant I interviewed shared very insightful comments on motherhood:

> I got my feelings from a mother and wherever you have seen it the mothers are most proud about nationalism, in folklore you will see that boys (I won't say men I say boys) get inspired from what they hear from their mothers. In the folklore about the heroes and the tales about the mujahids howsoever you describe it. So, you get the passion, you may not get the reason from the mother. That passion transferred from your mother is for everyone to see. If the mother is passionate about the cause, the cause will find more and more people joining the movement. (Interview 2008)

The movement becomes a legitimate cause as mothers become the gendered revolutionary bridges. The former militant who now works as an educationist further said:

Once you remove the mothers it affects the functioning of the militants, the pressure starts building upon them. So if you remove the mother you remove the social sanctity. If your mother is with you it is but natural that your sister is with you. If women folk are helping you in the cause, they are the most who push you and once they feel that the cause is of no worth they may help you to get back. (Interview 2008)

The motherhood narrative, therefore, plays a very important role in the mobilization of women by the militant groups operating in Kashmir. As Sjoberg and Gentry have suggested, 'the mother narrative describes women's violence as a need to belong, a need to nurture, and a way of taking care of and being loyal to men; motherhood gone awry' (2007: 13). Of all the militant groups that are actively targeting women in order to expand their support network for jihad, Lashkar-e-Toiba (Army of Pure) uses the motherhood narrative most effectively in its mobilization strategy. The Lashkar chief, Hafiz Saed, has often been heard in conventions and rallies appealing to the sacrifices of mothers in the cause of jihad. Motherhood provides greater justification for jihad, as appeals are made to the mothers of Islam to sacrifice their sons, those sons whose duty it is to protect their mothers (Haq 2007; Naim 2008). The sacrifice of the mother is held greater than the monetary contribution in jihad. Paradoxically, while these mother narratives are part of the public face of militancy and women are encouraged to have a political voice in jihad, their roles are constructed within accepted norms of femininity. Women, thus, gain access to public spaces in their gendered roles as mothers but the objective is to use that public space and legitimacy to reinstate traditional gender norms where women belong to the home and hearth (Haq 2007; Parashar 2011).

Apart from gendered deployments of motherhood that were quite common, women also aided the militancy through direct involvement. Muslim Khawateen Markaz (Muslim Women's Organization) was established in 1989 as a legitimate and organized channel for women to contribute in the militancy. There is also speculation that militant groups are training women to become ground operatives and vital intelligence links. Apart from these direct involvements there are also radical groups such as the Dukhtaran-e-Millat (Daughters of Faith) whose founder Asiya Andrabi is an open supporter of the militancy and the mujahideen. She advocates that women should perform the jihad at home by taking care of their families while the men go out as mujahideen to fight against the oppressive Indian state according to Islamic principles. She bases her arguments entirely on theological ground that, she claims, does not permit women to directly take up arms but expects women to support in whatever way they can, the holy war or jihad for a just cause. She denies that Kashmiri women would take up arms as there are enough men to do the job but also admits that if such a need arose women would not step back, like their Palestinian and Chechen sisters had shown before (Parashar 2011).

Kashmir is an interesting case study of a political conflict in which women's direct participation is denied on theological grounds on one hand and is expected along traditional notions of femininity on the other. Both men and women have been at the forefront of denying women any direct engagement with armed resistance and promoting a culture of silence and secrecy about women's past engagements with militancy. One interviewee, who has even served a jail term on charges of siphoning funds to militant groups, had this to say:

> I do not want to glorify the women by saying that we held guns and all that because this will create trouble for the women folk, for this reason only I do not want to say anything about women holding guns. Otherwise, I used to have a gun under my bed and there is nothing great about it. At that time every locality used to have two to three militant (women), they used to have guns and everyone used to know that, so, it is an open secret.

She further confided:

> The militancy cannot be so successful unless there is direct assistance and help of women. It is a fact that there was no way that militancy would have reached to the levels it did without the work done by the women. We used to carry guns; we have done work and contributed to the militancy. Now it is past so I do want to rake up all that now. Women had participated and made contributions to the movement. I am saying that I was positively involved with the movement. I was one of the first women participants of this movement. (Interview July 2008)

It is these silences about women's roles in the militancy that have further perpetuated women's exclusion from peace processes. Women are missing from any political talks between the governments of India, Pakistan and the Kashmiri leadership.

In Sri Lanka, despite some existing discourses on the Tamil militant women, the high degree of secrecy maintained by the LTTE has done little to forefront the different voices of the women in the movement. Sometimes their voices have been mediated through various external sources.[12] The government and the LTTE accounts have privileged the male leadership (of the LTTE leader, Prabhakaran) and the masculine discourse of the conflict based on military prowess. Many women combatants were at the battlefront, fighting for their leader, their homeland and their convictions. We will never get to hear their real stories especially as the government's military campaign finally defeated and killed the LTTE fighters, including their high-profile leadership, in May 2009. The highly centralized and secretive organization that the LTTE was allowed 'outsiders' virtually no access to its members and guerrilla fighters. In most of the available accounts there are embedded silences of their (women cadres') version of events and situation, their aspirations and their frustrations at the devaluation of their political labor.

The LTTE had an active women's wing from the late 1980s where women were trained not just for direct combat and guerrilla warfare but also for suicide bombings, intelligence gathering, communication networking and for other logistical work during the war years (Balasingham 1993, 2001; Schalk 1992; Narayan Swamy 1994). The inclusion of women was an intelligent political decision that not only served to enhance the popular legitimacy of the LTTE's separatist war but also won them the support of committed women cadres who were in many cases better fighters and strategically more effective suicide bombers. These women cadres have drawn a degree of scholarly interest over the years with scholars debating about their 'victim' or 'agent' status within the LTTE's patriarchal militant ideology. Whether these women were able to make independent choices has often been questioned in studies that indicated gender segregation within the LTTE as well as decision-making was tightly controlled by the top male leadership including major suicide operations such as that of Indian Prime Minister Rajiv Gandhi (Kartikeyan and Raju 2004). Feminist scholars have criticized the forced conscriptions of women and girls and of the LTTE's patriarchal and militarized political project that rendered women as 'cogs in the wheel' (Coomaraswamy 1997; de Mel 2001, 2007). Some scholarship attributes a sense of empowerment for these women, though, highlighting its ambivalent nature (Rajasingham-Senanayake 2001; Alison 2003, 2004; Gonsalves 2003).

I interviewed 16 former women cadres of the LTTE during my visit to Trincomalee and Batticaloa in August 2008. At the time of my visit, the LTTE was engaged in a war with the Sri Lankan Armed Forces in the North and by May 2009, the war was officially over with the massive defeat of the LTTE and the elimination of its top leadership, including chief Prabhakaran. The women I interviewed had already left the LTTE during the 2006 split between Prabhakaran and Colonel Karuna.[13] The women were keen to talk and to tell their stories and were even surprised that someone from outside was interested in talking to them. These women left the LTTE in the unprecedented circumstance of the split between Prabhakaran and Col. Karuna. Life after the LTTE had unleashed problems that were not just part of the conflict milieu but were also sociocultural and political responses and reactions to the disruption of the traditional feminine identity that occurred when women joined the militant group. A sense of 'homelessness' had come to haunt these former cadres. One of the interviewees said:

> Lots of girls are unable to marry. Some girls are disabled and the dowry expected of girls in the movement is very high. I have selected my companion but am still struggling. We expect society to rehabilitate us. I

had to change my mentality because I had worn the uniform for eight years. (Interview 2008)

However, it is their political labor that they had fond memories of and that to a great extent gave them a purpose in life. In my interviews with them, they spent considerable time describing the work they did, driving trucks and lorries, handling communicating equipment, being a bodyguard to Col. Karuna, whom they called Amman (uncle), participating in the battle or volunteering to be a suicide bomber. I met women who had lost a limb or an eye in the battle but they did not seem to regret their association with the LTTE even though some were coerced to join while a few were attracted to the ideology or compelled due to other reasons.[14] There seems to be consensus in accepting that the 2006 split within the LTTE ranks had caused great setback to the *Eelam* (homeland) plans and even though these women had served under Col. Karuna, they believed that only a united LTTE could make possible the dreams of a homeland for which they had all sacrificed.

The feeling of homelessness never ceases to exist in the lives of these women, before, within and beyond the LTTE. Having partly accepted this premise, I am still bothered by the fact that the multiple experiences of these women remain captured in binary discourses about agency and victimhood. This only serves to create discursive boundaries and sustains stereotypes about the lives of these women militants. Whether militancy should make them victims or should liberate them does not question the character of the militant projects, and instead limits the possibilities of discursive analogies that can capture, among other things, the politics of these women and their aspirations. The split in the LTTE brought about the end of the war for them, and they were disbanded and were forced to return home. This transition to the mainstream was not all a happy story. Most of the women I interviewed conveyed that being in the 'state of war' held more opportunities to experience joy and fulfillment than an enforced peace or being 'out of war.' The state of homelessness was unleashed on them in the absence of war. While documenting the lives of these women I have asked myself what purpose it would serve to deny these women their politics, their joy and sense of fulfillment and, instead, assign victimhood and/or empowerment in any 'scholarly' vocabulary.

The debate about agency and victimhood, thus, serves to treat women like objects of discursive practices as we discuss politics 'on' them and not 'by' them. I am conscious of any generalizations based on my interviews and fieldwork and do not wish to imply that the women I met are representative of all the women who have served in the LTTE. Each experience is special and unique and together they constitute a powerful voice of women's participation in the Tamil militant nationalist project. However, the varied experiences of these women also tell stories of the silences that are at work and that need to be countered while the narrative of the Tamil nation is still in the process of being constructed (given that the movement has entered a new phase after the defeat of the LTTE). The voices of these women are important, and when unpacked reveal the politics of exclusion and inclusion that is deployed in particular nationalist contexts; politics that subverts gender norms and roles and unleashes new social and cultural processes.

FEMINIST IR'S DILEMMA AND POSSIBILITIES OF NEW WAR STORIES?

Feminist IR continues to be troubled by women's violence and wars in general (Sylvester 2005; Parashar 2009). Having already pushed violence into the realm of militarized masculinity, IR feminists have engaged in scholarly censorship of women who participate in any kind of political violence. Women do not 'do' violence, at least not as autonomous agents or in the same way as men, has been the commonly held belief. Apart from militarized masculinities, peacekeeping and peace building are the other areas that feminist scholarship has contributed to. There are no feminist IR textbooks at this point that address women's political violence along with other topics.[15] The problem envisaged here is not that there are some militants who are women[16] but that there are women who 'choose' to be militants, support political violence and whose lives are closely entwined with the militant project in which they participate.

Feminists have, at best, claimed ambivalent agency for women who participate in any kind of political violence. Feminist ethical studies have suggested that agency is the freedom from violence or force and it is contradictory to assume that violence can be an ethical means to bring about freedom from violence (Hutchings 2007; Roy 2009). What is of significance here is that the subjectivity of women militants has often been subsumed in the debate about the (violent) act that is performed. Once again revisiting Butler (1988), we can argue that in the dual performance, of gender and of the political moment of war, it is the latter that is often deployed (in most scholarship) to suggest that it is not only a historical moment of exceptionality for women (participating in wars is not normal for women), but also that it does not empower women even as they gain access to public spaces and political means, and there is an 'everyday' experience of violence. This seems almost antithetical to feminist claims that the personal is political. Butler reminds us:

> subjective experience is not only structured by existing political arrangements, but effects and structures those arrangements in turn. . . . Systemic or pervasive political and cultural structures are enacted and reproduced through individual acts and practices, and the analysis of ostensibly personal situations is clarified through situating the issues in a broader and shared cultural context. (1988: 522)

Veena Das (in Cushman 2004) argues that in experiences of cultural (extended also to gender) repressions are also inherent experiences of freedom. Other scholars have also interrogated normative understandings of 'emancipation' and 'agency' in oppressive cultural regimes and religious practices (Mahmood 2001; Bucar 2010). I argue that to suggest that women are incapable of thinking, internalizing and acting out politics, especially of a violent nature, and to question the motivations of those who do is a disempowering feminist discursive strategy. In Kashmir, the personal is political as women participate in the militancy within the confines of traditional gender roles. Their jihad is performed at home, to keep the men (husbands, brothers and sons) ideologically motivated and to take charge of the home when the men go for jihad outside. In Sri Lanka, behind the politics of the LTTE women cadres are personal experiences of tragedy and triumph, of home and homelessness, of suffering and empowerment and of equality and discrimination. The personal and the political are not binaries and interact closely in the multiple experiences of these women.

I have tried to demonstrate in this chapter the processes of silencing that work to exclude the voices of women militants. I do not equate silence with voicelessness or with powerlessness. I recognize that silence does not imply a lack of speech imposed upon the powerless and neither is it inimical to politics (Parpart 2009; Ferguson 2003). Silence is not always absence and can be a powerful tool for politics and resistance. Ferguson (2003) has argued that silence does not merely reinforce or resist power, but can be used to constitute selves and even communities. Silence also takes multiple forms and its politics is not fixed and determined, nor can it be captured in binary discourses. Silence in the case of women militants is imposed in various ways and is also much nuanced in terms of the politics it captures; the politics of empowerment, survival and negotiation and of victimhood and disappointment, of freedom and also of fear, as I found in the two South Asian cases.

Jane Parpart (2009) raises an important question about why voice is often equated with agency and argues that 'silence' can be a subtle strategy of transformation and resistance. But while silence maybe a 'negotiated survival strategy' that could provide limited possibilities of resistance,[17] it is difficult to imagine that within all 'silences,' agency and choices are inherently being negotiated. Choosing 'silence' does not always mean an empowering and autonomous experience but is moderated or influenced by other factors. When IR feminists study war, locating and understanding such 'silences' become necessary in order to tell new war stories, previously unheard and yet powerful tales of gender subordination and performances. What, therefore, interests me is: Which voices are privileged in a war narrative and what do they tell us about the voices that are silent? Silencing and censoring the experiences of militant women only serves to legitimate the larger patriarchal politics of excluding and undermining women's political contributions and denying their political labor. Recognizing only certain kinds of women's political activities and voices is a problematic framework of gendered inquiry that strips women of difference and renders them powerless (Sjoberg and Gentry 2007; Hirsch and Spitzer 1993).

Christine Sylvester argues against overgeneralization and for recognizing multiple gender subjectivities that are produced in the context of wars and conflicts. Sylvester (1994, 2005) offers homesteadings for feminists within IR, but of a different nature. She argues, 'Homesteadings refers here to processes that reconfigure known subject statuses . . . but also the common places of human men and women—in ways that open up rather than fence in terrains of meaning, identity, and place' (1994: 2). I adopt this homesteading, for it provides an opportunity to engage with women's participation in militant projects while remaining cognizant of fluid identities and changing/shifting gender roles in militancy. Sylvester (1994) provides an insight we cannot ignore: Can we have meaningful categories of women and question them too? My feminist propositions, therefore, are first to study wars as important sociopolitical processes that impact the lives of women and men and to discover and narrativise war stories that are silent in dominant narratives as feminist war studies has already started doing (see Sylvester 2005, 2010a, 2010b; MacKenzie 2009, 2010; Parashar 2009, 2011; Sjoberg and Gentry 2007), and second to problematize women as 'women' and war as 'exception' and engage with the ways in which the two performances of war and gender interact with each other and impact the particular historical moments in which they are enacted.

It was the Touching War program (2008–2009) at Lancaster University, directed by Christine Sylvester[18] that offered a refreshing scholarly space to discuss the emotional and physical aspects of war; a space vital to any critical inquiry about women's participation in political violence and emerging feminist analytical frameworks. For the first time, there was a debate organized on the issue of Women: Armed and Dangerous,[19] a debate that offered new insights on gender and women engaged in political violence. Elina Penttinen was particularly persuasive as she argued that the feminist IR community should not be trapped in its puzzles and problems and should stretch boundaries of imagination and analysis. She concluded that if we did focus on the cheerful, happy (different) things in IR, we would contribute to a more hopeful, joyous world, something that we all need to survive. What we are leaving out in our quest for serious and problem-making scholarship are moments and events when IR is about fun and being alive. How can we be sure that the stories we tell of violence and oppressions and pain and sufferings are the only 'true' stories? As feminists we can be liberated social scientists to speak of life as joy, Penttinen argued. Even in this volume, where she critiques gender essentialization and argues for the transformation of the possibilities of gendered and ethnicized subjectivities in the case of Nordic women police officers, she speaks of a politics and agency that can influence the outcome, not merely 'passive' hope.[20]

Penttinen's scholarship does two important things. One, it forces us to question the boundaries of our own scholarship and interrogate discursive strategies we deploy to understand and analyze gendered outcomes in wars and conflicts. Second, it asks why and how certain topics have become taboo in IR, like women's violence. What if wars were to be positive experiences for some, especially women? What if women did more than just wail and mourn? What if there were other and 'different' stories to tell? I find her arguments exhilarating because they consider possibilities of discussing the multiplicity of experiences of women who participate in wars and militant projects. Sylvester (2010b), like Penttinen, but in a slightly different genre, highlights how the 'difference' discourse needs rescuing within feminism. Her concern is that feminists are abandoning their commitment and solidarity to women who speak with a 'different' voice and whose actions 'hold an unpopular line and politics.' Sylvester questions the feminist contempt for women like Ayan Hirsi Ali and Azar Nafisi whose works and lived experiences challenge cultural relativism and dominant worldviews. Militant women also speak/perform the non-negotiable difference that Sylvester mentions, and a hybrid of narratives within feminist IR can reconstruct the subjectivity of these 'difficult' women based on a variety of reference points such as nationalism, religion, ethnicity and militant violence. Thus, between the two ends of victimhood and agency there are stories of survival, hope, fulfillment and of the politics of subversion and purpose.

CONCLUSION

The stories of the LTTE women are stories of joining the movement to escape the hardships of poverty, of escaping to a better world, of reliving their dream of a homeland, of escaping the harshness of violence at home, of escaping homelessness to find a home, of avenging their humiliation by Sinhalese soldiers, of finding real joy in the war, where they could do what they were best at. In Kashmir, too, women had different stories to tell; of the romantic love and longing for the militant with the gun, of songs celebrating martyrdom, of hiding guns under their beds and militants in their homes, of nursing the wounded, of encouraging sons to fight, of creating and then shouting slogans against the enemy other, of holding on to their religious identity and of politics and activism that they believed would change their world.

I am not arguing that these 'different' and missing stories that I wish to tell are stories that can make the world better. What they can do is help interpret the world, help understand the gender coding in wars and conflicts and map the silences that are often enforced on women to uphold the legitimacy of the patriarchal nationalist project. Hence, telling these different stories constitutes a political act itself that reveals a whole new world where women have a stake and claim in war and further in peace. Scholars like Sylvester, Penttinen and MacKenzie give me hope that feminist IR has much to contribute if any alternative discourse must emerge, and if women are not to be seen merely as victims and mourners.

Politics and embedded power relations decide whose narratives are privileged and what kind of silences must be promoted in the construction of the nation and national identity. Excluding the voices of militant women is a process of creating gendered myths about their violent politics perpetuated through narratives of stereotypes, exceptionality and deviance (MacKenzie 2010; Parashar 2009; Sjoberg and Gentry 2007). Multiple processes of silencing ensure that women's voices remain subdued within the militant nationalist discourse. The women of Kashmir and Sri Lanka have been silent for too long. Their silences speak; they speak loudly and in multiple voices. Are we listening?

NOTES

1. A participant at the War Question in Feminism Workshop organized at the Orebro University in Sweden (September 2008) said this during a discussion session. She is a senior academic in the US and her statement also expressed the anxieties of several other academics and activists who had gathered for the workshop.
2. Founders of Al Qaeda and the Tamil militant group in Sri Lanka, the Liberation Tigers of Tamil Elam (LTTE), respectively.
3. Sjoberg and Gentry have made a study of Lynndie England and other violent women in various contexts in their 2007 book *Mothers, Monsters, Whores*. There are some studies of women in the state militaries also available but women in nonstate militant groups have not received any significant attention in the IR literature.
4. Like suicide bombings and jihad by certain Islamist groups is justified on the basis of Islamic identity and through Islamic theological arguments.
5. Terms like 'victimhood,' 'oppressive' and 'other' are all constructed at various points in the conflict discourse and are not static categories. Both state and nonstate actors use these terms to describe themselves and the perceived 'enemy.'
6. Veena Das (2007) has described violence not as an extraordinary phenomenon but as a 'descent into the ordinary,' which remains the case in most contemporary wars and conflicts.
7. The war (military clashes between the security forces and the LTTE) officially ended in May 2009 when the Sri Lankan armed forces defeated the LTTE and killed its top leadership, including its founding chief, Prabhakaran.

However, the conflict itself is far from over. The war has left several Tamils as internally displaced and the moderate Tamil parties are working towards negotiations with the government.

8. For example, 'Rising Kashmir'—a local Kashmiri newspaper ran a story on Syed Salahudin, the leader of the militant group Hizbul Mujahideen. This story glorified him and talked about his popularity in Kashmir. See http://www.risingkashmir.com/index.php?option=com_content&task=blogsection&id=6&Itemid=36&limit=9&limitstart=9 (accessed 1 August 2009).
9. Most of my male interviewees responded that way.
10. D'Costa discusses such silences in the case of raped women in Bangladesh during the 1971 war. Silences also do not mean that the women are voiceless, D'Costa argues. But she draws attention to how the politics of silence works and what sociopolitical processes are responsible for these silences. This can be extended to studies of women's experiences in militant movements like in Kashmir.
11. Militant attacks by Pakistani groups have spread to other parts of India, including the daring attacks by the Lashkar-e-Toiba at multiple targets in Mumbai on 26 November 2008.
12. Apart from scholarly discourses on the women militants in Sri Lanka, there is some writing that has emerged from the movement itself. Adele Anne Balasingham, the Australian wife of Late Anton Balasingham, the political adviser of the LTTE, has written an insider's account of the women in the LTTE and the transformative and emancipatory character of women in the guerrilla force. Then there are documentaries like the BBC *Inside Story on the Tamil Tigers* (1992) and *My Daughter: The Terrorist*, on the Black Tigresses (suicide squad), which were made with the LTTE's full permission and are, therefore, mostly official stories that LTTE leadership wanted to tell about their women cadres.
13. Vinagamoorthy Muralitharan, or Colonel Karuna, was Prabhakaran's bodyguard once and later was made head of the LTTE's eastern command. He rebelled against Prabhakaran in 2006, disbanded his cadres and formed his own political party in 2006. He is now a minister in the current government.
14. The reasons for joining the LTTE and 'compulsions' varied. One woman said she joined to prevent her younger brother from joining as he was the only male member. Another woman joined after she was harassed by the security forces at a checkpoint. Two women told me that they ran away from school after they were inspired by the LTTE members' talk in their school. Another woman said she joined the LTTE to escape her mother's beatings; another joined to escape the poverty at home.
15. One of the latest textbooks is Laura Shepherd's (2010) *Gender Matters in Global Politics: A Feminist Introduction to International Relations*. It discusses various issues related to violence, militarization, wars, peacekeeping, peace building and masculinities but makes no mention of women fighters or militants.
16. This is especially acknowledged in analysis of women suicide bombers and women as revolutionary warriors.
17. Bina D'Costa talks about the limited potential of silence as a resistance strategy. See D'Costa's chapter in Ackerly et al. (2006).
18. Touching War was an academic program directed by Christine Sylvester at Lancaster University, UK, between October 2008 and April 2009. Numerous workshops, panels, roundtable discussions and movie screening sessions were organized to discuss physical and emotional aspects of wars. Details

can be found at http://www.lancs.ac.uk/fass/events/touchingwar/ (accessed 11 January 2011).
19. The workshop on Women: Armed and Dangerous, as part of the Touching War program was organized on 20 March 2009, at Lancaster University, UK. Megan MacKenzie, Cristina Masters, Laura Sjoberg, Christine Sylvester, Elina Penttinen and I presented our research and debated the theoretical spaces within feminism to discuss women's violent politics.
20. See Penttinen's chapter in this volume.

13 In the Business of (In)Security?
Mavericks, Mercenaries and Masculinities in the Private Security Company

Paul Higate

> Washington's adoption of a policy of pre-emptive warfare has created ... a culture ... a world in which conflict [is] fought without rules and without regard to national sovereignty [this] has become the norm ... it is no coincidence that a new breed of freelance soldier has come into his own, maintaining traditional qualities of ruthlessness and *deniability* but employing a thoroughly modern modus operandi ... the freelance soldier has ... become part of a well-ordered corporate structure. (Geraghty 2009: 3; emphasis added)

INTRODUCTION AND BACKGROUND

While there is little new in the existence of 'guns for hire' or 'mercenaries'[1] for more critically inclined commentators, few predicted the extent to which these (mainly) men would come to supplant the activities of regular military personnel in the contemporary period. The invasion of Iraq and Afghanistan put this into sharp focus as these occupations involve many tens of thousands of contractors. Drawing on the labor of men from a range of countries including those in the global South (Maclellan 2006), this multibillion-dollar industry has become a key component in the management of conflict and its aftermath (Holmqvist 2005). A constellation of forces underpin the growth of the private security company (PSC) industry, including the dominance of post–Cold War free markets that have fueled a strong tendency to outsource traditional government functions (Krahmann 2003) and, simultaneously, regular armed forces have been downsized, providing a large number ripe for recruitment by PSCs (Holmqvist 2005). Of particular importance here is the observation that national militaries are increasingly redeployed away from second-line security roles for reasons linked in part to 'risk transfer militarism' (Shaw 2002), where body bags can be usefully exorcised from the political equation and the public opinion on which it rests. It has also been noted that 'massive arms stocks have become available to the open market' (Singer 2005: 54), which in turn has the potential to exacerbate intrastate conflict. Finally, there has been a 'decline of local state governance,' fueling greater overall insecurity around borders, markets and central bureaucratic authorities (Singer 2005: 55). As a consequence of these developments, the relative inability for national militaries to respond to insecurity compounds a cycle of instability that stimulates, and is stimulated by, the PSC sector. Companies are involved in a range of tasks, the performance of which has varying potentials to exacerbate host populations' insecurity (O'Brien 2009). For example, convoy protection duties are often associated with creating insecurity, whereas the close protection of dignitaries, static guarding of civilian and military installations, training of local personnel as part of security sector reform and provision of logistical and support functions to military peacekeeping operations tend not to have attracted such concerns (Singer 2005; Kinsey 2007). At the center of debates on PSCs is the 'strongly contested commodity of security . . . because providing it may involve the use of force and . . . decisions to kill or let live' (Leander 2009: 6). In this respect, two key developments turning on how the industry represents itself have contributed towards its increasing normalization. First, that security contractors are framed within the industry as either 'cowboys,' 'rogues' or 'professionals.'[2] This restatement of the 'bad apple' thesis in the first two categories turns on the amputation of social practice from its broader context (Plummer 1983), and as such diverts from the social-structural and cultural-generative characteristics of the private security industry. In this way, escalations of force resulting in the death and injury of members of the host population are frequently argued to be the result of exogenous factors, seemingly unrelated to the subcultures of violence in some parts of the industry within which they arise.[3] Second, the industry actively disavows inclusion of the word 'military,' and in so doing diverts attention from the militarized activities of some of its armed security contractors (Leander 2009: 11). In sum, the private security sector is framed as a benign response-led industry doing nothing more than meeting 'the security needs of states, organizations, private businesses and individuals' that are conceived of as 'pre-existing and independent from the companies they respond to' (Leander 2009: 14). Thus, disassociated from the profit/insecurity nexus, the industry is sold via its 'solution solving' pitch as just another 'client-driven' service.[4] However, it has been argued that the private security industry is energized by the business of armed conflict as a commodity that, most notably in the case of Iraq:

> Chimes perfectly with the current American approach, effectively controlled by commercial interests, notably the oil lobby. Oil—its acquisition and protection—is one of the major themes of this history, whether it is the care of BP in such disparate areas as Columbia, Algeria, Georgia and Pakistan, Shell in Nigeria or American assets elsewhere. (Geraghty 2009: 31)

In the broadest sense, it could be argued that the industry's role is to protect the hegemonic powers' various economic and political interests, through co-opting security services ranging from the mundane (static guarding of military and key civilian installations), through to the more spectacular—though less common suppression of insurrection where violent force is used. Seen in this way, private security has a key and growing role in facilitating neoliberalized processes of 'accumulation through dispossession,' as the scholar David Harvey might see it. Securing the interests of capital has a long and dark history of violent struggle that has sustained intra- and inter-gender and racial global orders configured around the subordination of women, young people and marginal men. The dramatic burgeoning of the private security sector has led commentators to describe it as the new business face of warfare in the contemporary period (Mandel 2002; Avant 2005; Kinsey 2007; Singer 2005), underscoring its significance both now and almost certainly into the future. Thus, the PSC sector should be seen as a critical subject of political inquiry as it engages international relations (IR), domestic politics and national/international legislative systems, alongside concerns of gender within the context of both ethical and moral questions concerning the use of violence.

Curiously however, scholars working within the fields of Political Science, Critical Security Studies, Law and Gender Studies have almost entirely overlooked the importance of masculinity in their analyses of this sector.[5] What do we miss when masculinity is ignored in analyses of PSC? It is not simply that the PSC industry has become increasingly important to how conflict is managed, but crucially—in contrast to regular militaries—their activities remain largely unregulated and their personnel almost entirely unaccountable[6] (Singer 2005; Leander 2009). When seen alongside the human rights abuses perpetrated by a small, but not insignificant number of private contractors—including most notoriously the shooting of 17 unarmed Iraqi civilians in Nisour Square in September 2007 (Scahill 2007a)—many have come to see the PSC sector as a regressive step in the drive to demilitarize and demasculinize the wider political, economic and social terrain. It is for this reason that the curiosity of gender scholars should be sparked since the mobilization of many thousands of men trained in the use of 'legitimate violence' can at times have an uneven impact on the security of civilian populations who have no choice but to host these corporate entities and their security contracting workforce. Understanding the institutional-identity dimensions framing this diverse corporate-gendered terrain are important for the war question in feminism since they can help explain the emergent conditions of violence, where triggers are pulled, cars rammed off roads, local men and women intimidated and countries occupied. While it is important to draw attention to social practices that can result in the death and injury of host populations and security contractors alike, it should also be acknowledged that this line of inquiry pursuing transgression diverts from the everyday, unremarkable instances of restraint exercised by contractors in their work.⁷ What is occluded in our concern to highlight the spectacular, the exotic, the abhorrent and the violent? It is crucial to note that the significant majority of security contractors do not perpetrate human rights abuses; rather they conduct themselves in a thoughtful, measured and respectful manner as they go about their work. Thus, it should be noted that security contractors are a heterogeneous community and carry diverse identities that could include, amongst others, father, brother, divorcee, ex-police, ex-military, US, Fijian, Nepalese, Chilean, British, divorcee and alcoholic. Yet, private security contractor identities and the social practices to which they give rise do nonetheless engage the embodied skill capitals of a majority of former military and police personnel, where professional repertoires are imbued with the capacity for instrumental violence warranting them an important subject of study.⁸ However, whilst this is the case, escalations of force resulting in the death and injury of host populations cannot be explained by individual pathology alone, as contingent-situational (Collins 2008) and more distant factors inflect contractor identity and their security work. For example, framed at the macro level, these privatized forms of violence are only made possible as a result of:

> Changes in the way our world functions, the vast expansion of commercial, privatised—and corporate—warfare that followed the invasions of Afghanistan and Iraq, where the freelance soldier, alongside the GI, was handed an elaborately written licence to kill, Wild West style, [which] needs to be examined carefully . . . the indefinite, undefined war on terror after 9/11, 7/7 and the invasions of Iraq and Afghanistan, fought without rules or mechanisms of international control, challenged everyone's values, including those of the professional warrior. (Geraghty 2009: 21)

Set against this ideologically constitutive backdrop where enemies are created, 'appropriate' security responses routinized and dollars generated, it can be argued that it is within the everyday practices of contractors 'that lurk some of the most potent geopolitical forces by which the geopolitical is translated into being' (Thrift 2000: 380, 384). Taking a critical look at how the everyday articulates with the international⁹ in the case of private security contractors is of pressing significance in the contemporary period. Yet, this is no easy task particularly when one seeks generalizable findings. Exacerbated by the challenges of inaccessibility and corporate sensitivity (Berndtsson 2009), the social world of the PSC remains largely closed to the research community thereby limiting the development of empirically informed thick-description of their gendered terrains.¹⁰ In a methodological sense then, following both David Morgan's (1992) text *Discovering Men* and Cynthia Enloe's strategy to apply a gender curiosity, this chapter provides fleeting glimpses of the taken-for-granted and naturalized role of militarized and masculinized social practice through secondary sources. The empirical focus for these lines of inquiry include scholarly contributions as well as texts written by war correspondents, historians, journalists and military-veteran authors. While the private security sphere is a world of complex morality, central to these corporatized institutions are their militarized-masculinized ways of seeing, doing, performing and embodying security. The process of identifying, analyzing and documenting these gendered (and racialized) fragments is the first step in engaging feminists in one modest, but growing element of the war question puzzle in respect of the privatization of violence.

LOCATING PRIVATE SECURITY CONTRACTORS: IDENTITIES OF THE 'IN BETWEEN'

How might we think through the institutional status of the private security sphere and, in turn, security contractor identity? Given the aim of making visible the militarized masculine identity of operatives, the most obvious point of departure is to consider the legacy of the regular military in their lives, since many of these men are veterans. In turn, this raises the central question of how to think through the articulation of former military identity with private security contractor identity: What kinds of transitional processes are at play here?[11]

Writing at the end of the 1950s, the sociologist Erving Goffman identified army barracks as 'total institutions.' In so doing, his emphasis on separateness, division, boundary and isolation between this (unique) institution and its host society dominated the ways that militaries have been framed. Here, there is a tendency to see military personnel as somewhat apart from their civilian hosts and, implicitly, as subjectively unique individuals. Presented in normative terms it is argued that soldiers, sailors, airmen and airwomen are not just different, but have a *'need* to be different' from their civilian counterparts (Dandeker 2000; emphasis added). The emphasis on difference and separation also shapes the political science and organizational studies' literatures where the unspoken exceptionality of the military persists by virtue of the institution's framing through its 'civil–military relations' and the 'civil–military gap.' Though proceeding on more critical terrain, the binary of civil/military, and by virtue soldier/civilian, also shapes feminist and pro-feminist critical men's studies and sociology literatures (Arkin and Dobrofsky 1978; Barrett 1996; Enloe 2000; Razack 2004; Whitworth 2004). Here, debates on military and militarized masculinities unfold on the basis of difference rather than similarity with 'civilian' masculinities. This dichotomous framing also influences media constructions of military men and women where reports in the British context concerning 'returned heroes—"our boys" killed in action'[12] jostle with commentary on 'Britain's own Abu Ghraib' involving human rights abuses made possible 'by bullying squaddies' who have killed, tortured and humiliated Iraqi citizens.[13]

Categorizing the military as a discrete sphere has undoubted utility for the analytical enterprise, and as such represents a useful way to think through the militarized, institutional-generative structures that give rise to violence. However, rather than boundary, difference and separation, it is perhaps more fruitful to conceive of the military–civilian interface as permeable and dialogic for the purposes of the current inquiry where:

> Civil–military relations [might not be seen as] two observable entities linked and separated at strategic points, but as the outcome of discursive practice, a constantly evolving network of ideas through which the ideas of the 'civilian' and 'military' are constructed, and through which the materiality of the armed forces are given meaning and brought into being. (Woodward and Winter 2007: 100)

Notwithstanding the military's path-dependent character through which gender norms shaping military cultures can remain tenacious, troubling the boundaries between civilian and military can help to foreground the unique status of the ex-military private security contractor. Thought of as neither soldier nor civilian, this diverse group could be said to inhabit a liminal, in-between, discursive space, since many of these individuals re-create military institutional cultures in the private security sphere, as well as (for a small number) move from regular service in national armed forces to the world of the private soldier and back again. The focus on identity rather than institution is—at times—better disposed to revealing the tenacity of militarized and masculinized selves as institutionalized (Higate 2001), where ability to handle weapons and use lethal force transcends the arbitrary military-institutional boundary. A focus on identity also fits with the apparent process of (re)allegiance affected by these men from military codes of loyalty to:

> Money . . . and the basic fact that any of them could walk away at any time. The sheer turnover—operators came and went, disappearing in the middle of the night . . . [they] muddle concepts like loyalty and cohesiveness. (Fainaru 2008: 60)

Though money is clearly important, it is the overall accountability gap signaled by lack of regulation and the impunity it provides for security contractors and gender-norm-bound performance that must surely feature in any explanation of human rights abuses perpetrated by these men. Given that the binary constructions of military/civil, soldier/civilian and good soldier/bad soldier limits the means by which it is possible to think through the anomalous category of the nonregular soldier or 'mercenary,' discussion now turns to one way in which to consider how militarized masculinities get rearticulated in the private security sphere.

SECURITY CONTRACTORS: MILITARIZED OR MAVERICK?

In responding to a point made earlier concerning the industry's disavowal of the word 'military' in labels attached to firms, it is useful to think of the private security sphere as constituted by a diverse range of private militarized security companies (PMSC) as a heuristic intended to highlight the gendered contexts in play here. This approach seeks to circumvent the endless typologizing of the industry in respect of company 'function' (Singer 2005; Kinsey 2007). Intuitively, it is reasonable to think of these companies as militarized, as not only are the majority of private security contractors ex-military, but also much of what they do supplants the work of regular militaries and involves allied military operating procedures and the use of firearms. Yet it appears that military values are modified in the private sphere in ways that unsettle the core tenets of what the concept of militarized is understood to signify (Enloe 2004, 2007). Thus, provisional indications of security contractor identity hint at the ubiquity of a tempered disobedience rather than obedience, coupled with a celebration of the altogether less rigid hierarchies directing their professional lives.[14] An excerpt from the Contractors Creed, though perhaps of significance to only a small number of contractors—is nonetheless an ironic reworking of the US Soldier's Creed. It includes the following lines:

> I am a US contractor. I look out for myself, the operators to my left and right, and no one else. I will always take advantage of the fact that I can finally tell military officers to pound sand, and will do so at every opportunity ... I am greedy. I care not for ribbons and awards for valor. I do this job for the opportunity to kill the enemies of my country, and to finally get that boat I've always wanted ... I will be in better shape that 99 percent of the active duty personnel, I will deploy on my terms, and if it ever gets too stupid, I will simply find another company that pays more. (Young-Pelton 2006)

Echoing this (relative) sense of freedom from rules, distancing from the regular military and superiority that could feed narcissist identities for some, it has been argued that:

> The military, for all its rigidity, was a culture of rules and accountability. That had been stripped away. In private security ... [it] was explained to me [by a contractor]: You got all the good things about the military—the camaraderie, the esprit de corps, you get to shoot things and blow things up—but with none of the other bullshit ... if you feel threatened you take a shot. (Fainaru 2008: 33)

In lifting the constraints of military life a small number of private security contractors might feel empowered to fight and kill 'the enemy' in ways that feed a sense of autonomous and empowered militarized masculinity. Here, possibilities for the use of force resonate with the idea of the frontier cowboy who, unfettered by rigorously enforced rules of engagement, directly pits his wits against a wily foe whose underhand tactics have served to liberate the 'rules of the game.'[15] Militarized identities played out in these frames could speak to nihilist masculinities considerably less likely to flourish in regular military settings (O'Brien 1993; Titunik 2007). Whilst pertaining to only a small part of the overall industry, nevertheless these hypermilitarized masculinities can exert a disproportionate impact on local people's experience and perception of the privatized occupations in both Iraq and Afghanistan.[16] A number of contractors who find the relative absence of rules and protocols liberating reaffirms the visceral appeal that violence may have for some individuals (Bourke 1999).[17] Numerous allegations point to the way legal immunity has encouraged a 'minority of mercenaries to kill civilians at random, or for target practice, from the armed public convoys they run on public roads in Iraq' (Geraghty 2009: 13). Seen in this light, the 'moral leash' on some contractors may turn on how they view themselves, rather than how they are seen by the intimidated local population (Young-Pelton 2006: 6).

PLAUSIBLE DENIABILITY AND COVERT OPERATIONS

There is a further empirical twist in this story of hybridized soldier-contractors operating in spaces of institutional and political exception signaled by the experiences of so-called 'plausibly deniable' freelance soldiers. These include British citizens who have been fighting alongside regular US Armed Forces and enjoying 'legal immunity from any consequences, including 'a massacre of civilians' (Geraghty 2009: 12). Militarized masculinities fostered in these contexts add another category to the traditional mercenary 'familiar since the wild days of the Congo in the 1960's' (Geraghty 2009: 2), and the modern-day private security operative discussed earlier. It is argued that the plausibly deniable warrior carries out missions for legitimate governments or their intelligence agencies and have a history spanning UK and US government-sponsored operations in Yemen, Oman, Afghanistan (during the Soviet occupation), Nicaragua, Sierra Leone and others (Geraghty 2009: 3). The phrase 'plausibly deniable' is worthy of particular attention since it too speaks to the nexus linking unaccountable militarized, masculinized violence with geopolitical concerns. These covert operations deploy militarized masculinities expert in the use of violence operating largely outside of formal institutional structures—in numerous cases involving unofficially 'seconded' regular national, military Special Forces personnel as noted here:

> From time to time the British government found it expedient to release SAS [Special Air Service] soldiers from regular service to serve as de-

niable guerrillas in a war aimed at regime change . . . some worked secretly, and deniably, against the Russians in Afghanistan in 1982, before [re]joining the regular army. In 2006 members of the same regiment were given leave of absence from regular army service to work in the private sector to 'load up' in Iraq . . . others were detached to work with [the British Secret Service] MI6. (Geraghty 2009: 7)

These unofficial soldiers were involved in 'deniable' work where their ambivalent status could deflect the British government's hidden agenda if missions were to go awry. Establishing the social norms guiding the militarized masculinities to be found in these contexts is considerably more problematic since the financial motive—unlike the traditional 'mercenary' or private security contractor counterpart—is less clear-cut. Rather, Geraghty's framing of these operative' identities touches on their 'exploits' and zeal for 'overseas adventure' that have more to say about a quintessential English masculine identity that plays down the lethal use of violence.[18] A more recent derivative of (privatized) plausible deniability involving covert operations has been exposed in the US media where in 2004, employees of Blackwater were alleged to be working alongside the US Criminal Intelligence Agency (CIA) as part of a secret strategy to locate and assassinate top operatives of Al Qaeda.[19] It is further believed that these private security contractors were involved in planning, training and surveillance with the CIA, funding the project to the tune of many millions of dollars. Despite this, it was reported that 'no terrorists were killed,'[20] since the 'Killing Program' began (Leander 2009).

NATIONALITY AND BROTHERHOOD

Whilst it is clear that private militarized security companies have the potential to create both security and insecurity, they are also sites of hierarchical masculine relations turning on the increasing presence of Third Country National (TCN) and Local National (LN) employees (Singer 2005; Schultz and Yeung 2005; Fainaru 2008; Geraghty 2009). Developing an analytical sensitivity to the national dimension of militarized masculinities in these contexts reveals narratives inflected with stereotype. These narratives frame the proficiency (or otherwise) of lethal force and, in so doing, give an insight into how violence is rationalized and normalized in these privatized contexts. For example, an article in the 'magazine for mercenaries' *Soldiers of Fortune* written by a former SAS Warrant Officer, relies on traditional British reserve even when shooting up 'insurgents' in a following car. Through a pall of fresh cordite and in a calm unruffled voice, the ex-Special Forces British contractor turns towards his clients, rudely awakened in the vehicle in which they were traveling by the incessant clattering of his AK-47, and urges them to 'go back to sleep, guys.' A recent documentary on the work of PMSC in Iraq by a Canadian filmmaker perpetuates national stereotypical portrayals of contractors where US operatives are loud and aggressive; Italian operatives are preoccupied with hairstyle and clothing; and the British remain understated, pragmatic and reserved (Bicanic and Bourque 2006). Alternatively, though suffused with journalistic flair, US contractors of Blackwater are constructed thus:

> T-boy stands off by himself 'zoning,' as he calls it, staying focused on the dangerous return trip to the Green Zone. T-Boy looks like he has adopted a style of generic death—black helmet, black shirt, black mask, black goggles, with a large skull and crossbones chalked on the back of his armor vest and another drawn on his Kevlar helmet. All the gear covers the skull tattoos. (Young-Pelton 2006: 8)

> A former LA cop from a tough inner-city beat, Miyagi speaks in a cool-guy Latino riff . . . short with a salt-and-pepper beard, his weapons and gear hang off him with the comfortable look typical of security contractors. . . . 'Bro,' Miyagi says, describing the look the contractors try to achieve. 'We call it CDI—Chicks Dig It.' When we pull in to the airport and stare at ourselves in those mirrored windows, all we say is 'Hey, Bro, CDI.' (Young-Pelton 2006: 75)

> Square jawed and built low, Pete resembles a real-life white-skinned version of the Incredible Hulk. In his early thirties, he originally hails from the Midwest and spent over a decade in the Special Forces as a weapons specialist. (Young-Pelton 2006: 75)

It is important to examine national framing, since these performances could be read by members of the host population as intimidating and hostile, with their ironic or perhaps 'deterrent intent' and 'hard stance' creating a sense of social distance and unease rather than safety, calm and reassurance (B. Shepherd 2008). Importantly, these intra-masculine relationships are played out in fratriarchal contexts, a topic to which we briefly turn.

INTRA-MASCULINITY: GETTING NAKED, BONDING AND EXCLUDING

On 1 September 2009, the US-based Project on Government Oversight (POGO) drafted a letter for the Secretary of State, Hillary Clinton 'regarding the US Embassy in Kabul.'[21] It started with a brief description of the insecure context of Kabul describing the firing of rockets and a suicide bombing—both aimed at the US Embassy—that whilst killing civilians, failed to reach their targets. The opening of the letter sets the tone for its principal narrative, that the security of the US Embassy should be called into question because of the behavior of its private security guard force employed by ArmorGroup. The text then details the concerns about 'blatant longstanding violations of the security contract,' a 'pervasive breakdown in the chain of command guard force discipline and morale' (Brian 2009: 1). The high turnover of staff is alleged to have weakened team cohesion and those involved in misconduct are 'not being held accountable' (Brian 2009: 2). Guard force shortages have led to chronically sleep-deprived personnel and a breach of contract over leave entitlement. Other problems identified by the report included the inability for many of the Ghurka guards to 'speak adequate English' (Brian 2009: 4) and allegations of hazing and drunken brawls. Incidents believed to put the security of the Embassy in jeopardy include unauthorized:

> Reconnaissance missions outside the perimeter for which guard force supervisors took weapons, night vision goggles ... photographs posted on the internet show Embassy guards hiding in abandoned buildings in Kabul ... engaged in a mission for which they had never trained. (POGO 2009: 6)

It was further alleged that prostitutes were brought to Camp Sullivan for 'birthday celebrations' with the complicity of the guard force supervisors and finally, the letter goes on to detail a series of recommendations culminating in the 'suspension and debarment proceedings against the companies ArmorGroup North America, INC.' (Brian 2009: 8).

The most eye-catching aspect of the report that speaks directly to (militarized) and masculinized identity making practices, concerned the 12 'graphic' images and one brief video clip accompanying the POGO report.[22] These were picked up by all of the major US media outlets and posted on their respected websites. They depicted a series of photos featuring naked or partially clothed men consuming alcohol, dancing around a fire, posing for the camera and, most widely reported, 'drinking vodka from the butt crack,' as noted in the video footage. Overall, the images spoke to a fascination with the male buttocks as well as nakedness more generally in ways that chime with hazing across a number of contexts from fraternity houses through to the military[23] (Nuwer 2004; Pershing 2003). Hazing is a deeply masculinized practice not least in regard to its strong homosocial and homoerotic dimensions and use of violence, abuse and humiliation—the extremes of which have not been reported amongst all female groups (Allan 2004). The argument I make here is that this particular instance of what might be seen as a form of pseudo-hazing, where those in the images and video appear to consent to the various celebrated and ritualized practices, has the potential to offer an insight into the specific intra-masculine and intra-racialized fraternal relations of the US Embassy private security guard force in Kabul. Interpreting these so-called 'lewd practices'—as they were described (Brian 2009: 2) is important, for it throws light on the fratriarchal conditions of gendered possibility that prevailed in the particular context of the Kabul guard force. This line of inquiry is most fruitfully addressed using the work of the sociologist Jay Mechling, who has drawn attention to the ironic, the humorous and the consensual in hazing practice (characteristics of the Kabul Embassy guard force) in opposition to the more widely held assumption that hazing can only ever be about humiliation, bullying and initiation (Nuwer 2004). Mechling's point of departure is the symbolism of the naked buttocks where the act of 'paddling' (striking of the initiate or pledge on the bare bottom)—like the Kabul incident—also involves the buttocks, but in this case 'drinking vodka and eating chips from the butt crack.' What is the significance of this idiosyncratic social practice taking place in a war zone, and what might it tell us about the nexus linking masculinities, bonding and heteronormativity?

Presented here in a drastically simplified form, and drawing on the work of Freud, Mechling's argument starts by challenging the dominant reading of paddling where the pledge is widely held to be infantilized through a ritual spanking by the 'parent-authority' of the more senior fraternity member. Rather, Mechling sees this ritual as altogether more complex in ways that frame the male buttocks as a site of both weakness and strength. His interpretation of paddling starts with the vulnerability of the pledge (or Embassy guard force contractor) in presenting his naked buttocks to the senior/other member. In so doing the (junior) member experiences—albeit pre-reflectively—the threat of being penetrated and incurring the feminizing stigma accompanying this potential act.[24] That the more powerful player (or in the Kabul case, other team member) does not penetrate the weaker party serves to solidify the heterosexuality of both males. In other words, whilst the opportunity for penetration was available—it, and by implication homosexuality—is actively rejected. Skillfully, and with unspoken mutual consent fostered at the pre-discursive level, this heteronormative interaction is boundary making. It steers a careful course between the homoerotic and the homosexual where the latter is rejected in favor of a norm-bound ritual by which heterosexual resolve is found to be resilient in the face of the 'test.' Set against the backdrop of high levels of risk and danger, and coupled with the consumption of alcohol, the images derived from the private security guard force in Kabul begin to make sense. These activities provided an opportunity to 'let off steam,' as well as foster fratriarchal bonds amongst the private guards within the context of stylized hazing practice. Closely linked, and within the context of the POGO report (since it is not clear that the images and video support this assertion), is the argument that pseudo-hazing or stylized hazing practices sought to reaffirm the intra-masculine gender hierarchy amongst the multinational and multifaith guard force. Allegations that LN Afghan men were coerced to take part in this stylized hazing were understood to affront Muslim identity where nudity, sexual humiliation and the consumption of alcohol are prohibited. In a more speculative sense, the nakedness of US members of the guard force can be seen as a challenge to Afghan men perceived, perhaps, to be 'out of touch' with their masculine selves, or in a more obviously neocolonial sense, as feminized and in need of gendered enlightenment, providing for a reconnection with 'authentic' masculinity (Seidler 1997). In this way, the ritual could be seen as an invitation into manhood, to transform an impoverished (national-marginal) gender identity into a liberated, robust, virile, resilient and superior (Western) masculinity. This gendered fusion of paternalism and fraternalism is important since it replicates in microcosm numerous anecdotes around how TCN and LN men are constituted as subalterns more widely in the PMSC sphere, where their pay is lower, they are subject to greater risk and are treated poorly by companies (Scahill 2007b).

CLOSING COMMENTS

Where do our preceding discussions leave us in respect of the war question for feminism? First, I would encourage critical IR scholars of gender to make visible the militarized and masculinized practices central to the cultural terrains of PMSC, as light can be thrown on the ways that a small but not insignificant number of contractors can exacerbate the insecurity of host populations. This requires us to understand what kinds of identities and allied social practices emerge at the military–private interface set against the backdrop of the industry's accountability gap. Second, what can be said about PMSC impact on women, young children and men, as particular groups who have necessarily to host this corporate presence? It is not clear that escalations of violence have specific gendered outcomes, since there appears to be a sense of randomness framing shootings by personnel on convoy protection duties, for example. Third, what of the other gender silences here, concerning the wives and girlfriends of contractors who may have to negotiate the increased threat of violence from psychologically damaged men returning to their homes, post-deployment? Fourth, how important might it be to shine a light on the fratriarchal subcultures shaping PMSC life and how do they shape the conditions of possibility for violence? Though important for a feminist agenda, these questions should be considered within the broader context of complexity and contradiction in the social practices of contractors, where violence and restraint run alongside one another. To bring this discussion to a close, then, gender/IR theory can benefit from further considering the topics engaged in this chapter. Though the field is at an early stage of development, it does nonetheless remain central to the 'man question' (Parpart and Zalewski 2008). Not only might PMSC become a vibrant site of gender-based research, but in addition critical interest in the industry and its many ex-military men might serve as a catalyst to expand the feminist purview to include veterans. While little is known about this diverse but important group, there is much to be said about their key role in contemporary militaristic capitalism, and, in turn, strategies to reform the increasingly privatized war-system now and into the future.

NOTES

1. The term 'mercenary' polarizes audiences, some of whom may question the legitimacy of the PSC sector. Use of the term is therefore a strategic concern, and in this chapter, the more neutral term 'contractor' is used throughout.
2. This narrative has been conveyed by private security contractors interviewed by the author as well as spokespeople from within the industry.
3. The second chapter in Steve Fainaru's book *Big Boy Rules* (2008) is entitled 'I Want to Kill Somebody Today.' It documents the story of 'Jake' who relayed this sentiment to Fainaru during his time in Iraq whilst researching the book. 'Jake'—though framed as a dangerous man—should not be seen in any way as representative of the wider contracting community, though the fact he is able to work in the industry is telling.
4. Which is of course exemplary of late modern capitalism where 'sovereign consumers' have 'needs' to which 'free markets' respond in a purely 'reactive' sense.
5. With the exception of Schultz and Yeung (2005) who have argued that private military security companies should be 'gender mainstreamed.'
6. Though, as Carl Boggs argues: 'Compared to the barbaric policies and actions of the US military itself, the [Private Military Company] record must be considered peripheral to the larger history. It is worth remembering that the US invasion and occupation of Iraq was itself illegal, a crime against peace, meaning that five years of death, destruction, and chaos can be laid squarely at the doorstep of Washington. The entire criminal enterprise has brought daily, virtual routine, horrors and misery to the Iraqi people: takeover of national institutions and resources by force, mass killings, torture, exiled populations, infrastructure devastation, large-scale arrests and detentions, use of inhumane weapons (depleted uranium, white phosphorous, anti-personnel and blockbuster bombs), local atrocities against civilians.' See http://www.uta.edu/huma/agger/fastcapitalism/4_1/boggs.html (accessed 20 November 2009).
7. I would like to thank Eric Herring and Joanna Tidy for reminding me of this complexity.
8. Yet, being trained in violence may also encourage its use as a last resort, as individuals are experienced in and familiar with the potential lethality of this particular skill capital.
9. I am indebted to Cynthia Enloe's canon of work in this respect.
10. However, at the time of writing, the author is supervising a PhD student carrying out an ethnographic study of a private security company in Kabul, Afghanistan, with a focus on the racialization of Ghurka contractors.
11. Thanks to Amanda Chisholm for sensitizing me to these processes.
12. As one of many examples, see http://news.bbc.co.uk/1/hi/uk/8353290.stm (accessed 20 November 2009).
13. See http://www.independent.co.uk/news/uk/home-news/britains-abu-ghraib-did-britain-collude-with-us-in-abuse-of-iraqis-1820545.html (accessed 20 November 2009).

14. Though it should be said that the wider literature dealing with military/militarized masculinities signally overlooks the resistance of (mainly) soldiers even within the most intense, disciplined period of infantryman training and beyond during regular military service (cf. Hockey 1986; Kirke 2010). The belief that soldiers are 'stripped of their agency' and said to be 'blindly obedient, unthinking automatons' (Jolly 1996; Whitworth 2004) is not borne out in the empirical record.
15. The 'War on Terror' discourse, itself fading from popular use, has nevertheless resonated strongly with the sentiment that 9/11 'changed everything,' including the 'rules of the game.' Tony Blair also invoked a change to the 'rules of the game' in his speech on security in 2005. See http://www.number10.gov.uk/Page8041 (accessed 20 November 2009).
16. On Afghanistan in particular, see http://www.privatesecurityregulation.net/files/Impact percent20in percent20Human percent20Rights percent20of percent20Private percent20Military percent20and percent20Security percent20Companies' percent20Activities.pdf (accessed 20 November 2009).
17. Though Bourke's thesis is controversial; see Collins's (2008) alternative explanatory framework that shifts from the individual to the social context or interactional-situation of killing.
18. The 2009 movie *Hurt Locker* set in Iraq and dealing with the lives of US army bomb disposal personnel features a scene where the central characters stumble upon what appear to be British Special Forces personnel operating in the desert. These men, disguised as locals through their dress and bearded appearance, are cool and collected in contrast to their jittery US counterparts. Their mission is framed in terms of an adventure and the actor Ralph Fiennes presents a sophisticated, well-spoken exemplar of this English derivative of military masculinity.
19. Two of the 9 CIA operatives killed by a 'double agent' in Afghanistan were employees of Xe (formerly known as Blackwater). See http://edition.cnn.com/2009/WORLD/asiapcf/12/31/afghanistan.us.casualties/index.html (accessed 3 March 2010).
20. See http://www.nytimes.com/2009/08/20/us/20intel.html (accessed 20 November 2009).
21. For a full transcript of the letter, see http://www.pogo.org/pogo-files/letters/contract-oversight/co-gp-20090901.html (accessed 20 November 2009).
22. For some but not all of the images and the video footage, see http://www.cbsnews.com/stories/2009/09/01/eveningnews/main5280465.shtml (accessed 20 November 2009).
23. For an exemplary instance of military hazing where naked male buttocks play a central role see http://www.youtube.com/watch?v=ROfBuyTQn04 (accessed 20 November 2009). Hazing rituals have been reported as significant in the lead-up to the deployment of the Canadian Airborne Regiment's perpetration of human rights abuses in Somalia (Whitworth 2004), and have also played a role in the interpretation of images generated from Abu Ghraib.
24. This is not to say that penetration never occurs during hazing rituals. The brutal torture and murder of Shidane Arone in Somalia (see note 17) involved sodomy, and more broadly, reports of penetration of pledges—including US Coastguard men.

14 Reenvisioning Masculinities in the Context of Conflict Transformation
The Gender Politics of Demilitarizing Northern Ireland Society

Fidelma Ashe

Processes of demilitarization are often central aspects of societies emerging from violent ethnic conflicts. As feminist scholars have illustrated, both the militarization and demilitarization of societies are highly gendered processes that are interlinked with particular manifestations of masculinities (see Enloe 2000; Cockburn, this volume). Northern Ireland is going through a period of conflict transformation, and the processes of demilitarization that have emerged in that region offer insights into the constitution and reconstitution of masculinities in militarized societies more widely.

The chapter begins by exploring how Northern Ireland's ethnic conflict provoked particular constitutions of masculinities that have been both challenged and reconstituted during the period of conflict transformation. Throughout, this chapter attempts to expose the gendered power effects of the relationships between masculinities, militarization and demilitarization in Northern Ireland.

GENDERED IDENTITIES AND THE NORTHERN IRELAND CONFLICT

To understand the reenvisioning of masculinities during the period of conflict transformation it is necessary to examine men's identities and gendered relationships during the period of the Northern Ireland conflict, colloquially known as the Troubles. Exploring this period highlights the prominence of what could be termed 'warrior' identities during the Troubles and illustrates the gendered power relationships created by those identities.

Ethno-nationalist discourses tend to frame women's roles as maternal and domestic (see Yuval-Davis and Anthias 1989). In Northern Ireland feminists have attempted to expose how women became positioned as symbols of the nation, for example, in the form of Mother Ireland (see Ashe 2008 for overview). Traditionally, ethno-nationalist discourses in Northern Ireland have associated women with the private sphere, and women in the region have often embodied the cultural values of both ethno-nationalist groups (see Ashe 2006a, 2006b, 2006c; Davis and Roulston 2000; V. Morgan 1995). While nationalist politics constituted maternal roles for women and attempted to restrict women's agency to the private sphere, women contested this constitution in a variety of ways.

Northern Ireland's ethno-gendered regime, as Racioppi and O'Sullivan See (2001) term it, limited women's political activity but also provoked women's engagement in community politics. Men's dominance of political life meant that it was difficult for women to enter formal politics. Only one woman was elected to the British Parliament during the period of conflict. Moreover, engaging in formal politics in Northern Ireland involved a degree of danger and the combative nature of politics meant that involvement in formal political arenas held little appeal for many women (see Davis and Roulston 2000). However, a few women did become elected representatives during the Troubles. Between 1977 and 1993 the percentage of women elected in local elections rose from 7.2 percent to 12 percent, but women's formal political representation remained limited (Racioppi and O'Sullivan See 2001: 98).

Women tended to be more politically active in civil society organizations dealing with welfare issues, which constituted a safer political arena (see Davis and Roulston 2000). As Racioppi and O'Sullivan See (2001: 99) argue, the 'informal sector afforded women an opportunity for women as political outsiders to disrupt the ethno-gendered regime.' For example, women engaged in cross-community efforts to tackle issues of poverty and social exclusion (see Cockburn 1998). Researchers have argued that women in the Irish Republican community have tended to be more politically engaged as women in this community became highly politicized through struggles around ethno-nationalist equality issues (see Aretxaga 1997; Ashe 2007a; McWilliams 1995). However, women in the Unionist community also engaged in work in the voluntary sector, and some worked behind the scenes to support men's election campaigns (Urquhart 2000: 77–84). As women tended to express political agency through community work and through their involvement in supporting men's electoral campaigns, two gendered spheres of political activity emerged in Northern Ireland with women being located primarily in civil society organizations and men dominating the sphere of formal politics.

Other expressions of women's political agency were provoked by the everyday effects of sectarian conflict. During the conflict, sectarian attacks on homes and neighborhoods were commonplace. The boundary between the home and the street became increasingly fluid during times of high sectarian street violence (see Aretxaga 1997). Attacks on the family often generated public political activity by women in Northern Ireland. For example, the catalyst for the emergence of the peace people in the 1980s, a campaign led by two women, was the accidental killing of three children by paramilitaries.

The ethno-gendered regime that emerged in Northern Ireland also restricted women's political involvement in paramilitary activity. Valorized ideologically for their roles as mothers and symbols of the nation, women in Northern Ireland like women in other nationalist societies became, as Peterson (1999) observes, positioned as the 'soft interior' of the nation requiring protection and defense from 'the enemy.' As in other societies, some women transcended their traditional roles as mothers and symbols of the nation and took up combatant roles (see Alison 2004; Aretxaga 1995, 1997; Dowler 1998). However, these women were small in number. Moreover, as a number of researchers have noted, men and women combatants were treated differently by paramilitary groups and the broader society (see Aretxaga 1995; Dowler 1998). In summary, ethno-nationalist discourses in Northern Ireland constituted normative femininity as primarily orientated around the private sphere. Subsequently, much of women's political activity revolved around addressing welfare issues in communities, protecting their families from the effects of ethnic conflict and supporting men's political agendas.

In general, formal politics and the 'call to arms' in Northern Ireland were very much a 'call to manhood.' Nationalist communities in Northern Ireland positioned men as defenders of the political interests of both communities in the form of elected representatives or as men prepared to engage in violence to protect the political, cultural and social rights of their respective ethnic groups. In the 1960s the first statement of the paramilitary organization the Provisional Irish Republican Army (PIRA) read: 'We will show by our actions that we are the essence of Irish manhood' (Frontline Online 2005: 7). Such declarations constituted the arena of ethno-nationalist political violence as a normative arena for men. As Nagel (1998) observes, the manly virtues required in this arena reflect those traits associated with traditional masculinity, which include bravery, physical strength and violence. Nagel (1998: 252) points out that terms like *honor, patriotism, cowardice* and *duty* are hard to distinguish as either nationalist or masculinist, since they seem so 'thoroughly tied both to the nation and to manliness' (see also Mosse 1996). The valorization of these masculinities reinforces the ideology of sexual difference in nationalist societies such as Northern Ireland and, in the case of Northern Ireland, operated to support a range of gendered inequalities. The rigid ideals of gendered identities that ethno-nationalist politics created in this region are reflected in the kinds of masculinities that emerged during the period of overt ethnic conflict. The constitution of men's identities as the primary defenders of the community enabled men to gain power in both public and private life in the region (McWilliams 1995).

The constitution of masculinities in Northern Ireland has been both multiple and fluid. However, in the arena of nationalist politics men who refuse to negotiate with the enemy or have had the capacity to perpetrate violence have been supported and glorified as leaders of the communities by nationalist ideologies. For example, the narrative of the 'hard man' has always been an element of Irish Republican masculinity (see Ashe 2007a). Those men who challenged the enemy through violent campaigns are still celebrated and commemorated on the wall murals of nationalist areas of Belfast and Derry City (see McDowell 2008). On the Loyalist side, similar ideals of identity emerged that challenged Loyalist men to protect a Unionist community that viewed itself as under siege from Irish Republicans intent on securing a united Ireland. Loyalist paramilitarism was constituted as the preserve of 'Ulster's loyal sons.' As Racioppi and O'Sullivan observe, Ulster's 'daughters appeared to serve as helpmates to the male defenders of the Union' (2001: 94). In a discussion of Loyalist masculinity in Northern Ireland, Bairner (2008) notes the attraction of Loyalist paramilitaries to body building; an attraction that is reflected in the models of hypermasculinity practiced by prominent Loyalist paramilitaries. In short, men have been viewed as natural combatants and the intersection of notions about masculinity and the defense of the nation were part of the ideological narratives that constituted sexual difference in the region.

The constitution of militarized models of masculinities has been central to the generation of violent expressions of nationalist struggles in both communities. While scholars working in the area have viewed 'the men of violence' as a political problem that they have sought to address with either political or military solutions, they have not assessed the impact of military identities on gender relations within communities. Therefore, the gendered effects of militarism have not been framed as a problem by the mainstream that requires analysis and 'solutions' (see Dunn 1995 for analysis of mainstream solutions to the conflict). As already noted, in Northern Ireland men's identities as leaders of both ethno-nationalist communities and as combatants engaged in political violence impacted significantly on gender relationships. Women's influence in formal political decisions, styles of political engagement and in military campaigns was limited. However, the 'peace process' disrupted both men's military masculinities and men's styles of political leadership. Subsequently, new expressions of masculinities emerged in the region. The next section examines how traditional masculinities in the region have been disrupted in the context of demilitarization and conflict transformation.

CHALLENGING MEN'S DOMINANCE IN THE CONTEXT OF DEMILITARIZATION

Gender relationships are dynamic and continually modify in relation to changing political, social and political conditions. Often, periods of social change can prompt feminist activism or activism by women who do not identify as feminists, but whose agency generates feminist outcomes (see Ashe 2006a). Attempts to demilitarize Northern Ireland society through the development of conflict transformational processes have provoked interventions by women in political arenas in Northern Ireland that attacked militaristic and machismo masculinities.

One of the most public challenges to men's machismo political identities and forms of political engagement emerged through the formation of the Northern Ireland Women's Coalition (NIWC). The NIWC was an effect of the political developments that followed the paramilitary ceasefires of 1994. The original aim of the coalition's agenda was focused on improving women's substantive political representation in the peace talks that followed (Fearon and McWilliams 2000). At the time, women working in community organizations and academics had attempted to lobby political parties to increase the representation of women in the peace talks. Finding many of the parties lukewarm in relation to women's representation, women from both communities created their own political party. The NIWC gained two seats in the Northern Ireland Forum elections in May 1996, which enabled them to participate in the multiparty talks that began in June 1996 and paved the way for the Belfast/Good Friday Agreement (1998). The NIWC also had two members elected to the Northern Ireland Assembly in June 1998.

While the coalition increased women's representation in the peace talks and in the new Northern Ireland Assembly, the NIWC agenda expanded far beyond the goal of increasing women's participation in the peace talks (Fearon and McWilliams 2000). The NIWC felt that it had to develop a response to the constitutional conflict to justify its place at the negotiating table. Otherwise, the other political parties in Northern Ireland would claim that it was a single-issue party with little to contribute to the problem of conflict resolution (Fearon and McWilliams 2000; see also Ashe 2006c).

As it was a cross-community party the NIWC could not take a partisan position in the peace talks and instead developed a more dialogic approach to the difficult issues raised in the peace talks. The coalition's ethics were based around a number of ideals such as inclusion, open dialogue and difference. For Porter (1998, 2000), the coalition's practices met a number of criteria required for the accommodation of difference and the emergence of an agreed consensus in a deeply divided society, for example, open debate, the ability to negotiate issues and a willingness to understand the position of others in the dialogic process (Porter 2000: 149–161). Porter (1998, 2000) claims that these processes constitute the foundations of participatory democracy wherein all voices can be recognized, listened to and heard (see also Ashe 2006c).

The NIWC therefore challenged male hegemony in the political realm through increasing women's representation in the peace talks and also challenged the hypermasculine style of politics in the region that revolved around an attitude of 'not giving an inch' in terms of the constitutional question. While the NIWC received some public support for its dialogic agenda, during the negotiations leading up to the Good Friday Agreement, men treated the women in highly sexist ways that exposed the deep gendered antagonisms in Northern Ireland politics. However, the coalition's challenge to the traditional 'macho' style of politics in Northern Ireland was short-lived. The party lost its two seats in the 2003 Assembly elections and the party was officially 'wound down' in 2006. However, the intervention of the NIWC illustrated that compromise, negotiation and political movement were possible in formal politics, and also that women could challenge men's right to dominate political decisions and political life in a very public way.

While the NIWC challenged men's dominance and styles of political engagement at the formal level of politics, another campaign by women challenged the dominance of men in paramilitary organizations. The McCartney campaign hit the headlines in Northern Ireland in 2005. This campaign was provoked by the murder of a Catholic man, Robert McCartney, in a Belfast bar. McCartney's family claimed that members of the PIRA had been involved in the murder, and his sisters led a very public campaign to bring the alleged murder(s) of their brother to justice. Throughout the campaign the sisters claimed that Sinn Fein had colluded in protecting the alleged murderer(s). The allegation was harmful politically given that Sinn Fein, the political wing of the PIRA, had signed up to the Belfast/Good Friday Agreement (1998), which committed the organization to a process of decommissioning weapons and eventually the disbandment of PIRA. Bringing their brother's murderer(s) to justice through gaining information about those involved in his murder from members of the Irish Republican movement was the public goal of the sisters' campaign. However, the McCartney sisters also engaged in challenging traditional Irish Republican narratives of military masculinities.

Commentators and the media gave less attention to the sisters stated aim of wanting to tear down the romanticism of the PIRA (see Ashe 2006b). Irish Republicanism had produced a narrative of military masculinity as disciplined, noble, self-sacrificing and therefore as worthy of protecting and leading the community (see O'Malley 1990). In an interview in *The Times* Paula McCartney is quoted as saying that 'even without the Troubles these people would be scum.' This statement illustrates how the sisters' campaign attacked the narrative of 'noble' Irish Republican masculinity. Challenging the rights of Republican men to 'police' or represent the ideals of the community, Paula McCartney argued that their activities in the community represented the 'abuse of power' in 'idle hands' (Lister 2005: 30). The sisters labeled militarized men throughout their campaign as 'psychopaths' and 'cowards' (Lister 2005: 29). The McCartney sisters therefore contested militarized masculinities in their community and rejected the right of these men to control working-class communities. The McCartney sisters' campaign challenged and attempted to shame the Irish Republican movement. More specifically, the sisters tried to shame militarized masculinities in that movement. During this period it had also become clear that some Loyalist combatants were also turning more towards 'gangsterism,' which placed pressure on the rights of Loyalist military masculinities to lead and control their communities (see Howe 2005).

REINVENTING MASCULINITIES

Challenges to traditional masculinities in Northern Ireland, such as those analyzed in the previous section, were both provoked and reinforced by a changing political culture. As traditional masculinities became less legitimate and sustainable during the period of conflict transformation men began to reformulate new expressions of masculinities. Several men who held positions in the hierarchy of paramilitary organizations turned towards more intellectualized models of masculinities that involved a commitment to democratic processes and negotiations. Other ex-combatants attempted to formulate nonviolent models of masculinities through community-level activism. Community-level restorative justice schemes have been key sites in the development of these forms of masculinities in Northern Ireland.

This development of community-based restorative justice schemes has been one site where there have been transitions from military masculinities to nonviolent models of masculinities based around dialogue, mediation, reparation and forgiveness. One of the effects of military models of masculinities has been that the men involved in paramilitary groups began to 'police' their respective communities. The models of informal paramilitary justice that emerged involved brutal beatings, kneecapping and the exiling of individuals from Northern Ireland (see Shirlow and McEvoy 2008 for analysis). Young men involved in antisocial behavior became a central target for paramilitary punishments. Rather than rescinding in the context of conflict transformation, paramilitary punishment beating and shootings continued, exposing the barriers to conflict transformation at the local level in Northern Ireland (Knox 2002).

The community-level experimentation with new forms of informal justice, such as restorative justice, offered an alternative to paramilitary justice, and was developed by ex-combatants who had been involved in political violence. Indeed some of these men had been incarcerated for murder. Marshall (1996: 37) defines restorative justice practice as 'a process whereby all parties with a stake in a particular offence come together to resolve collectively how to deal with the aftermath of the offence and its implications for the future.'

Restorative justice often involves victim and offender engaging in face-to-face dialogue to address the harm done by an offense, and the offender often provides reparation to the victim (see, e.g., McCold 2006). Restorative justice practice also acknowledges the social causes of the offense, and places a premium on the offender remaining within the community (Zehr 1990). Advocates believe that as the community becomes more involved in restorative justice practices, it builds up greater competence in resolving community conflicts in nonviolent ways. Developing restorative justice projects to act as alternatives to paramilitary modes of justice became part of a broader political process, and the projects 'were designed to allow such paramilitaries to (in their terms) 'disengage responsibility' for such acts, handing dispute resolution back to the communities from which the conflicts emanate' (McEvoy and Mika 2002: 535).

Ex-combatant men's development of these schemes signaled both a rejection of 'warrior' masculinities and the cultivation of new models of subjectivity by ex-combatant men centered on a dialogic and nonviolent practice and philosophy. This process of reconstructing identity was both complex and shaped by broader political changes generated by a society emerging from conflict (see Shirlow and McEvoy 2008). This shift exposes masculinities as fluid, and demonstrates how masculinities modify as political cultures change. However, these new forms of masculinities may not necessarily mean that historical gender inequalities become challenged. Feminists have suggested that a decrease in levels of political violence benefits women as women bear much of the stress, trauma and effects of conflict and war. However, as El-Bushra (2000: 82) reminds us, 'turning some "bad" men into "good" men may reduce incidences of violence, and so help cut into the vicious cycle, but may in the long term fail to solve the gender axis of hegemonic power.'

In the analysis and practice of community-based restorative justice, issues of gender power have not been examined. Men have reinvented their identities in the conflict transformational period through philosophies such as restorative justice. However, men's dominance in the organization, development and delivery of restorative justice means that men still retain hegemonic status in working-class communities in Northern Ireland in the conflict transformational period. Perhaps one of the most telling manifestations of the elision of issues of gendered power in the community restorative justice literature emerges in the following assertion by community based restorative justice scholars in Northern Ireland: 'Their [ex-combatants] rejection of the efficacy of violence as a strategy is itself a powerful exercise in both moral leadership and community capacity building' (Shirlow et al. 2005: 122).

The effects of men's positioning as moral leaders in communities have not been questioned in terms of the effect on gendered relationships within those communities. As earlier sections of this chapter have illustrated, men in Northern Ireland have always been in positions of influence and have taken up the majority of leadership roles within communities. How do these new forms of masculinities affect gender relationships within communities? Are women's voices being heard in the restructuring of new modes of justice? Academic analysis has not engaged with these questions or assessed the contribution of women to the development of community-based restorative justice initiatives.

This kind of erasure of women in assessments of conflict transformational processes such as community-level restorative justice is easily explained. The relationship between political change and changes in gendered identities, particularly men's identities, has been ignored by mainstream scholarship in Northern Ireland. Therefore, developments such as community-level restorative justice have been assessed through a gender-blind lens by mainstream researchers. While mainstream researchers have rejected frameworks such as critical studies of masculinities as irrelevant in terms of examining ethnic conflict or conflict transformation processes, this framework offers the conceptual resources through which the gendered effects of conflict transformational processes can be assessed.[1]

Critical studies of masculinities challenge scholarship that positions men as nongendered subjects and provide the conceptual tools both to explore the constitution and reconstitution of masculinities and the power effects of these identities. Moreover, critical studies of masculinities encourage researchers to explore the occlusion of women from explorations of men's agency. To grasp the gender effects of Northern Ireland's conflict transformation, researchers must examine changes in masculinities and their impact on historical matrices of gender inequality in the region.

CONCLUSIONS

The Belfast/Good Friday Agreement and the processes of conflict transformation that it provoked have generated changes in masculinities in Northern Ireland. Warrior models of masculinities no longer 'fit' the region's political contours. New models of masculinities have emerged due to changes at the political, social and personal level. However, as masculinities modify, so too do relationships of gender power. Tracing shifts in men's identities must be accompanied by an analysis of how these shifts change inequalities in the arena of gender. Mainstream political analysis of shifts in Northern Ireland politics has worked with limited theoretical and empirical frames that have failed to engage with issues of both gender equality and power. However, Northern Ireland provides a fertile context for examining how masculinities can become modified in conflict transformational zones, and exposes the gender issues that such modifications generate for those interested in gender politics and gender justice.

NOTES

1. Hearn and Morgan (1990) set out a template for critical studies of men/masculinities to differentiate pro-feminist forms of analysis from men's studies. Hearn later developed this approach (see, e.g., Hearn 1997; Hearn, this volume). A range of other writers have also developed critical approaches to studying men, including Kimmel (see, e.g., 1996) and Connell (e.g., 1997). All these writers frame critical studies of men/masculinities as involving an analysis of men's power and its impact on women.

Conclusions

15 Is Feminism Being Co-Opted by Militarism?

Annica Kronsell and Erika Svedberg

From the outset of this project we were motivated by a wish to contribute to feminist research; to show how the gender study/feminist toolbox may indeed deepen our understanding of how gender, as norms and practices, are embedded in war making and peace building. We wanted to learn about how other contemporary researchers in what we have come to know as Feminist Security Studies have found ways to analyze and further understand the zones of overlapping and uncertainty in these practices. These zones are places of metaphorical intersections, where women and men behave in ways that do not fit the mold, where they do not behave in obvious ways. Or if they do behave in expected, obvious ways, performing the dichotomous gender relations that we are so used to seeing (i.e., boys/men as violent/active protectors; girls/women as peaceful and passive receivers of protection) Hearn urges us to ask ourselves why we stopped questioning the obvious (thereby contributing to making the obvious strangely invisible). When women's heroic acts in conflict are acts of violence, this tends to be 'forgotten' in post-conflict times, as discussed by Parashar. Along the same lines, many of our contributors want to leave behind simplified notions of masculinity as the cause of violence. As Higate says, post facto analysis of masculinity's apparent 'cause' of violence can obscure nonviolent masculinities that should be harnessed, better understood and learned from as a key element of a strategy for change towards a more peaceful world. We need to further reflect upon the complex links between masculinities and violence. Cockburn impels us to go to the root cause of the problem: the incessantly re-created structural power relations between men and women; women's constant subordination to men.

Several chapters discussed gender in relation to constructions or notions of national identity. This entails different roles, institutional practices and places to be for men and for women vis-à-vis the state. In this book we explore in much detail the important connection between military practices and nation building. Here, the chapters also analyze masculinity constructions in relation to so-called new war-making and military practice. The question addressed is: How is gender made when nations are remade in the context of new military practices? Eduards, Jukarainen, Penttinen and

Haaland all look at the politics of gender constructions and national identity surrounding these Nordic states' engagement in international peacekeeping. A common theme here seems to be that, on the part of the Nordic, peacekeeping helps to carve out a clearer sense of the national (male) self in a quite turbulent post–Cold War context.

There are, as we see it, two additional strands of congruence in this re-created Cold War self between the Nordic military organizations. First, all three attribute great importance to international peacekeeping as a continuance with the past sense of self as the good man; a Nordic male who is just and does the right thing. Taking part in international peacekeeping is thus of utmost importance because it enables this benevolent Nordic masculinity to come into being even without a national territory to protect (as the Soviet Union is no longer there to impose a threat to the Nordic). Second, as shown in these chapters, women are either invisible or are viewed as a security problem when entering the space of the masculine protector. At least in Sweden and Finland, the military organizations' behavior seems to convey a similar message: 'Leave it to us—leave it to the boys.' The redefinition of what security entails, then, is simultaneously an exercise in the search for an up-dated definition of national masculinity. Eduards finds it curious how the Swedish take on SCR 1325 is bluntly omitting important aspects of the resolution's intention: the involvement of women in decision-making on all levels of conflict resolution and peace building. Yuval-Davis's words on how women 'carry the "burden of representation", as they are constructed as the symbolic bearers of the collectivity's identity and honor, both personally and collectively,' comes to mind in Eduards's analysis of women's special role and purpose in the Swedish military (Yuval-Davis 1997: 45).

We acknowledge, in line with Tilly (1990), that historically, the forming of a military organization is the basis for the creation of the state. Without the basic agreement of a common enemy out there, people would not have come together to form nations and eventually unite to form states. In other words, the military organization is for historical reasons closely intertwined with the construction of the state. Today, however, the state has far more complex underpinnings than protection through violent means. In today's globalized world, we find that the state gains legitimacy through other means altogether. Analogous to this, we find that there are grounds for envisioning engagement in peace building missions where reconstructions of unjust gender power relations have no part to play. Could we not have peace building missions that are democratic institutions with men and women working side by side, without sexism? (See Cockburn and Hubic 2002.)

Postwar moments are known for being times when the patterns of domination from wartimes are replicating in postwar civilian life (Pankhurst 2008). This is echoed in Ashe's chapter, where she shows how understanding of the forming and reforming of masculinities in post-conflict

Northern Ireland is central to building a more just postwar society. Focusing as she does on femininities and masculinities is therefore key to seeing how conflicts go through processes of transformation where gender plays a crucial part.

Moreover, we looked at how feminist theory and concepts travel (see Hawkesworth 2009). The concept of traveling refers to processes of interpretation when concepts are to be implemented and put into practices somehow, by the workings of state institutions as well as international organizations that deal with war and gender. As pointed out by Hebert, there is an instrumentalism underlying gender mainstreaming policies promoted by national military systems and international organizations such as the UN and NATO. How does the UN's or NATO's utilization of the concept gender differ from other uses, such as the women's movement? McLeod's analysis shows how there are conscious strategic usages of SCR 1325 by certain actors, such as a post-Yugoslavian local women's group.

The potential of gender mainstreaming is being diminished due to lack of resources and proper coordination of gender-related efforts. It is troubling that feminist contributions to theorizing on gender and the feminist call for attention to gender in relation to military systems and situations of armed conflict have been co-opted. It is doubtful whether gender mainstreaming as a practice is still about advancing the ability of women to enjoy their human rights, instead it seems to have become a venue to harness and exploit capabilities and qualities associated with women, so as to improve the operational effectiveness. What is clearly needed is a 'thick' approach to gender mainstreaming, one that seriously attends to the relational construction of masculinities and femininities, rather than reducing 'gender' to 'women' or feeding into stereotyped characteristics associated with women. But what does this look like in practice? And is it even feasible to imagine a thick approach to gender mainstreaming that will not be similarly co-opted, thus having the effect of reinforcing rather than challenging militarism? Is feminism being co-opted by militarism?

Our special take on the war question for feminism in this book was with a focus on institutions and norms, i.e., the war-and-military-machinery. Gender relations are complex and multifaceted. The war question for feminism is thus a call to feminist/gender researchers to engage in a research program seeking to uncover how gendered norms and practices are institutionalized to reaffirm a sex/gender system of the male-as-norm, or, in other words, of male dominance and female subordination (a hierarchical system where children are the lowest). While gender in itself may be considered a social institution, our approach is narrower and we have a stricter understanding of institutions here. In this book, our aim has been to show how gendered practices may be found in institutions that are also physical organizations, for example, the state apparatus, the military, in the actual war-making, in international organizations, in guerrillas or liberation armies, etc. We have paid particular attention to how gendered norms are institutionalized, upheld and re-created. Some authors of this volume look at how practices of resistance are being developed and fought for, in different places and contexts: before, during and after the war, for example, by potential conscripts vis-à-vis the Turkish military and state, among Finnish female peacekeepers as well as by women in the armed movements of Kashmir and Sri Lanka.

The research program calls for work that runs theoretically deeper while at the same time being clearly empirically based, into questions relating to violence, masculinity and femininity, the institutionalized praxis of traditional patriarchal organizations such as the military and their relations with society and the state, resistances to violence on an individual as well as collective basis, relations between state institutions and arm's manufacturing, the international political economy and its influences on the choices and decisions made by women and men in their everyday lives in their respective contexts around the world. We propose that the war question for feminism is as much of a challenge to what constitutes good feminist research in today's globalized world as it could become a potential challenge to the construction of militarized patriarchal gender relations that rule much of the world today.

Cockburn argues for the perception of gender, violence and war as a continuum, where violence runs through it and predisposes our societies to war. Cockburn's insightful and well-grounded analysis leads us to conclude that any theory that discusses and analyzes war, organized violence and militaries is simply flawed if it lacks a gender dimension. When juxtaposed with Hearn's well-developed exposé of the many ways that masculinity impacts war–making, it pushes us to think of gender relations in terms of various masculinities and femininities, themselves imbued with power orders, hegemony and marginality, that all come to work almost like a resource in the potentiality of war-making. Two important insights come out of this. One is that gender relations are highly complex and any attempt to naturalize, or essentialize, men and women blinds us to the complexity of gender-power relations and seduces those who buy the message that men simply 'are' the protectors and soldiers while women 'are' those in need of protection. Secondly, every single strategy that has as its aim to end war in the benefit of peace must include not only an analysis of gender relations and gender effects, but perhaps more importantly, a plan for how to change gender relations.

Questions of agency on the part of individual women and men are of importance to our proposed research program. Freedman notes in this volume how a huge bureaucracy like UNHCR not only is there to protect the interests of refugees but that they also hold tremendous discursive and institutional power over refugees. This power can be seen to take away possibilities of agency from refugees and displaced people, limiting their participation in any form of planning, implementation or management of operations (Baines 2004). This critique might be particularly relevant to operations designed to overcome gender inequalities, which are often designed and implemented without any input from women and men refugees themselves as to what their needs or desires might be, which can be criticized for their framing of women merely in terms of their vulnerability. Gender mainstreaming is today a traveling concept with global reach, via UN agencies such as UNHCR. As such, the meaning of gender mainstreaming will need to be examined in each institutional setting, and the success of implementation will also be dependent on institutional characteristics. As Freedman points out, what is needed are policies to protect women that push the institutions to move beyond a mere focus on 'vulnerable' groups and towards a real integration of a gendered understanding of the global processes that produce refugees, and of the protection needs of these refugees. To apply gender mainstreaming as an institutional strategy is more demanding than what it appears to be. Real gender mainstreaming within these institutions would perhaps mean no less than the daunting task of setting in motion an entire overhaul of the institution's unquestioned assumptions regarding women, men and power relations.

What can we learn about intersections of power and gender subjectivities in the context of making war and building peace? According to Nina Lykke (2010), the principles of transnationalism are intersectional when women activists network across the globe. On the one hand, they include the challenge of universalism and constant attention to difference; on the other hand, there is the heuristics of mixed investigation in the extra-European context, which allows one to see different sides of the subject and to see the specific and the fragmented—the dialogue with one's subject and reflexivity of the researcher's own position in order to overcome the illusion of the omnipotence of knowledge. Transnational feminism involves a constant taking into account of different dimensions of gender inequality and their intersections. In line with this, the contributing authors of this volume have pointed to the complexity of gender subjectivities that go far beyond the simplifying tendencies that often surface in scholarship, policy circles and in local contexts, i.e., associating women with peace and men with violence and war. Such thinking lacks reflection, which in turn silences and delimits the critical discussion and scrutiny of war and violence.

Contributors

Fidelma Ashe is a lecturer in political theory in the School of Criminology, Politics and Policy Studies at the University of Ulster and is a member of the Social and Policy Institute. She is coauthor of *Contemporary Social and Political Theory* (Open University Press, 1999) and author of *The New Politics of Masculinity: Men, Power and Resistance* (Routledge, 2007) and *Gendering Conflict Transformation in Northern Ireland: New Themes, Old Problems* (Routledge, forthcoming). She has published several articles on gender and nationalism.

Alp Biricik is a PhD candidate at the Department of Gender Studies, Linköping University, Sweden. His current research explores the production of LGBT places since the 1970s in Istanbul. His publications include 'This Is Not an (Academic) Paper (on Ethnography),' in C. Asberg et al. (eds), *Gender Delight: Science, Knowledge, Culture and Writing . . . For Nina Lykke*, Linköping University, and 'A Bedroom of His Own: Intersections of Webcams, Surveillance and Male Sexuality,' in J. Hearn (ed), *GEXcel Work in Progress Report Volume 5*, Linköping University.

Cynthia Cockburn is Professor of Sociology at City University, London. Her books include *Brothers. Male Dominance and Technological Change* (1991); *In the Way of Women. Men's Resistance to Sex Equality in Organizations* (1991); *The Space between Us: Negotiating Gender and National Identities in Conflict* (1998); and with Dubravka Zarkov, *The Postwar Moment. Militaries, Masculinities and International Peacekeeping* (2002); *The Line: Women, Partition and the Gender Order in Cyprus* (2004); *From Where We Stand. War, Women's Activism and Feminist Analysis* (2007).

Maud Eduards is Professor of Political Science at Stockholm University. Her recent publications include *Kroppspolitik. Om Moder Svea och andra kvinnor* (2007); *Förbjuden handling. Om kvinnors organisering och feministisk teori* (2002); and (with Gunnel Gustafsson and Malin Rönnblom) *Towards a New Democratic Order? Women's Organizing in Sweden in the*

1990s (1997). Her current research focuses on gender, nation and security, and how women and feminist ideas are appropriated for war and peace.

Jane Freedman is a Professor at the Université de Paris 8, Saint-Denis and member of the Centre de Recherches et d'Etudes Sociologiques et Politiques de Paris (CRESPPA). Her research focuses on gendered issues in asylum and refugee policies. Publications include *Gendering the International Asylum and Refugee Debate* (Palgrave Macmillan, 2007), and, with Jérôme Valluy, *Persécutions des Femmes: Savoirs, Mobilisation, Protections* (Editions du Croquant, 2007).

Dr. Torunn Laugen Haaland is a Fellow at the Norwegian Institute for Defense Studies (IFS) in Oslo and lecturer at the Norwegian Defense University College. She specializes in Norwegian military reform, professional identities in the Norwegian Armed Forces and experience-based learning in the military. Recent publications include: 'The Development of Military Doctrine: The Particular Case of Small States,' *Journal of Strategic Studies* (2010, coauthor Kjell Inge Bjerga); 'Still Homeland Defenders at Heart? Norwegian Military Culture in International Deployments,' *International Peacekeeping* (2010); and *Small Armed Forces with a Global Outreach: Role Perceptions in the Norwegian Armed Forces after the Cold War* (Unipub forlag, 2008).

Jeff Hearn, AcSS, is Professor of Gender Studies (Critical Studies on Men), Linköping University, Sweden; Professor in Sociology, University of Huddersfield, UK; and Professor, Hanken School of Economics, Helsinki, Finland. He has worked on questions of gender, sexuality and violence for many years. His books include, for example, *The Gender of Oppression* (1987); *The Sexuality of Organization* (1989); *Men, Masculinities and Social Theory* (1990); *Violence and Gender Relations* (1996); *Men as Managers, Managers as Men* (1996); *The Violences of Men* (1998), *Gender, Sexuality and Violence in Organizations* (2001); *Handbook of Studies on Men and Masculinities* (2005); *Men and Masculinities in European Perspective* (2006); *Sex, Violence and the Body* (2008). He is managing co-editor of the series *Routledge Advances in Feminist Studies and Intersectionality*.

Laura A. Hebert is Assistant Professor of Diplomacy and World Affairs at Occidental College. Her research and teaching focus on gender and human rights, with a particular focus on gender-based violence. She is the author of articles appearing in the *International Journal of Human Rights*, the *Journal of Gender Studies* and *Human Rights and Human Welfare*, and has a book manuscript under publication review titled *The Politics of Women's Rights Advocacy: Lessons from Malaysia & South Africa*.

Paul Higate is Reader in Gender and Security in the School for Sociology, Politics and International Studies (SPAIS) at the University of Bristol. His publications include: *Military Masculinities: Identity and the State*, (2003, with Greenwood Praeger); 'Peacekeepers, Masculinities, and Sexual Exploitation,' in *Men and Masculinities* (2007); *Insecure Spaces: Peacekeeping, power and performance in Haiti, Kosovo and Liberia* (2009, with Marsha Henry); and the forthcoming 'Martial Races and Enforcement Masculinities of the Global South: Weaponizing Fijian, Chilean and Salvadoran Postcoloniality in the Mercenary Sector,' *Globalizations* (2011). He is currently a Fellow of the ESRC/AHRC Global Uncertainties Program with a project on Mercenary Masculinities.

Pirjo Jukarainen is a Senior Research Fellow at the Tampere Peace Research Institute, and Associate Professor of Regional Studies at the Tampere University, Finland. She is currently leading the project Gendered Agency in Conflict: Gender Sensitive Approach to development and Conflict Management Practices, funded by the Academy of Finland. She has been active in developing and monitoring (as a member of steering group) Finland's National Action Plan for implementing UN SCR 1325, Women, Peace and Security. Her publications include the articles: 'Definitely Not Yet the End of Nations—Northern Borderlands Youth in Defence of National Identity,' *Young: Nordic Journal of Youth Research*, and 'Norden is Dead—Long Live the Eastwards Faced Euro-North,' *Cooperation and Conflict*.

Annica Kronsell is Associate Professor of Political Science at Lund University, Sweden. Her teaching and research is in the fields of international relations, peace and conflict studies, feminist theory and environmental politics. Her publications include *Gender, Sex and the Post-National Defense* (Oxford University Press, 2011); 'Gender and Governance,' in *The International Studies Compendium Project* (2009); 'Methods for Studying Silences: Gender Analysis in Institutions of Hegemonic Masculinity,' in *Feminist Methodologies for International Relations* (2006); 'Gendered Practices in Institutions of Hegemonic Masculinity—Reflections from Feminist Standpoint Theory,' in *International Feminist Journal of Politics* (2005).

Laura McLeod is Lecturer in Politics at the University of Manchester, UK. She has recently completed her ESRC-funded PhD at the University of Sheffield. Her thesis explored competing modes of thought about 'gender security' within feminist and women's organizations in Serbia, highlighting how perceptions about conflict and post-conflict in ex-Yugoslavia continue to affect configurations of 'gender security.' Her current research and teaching interests are in the area of security studies and post-conflict reconstruction.

Swati Parashar (PhD Lancaster University) is Lecturer of Feminist International Relations and Development at the University of Limerick, Ireland. Her work focuses on gender, conflicts and development issues in South

Asia. Her recent publications include 'Gender Jihad and Jingoism: Women as Perpetrators, Planners and Patrons of Militancy in Kashmir,' in *Studies in Conflict and Terrorism* (2011); 'The Sacred and the Sacrilegious: Exploring Women's "Politics" and "Agency" in Radical Religious Movements in South Asia,' in *Totalitarian Movements and Political Religions* (2011); 'Feminist IR and Women Militants: Case Studies from South Asia,' in *Cambridge Review of International Affairs* (2009); (coauthored with Christine Sylvester) 'The Contemporary Mahabharata and the Many Draupadis: Bringing Gender to Critical Terrorism Studies,' in Richard Jackson, Marie Breen Smyth and Jeroen Gunning (eds), *Critical Terrorism Studies: A New Research Agenda* (2009). She is also the editor of *Maritime Counter Terrorism: A Pan Asian Perspective* (2007) and coeditor (with Wilson John) of *Terrorism in South Asia: Implications for South Asia* (2005).

Elina Penttinen (PhD) is a University Lecturer in World Politics, Faculty of Social Sciences, University of Helsinki. Her current research interests are in the ethical competence of security agents in the context of comprehensive crisis management. She is currently working on a book manuscript titled *Joy and International Relations: A New Methodology* to be published in 2012, in which she develops the potential of joy as a starting point for research on experiencing and witnessing war and develops the research practice of IR from the point of compassion and heartfelt positivity. Her recent publications in the field of crisis management include 'Enhancement of Expertise in Civilian Crisis Management: Positivity as a Key toward Personal Dedication for Comprehensive Approach,' *Crisis Management Studies: CMC Finland Yearbook* (CMC Finland, 2010). Her earlier work has been on globalization, prostitutions and sex trafficking.

Erika Svedberg is Assistant Professor in International Relations at Malmö University. Her publications include 'Feminist Theory and International Negotiations,' *International Studies Perspectives* (2002); (with Annica Kronsell) 'The Swedish Military Manpower Policies and their Gender Implications,' in *The Changing Face of European Conscription* (2005); and 'The Duty to Protect: Gender and the Swedish Practice of Conscription,' in *Cooperation and Conflict* (2001).

Christine Sylvester is Professor of International Relations and Development, Lancaster University, UK, and holder of Kerstin Hesselgren Chair placed at the School of Global Studies, University of Gothenburg Sweden. Her publications include *Feminist International Relations: The Key Works* (2010); *Experiencing War* (2010); *Art/Museums: International Relations Where We Least Expect It* (2009); *Feminist International Relations. An Unfinished Journey* (2002).

Bibliography

Aamulehti. (2010) 'Afganistanin operaatio ei ole houkutellut naisia' [Afghanistan Operation Has Not Appealed to Women], *Uutiset* [News], 17 March 2010.
Ackerly, B., Stern M. and True, J. (eds) (2006) *Feminist Methodologies for International Relations*, Cambridge: Cambridge University Press.
Advisory Board for Defense Information. (2009) *Finns' Opinions on Foreign and Security Policy, Defense and Security Issues*. Online. Available HTTP: <http://www.defmin.fi/?641_m=4159&l=en&s=26> (accessed 18 April 2010).
Ag, L. (2008) 'Du ignorerar kvinnorna i allt du gör, Carl Bildt' ['You Ignore Women in Everything You Do, Carl Bildt'], *Dagens Nyheter*, 24 May. Online. Available HTTP: <http://www.dn.se/debatt/du-ignorerar-kvinnorna-i-allt-du-gor-carl-bildt-1.603087> (accessed 24 May 2008).
Akça, İ. (2004) 'Kolektif bir sermayedar olarak Türk Silahlı Kuvvetleri,' in A. İnsel and A. Bayramoğlu (eds), *Bir Zümre, Bir Parti: Türkiye'de Ordu*, Istanbul: Birikim.
Allan, E.J. (2004) 'Hazing and Gender: Analyzing the Obvious,' in H. Nuwer (ed), *The Hazing Reader*, Indiana: Indiana University Press.
Allred, K.J. (2006) 'Peacekeepers and Prostitutes: How Deployed Forces Fuel the Demand for Trafficked Women and New Hope for Stopping It,' *Armed Forces and Society* 33(5): 5–23.
Allukian, M. and Atwood, P.L. (2000) 'Public Health and the Vietnam War,' in B.S. Levy and V.W. Sidel (eds), *War and Public Health*, Washington, DC: American Public Health Association.
Alison, M. (2003) 'Cogs in the Wheel? Women in the LTTE,' *Civil Wars* 6(4): 37–54.
Alison, M. (2004) 'Women as Agents of Political Violence: Gendering Security,' *Security Dialogue* 35(4): 447–463.
Altinay, A.G. (2004a) 'Human Rights or Military Ideals? Teaching National Security in High Schools,' in Denis Tarba Ceylan Tarba and Gürol Irzik (eds), *Human Rights Issues in Textbooks: The Turkish Case*, Istanbul: History Foundation.
Altinay, A.G. (2004b) *The Myth of the Military-Nation: Militarism, Gender and Education in Turkey*, New York: Palgrave MacMillan.
Andreassen, B., Holan, S. and Skotnes, B. (2009) 'The Norwegian PRT in Meymaneh,' in L. Olsson and J. Tejpar (eds), *Operational Effectiveness and UN Resolution 1325—Practices and Lessons from Afghanistan*, Stockholm: FOI.
Anıl, E., Arın, C., Berktay hacımirzaoğlu, A., Bingöllü, M., İlkkaracan, P. and Ercevik Amado, L. (eds) (2005) *Turkish Civil and Penal Code Reforms from a Gender Perspective: The Success of Two Nationwide Campaigns*, Istanbul: Women for Women's Human Rights Publication.
Anthias, F. (1998) *Sociological Debates: Thinking about Social Divisions*, London: Greenwich University Press.
Appadurai, A. (2006) *Fear of Small Numbers: An Essay on the Geography of Anger*, Durham, NC: Duke University Press.

Aretxaga, B. (1995) 'Dirty Protest,' *Ethos* 23(2): 123–148.
Aretxaga, B. (1997) *Shattering Silence: Women, Nationalism, and Political Subjectivity in Northern Ireland*, Princeton, NJ: Princeton University Press.
Arkin, W. and Dobrofsky, L.R. (1978) 'Military Socialization and Masculinity,' *Journal of Social Issues* 34:151–168.
Armstrong, S. (2008) *War PLC: The Rise of the New Corporate Mercenary*, London: Faber.
Åse, C. (2000) *Makten att se: om kropp och kvinnlighet i lagens namn*, Malmö: Liber.
Ashe, F. (2006a) 'Gendering the Holy Cross School Dispute: Women and Nationalism in Northern Ireland,' *Political Studies* 54(3): 147–164.
Ashe, F. (2006b) 'The McCartney Sisters Search for Justice: Gender and Political Protest in Northern Ireland,' *Politics* 26(3): 161–167.
Ashe, F. (2006c) 'The Virgin Mary Complex: Feminism and Northern Ireland Politics,' *Critical Review of International Social and Political Philosophy* 9(4): 573–588.
Ashe, F. (2007a) 'Gendering Ethno-Nationalist Conflict in Northern Ireland,' *Ethnic and Racial Studies* 30(5): 766–786.
Ashe, F. (2007b) *The New Politics of Masculinity*, New York: Routledge.
Ashe, F. (2008) 'Gender and Ethno-Nationalist Politics in Northern Ireland,' in C. Coulter (ed), *Northern Ireland after the Troubles*, Manchester: Manchester University Press.
Ashe, F. (2009) 'From Paramilitaries to Peacemakers: The Gender Dynamics of Community-Based Restorative Justice in Northern Ireland,' *British Journal of Politics and International Relations* 11(2): 298–314.
Aurén, V. (2007) 'Minkä ei pitäisi koskaan tapahtua, on tapahtunut. Suru ja kipu ovat iskeneet sydämiimme' [What Should Never happen Has Happened. Sorrow and Pain has Stuck to Our Hearts], *Sinibaretti* 29. Online. Available HTTP: <http://www.rauhanturvaajaliitto.fi/lehti/3_07/isop.html> (accessed 1 June 2011).
Avant, D. (2005) *The Market for Force: The Consequences of Privatizing Security*, Cambridge: Cambridge University Press.
Bailey, K.D. (1994) *Sociology and the New Systems Theory: Toward a Theoretical Synthesis*, New York: State of New York Press.
Baines, E.K. (2004) *Vulnerable Bodies: Gender, the UN and the Global Refugee Crisis*, Aldershot: Ashgate.
Bairner, A. (2008) 'The Ulster Boys: Reflections on Masculinity within Northern Ireland's Protestant Community,' Hitotsubashi Invited Fellow Program Discussion Paper Series No. 6, Hitotsubashi University.
Balasingham, A.A. (1993) *Women Fighters of Liberation Tigers*, Jaffna, Sri Lanka: Thasan.
Balasingham, A.A. (2001) *The Will to Freedom*, Mitcham: Fairmax.
Barnett, M. and Finnemore, M. (2004) *Rules for the World. International Organizations in Global Politics*, Ithaca, NY: Cornell University Press.
Baron, I.Z. (2010) 'Dying for the State: The Missing Just War Question?,' *Review of International Studies* 36:215–234.
Barrett, F.J. (1996) 'The Organizational Construction of Military Masculinity: The Case of the US Navy,' *Gender, Work and Organization* 3(3): 129–142.
Barrett, F.J. (2003) 'The Organizational Construction of Hegemonic Masculinity: The Case of the UN Navy' in P. Higate (ed), *Military Masculinities. Identity and the State*, Westport, CT: Praeger.
Barrow, A. (2009) '"[It's] Like a Rubber Band." Assessing UNSCR 1325 as a Gender Mainstreaming Process,' *International Journal of Law in Context* 5(1): 51–68.
Başaran, O. (2007) 'Militarized Medical Discourse on Homosexuality and Hegemonic Masculinity in Turkey,' MA thesis, Istanbul, Boğaziçi University.

Bibliography 221

Bass, G.J. (2004) 'Jus post bellum,' *Philosophy and Public Affairs* 31:384–412.
Basu, A. (ed) (2005) *The Challenge of Local Feminisms: Women's Movements in Global Perspective*, Boulder CO: Westview Press.
Belgrade Fund for Political Excellence. (2010) *United Nations Security Council Resolution 1325 in Serbia—On Women, Peace and Security: Recommendations for Drafting National Action Plan for Implementation of UN Security Council Resolution 1325 in Serbia*, Belgrade: Belgrade Fund for Political Excellence.
Berdal, M. and Malone, D.M. (eds) (2000) *Greed and Grievance: Economic Agendas in Civil Wars*, Boulder, CO: Lynne Rienner Publishers.
Bergoffen, D.B. (2008) 'The Just War Tradition: Translating the Ethics of Human Dignity into Political Practices,' *Hypatia* 23(2): 72–94.
Berndtsson, J. (2009) 'The Privatisation of Security and State Control of Force,' PhD thesis, Gothenburg, University of Gothenburg.
Bicanic, N. and Bourque, J. (2006) *Shadow Company*, DVD, Canada: A Purpose Built Film.
Birand, M.A. (1991) *Shirts of Steel: An Anatomy of the Turkish Armed Forces*, trans. S. Paker and R. Christie, London: I.B. Tauris.
Birch, N. (2009) 'Gay Referee Gets Red Card in Turkey,' *The Independent*, 25 June. Online. Available HTTP: <http://www.independent.co.uk/news/world/europe/gay-referee-gets-red-card-in-turkey-1718056.html> (accessed 5 January 2011).
Biricik, A. (2008) *Rotten Bodies/Idealized Masculinities: Reconstructing Hegemonic Masculinity through Militarized Medical Discourse in Turkey*, Saarbrucken, VDM Verlag Dr. Muller Aktiengessellschaft & Co.
Biricik, A. (2009) 'Rotten Report and Reconstructing Hegemonic Masculinity in Turkey,' in O.H. Cinar and C. Üsterci (eds), *Conscientious Objection: Resisting Militarized Society*, London: Zed Books.
Bloch, A., Galvin, T. and Harrell-Bond, B. (2000) 'Refugee Women in Europe: Some Aspects of the Legal and Policy Dimensions,' *International Migration* 38(2): 169–190.
Blum, W. (2003) *Killing Hope: US Military and CIA Interventions since World War II*, London: Zed Books.
Boëne, B., Callaghan, J. and Dandeker, C. (2004) 'Warriors in Peacekeeping: An Overview of Themes and Issues,' in J. Callaghan and M. Schönborn (eds), *Warriors in Peacekeeping: Points of Tension in Complex Cultural Encounters. A Comparative Study Based on Experiences in Bosnia*, New Brunswick, NJ: Transaction Publishers.
Bohm, D. (2008) *Wholeness and the Implicate Order*, London: Routledge.
Boorstin, R. and Nolan, S. (eds) (2004) *Iraq in Transition: Post-Conflict Challenges and Opportunities*, Open Society Institute and United Nations Foundation. Online. Available HTTP: <http://www.soros.org/initiatives/washington/articles_publications/publications/iraq_20041112/iraq_Transition.pdf> (accessed 12 November 2004).
Booth, K. (2005) *Theory of World Security*, Cambridge: Cambridge University Press.
Bora, T. (2004) 'Nationalism in Textbooks,' in Denis Tarba Ceylan Tarba and Gürol Irzik (eds), *Human Rights Issues in Textbooks: The Turkish Case*, Istanbul: History Foundation.
Bourke, J. (1999) *Intimate History of Killing: Face-to-Face Killing in Twentieth Century Warfare*, London: Basic Books.
Bowen, Jr., S.W. (2009) *Hard Lessons: The Iraq Reconstruction Experience*, Inspector General Draft Document, 2 February. Online. Available HTTP: <http://graphics8.nytimes.com/packages/images/world/20081213_RECONSTRUCTION_DOC/original.pdf> (accessed 2 February 2009).

Boyd, M. (1993) 'Gender Concealed, Gender Revealed: The Demography of Canada's Refugee Flows,' Working Paper, Center for the Study of Population, Florida State University.

Brian, D. (2009) Project on Government Oversight Letter to Secretary of State Hillary Clinton regarding U.S. Embassy in Kabul. Washington DC. Online. Available HTTP: <http://www.pogo.org/pogo-files/letters/contract-oversight/co-gp-20090901.html> (accessed 1 September 2009).

Brzezinski, Z. (1993) *Out of Control*, New York: Scribner's.

Bucar, E.M. (2010) 'Dianomy: Understanding Religious Women's Moral Agency as Creative Conformity,' *Journal of the American Academy of Religion* 78(3): 662–686.

Bunch, C. (1995) 'Transforming Human Rights from a Feminist Perspective,' in J. Peter and A. Wolper (eds), *Women's Rights, Human Rights: International Feminist Perspectives*, New York: Routledge.

Burnham, G., Lafta, R., Doocy, S. and Roberts, L. (2006) 'Mortality after the 2003 Invasion of Iraq: A Cross-Sectional Cluster Sample Survey,' *Lancet* 368:1421–1428.

Butler, J. (1988) 'Performative Acts and Gender Constitution: An Essay in Phenomenology and Feminist Theory,' *Theatre Journal* 40(4): 519–531.

Butler, J. (1990) *Gender Trouble: Feminism and the Subversion of Identity*, New York, Routledge.

Çakır, B. (2009) 'Gay Football Referee's Rights Restored, But . . . ,' *Bianet: News in English*. Online. Available HTTP: <http://bianet.org/english/freedom-of-expression/115124-gay-football-referees-rights-restored-but> (accessed 8 December 2010).

Cammermeyer, M. (1995) *Serving in Silence*, Harmondsworth: Penguin.

Can, H. (2009) 'Eşcinsel hakem düdüğünü istiyor, *Fanatik*, 13 May. Online. Available HTTP: <http://fanatik.ekolay.net/Default.aspx?aType=GazeteArsiv&Date=13.05.2009> or <http://fanatik.ekolay.net/Boylesi-gorulmedi!_3_Detail_27_133218.htm> (accessed 5 January 2011).

Carlton, E. (2001) *Militarism—Rule without Law*, Aldershot: Ashgate.

Carpenter, R.C. (2005) '"Women, Children and Other Vulnerable Groups": Gender, Strategic Frames and the Protection of Civilians as a Transnational Issue,' *International Studies Quarterly* 49:486–500.

Carpenter, R.C. (2006) *'Innocent Women and Children': Gender, Norms and the Protection of Civilians*, Aldershot: Ashgate.

Charlesworth, H. (1994) 'What Are "Women's International Human Rights"?,' in R. Cook (ed), *Human Rights of Women. National and International Perspectives*, Philadelphia: University of Pennsylvania Press.

Checkland, P. (1997) *Systems Thinking, Systems Practice*, Chichester: John Wiley and Sons.

Çınar, Ö.H. and Coskun, U. (eds) (2009) *Resisting Militarized Society: Conscientious Objection*, London and New York: Zed Books.

Çınar, Ö.H. and Üsterci, C. (eds) (2009) *Conscientious Objection: Resisting Militarized Society*, London: Zed Books.

Cockburn, C. (1998) *The Space between Us: Negotiating Gender and National Identities in Conflict*, London: Zed Books.

Cockburn, C. (2004) 'The Continuum of Violence: A Gender Perspective on War and Peace,' in W. Giles and J. Hyndman (eds), *Sites of Violence: Gender and Conflict Zones*, Berkeley: University of California Press.

Cockburn, C. (2007) *From Where We Stand: War, Women's Activism and Feminist Analysis*, London: Zed Books.

Cockburn, C. and Hubic, M. (2002) 'Gender and the Peacekeeping Military: A View from Bosnian Women's Organizations,' in C. Cockburn and D. Zarkov (eds), *The Postwar Moment*, London: Lawrence and Wishart.

Coghlan, B., Brennan, R.J. and Ngoy, P. (2006) 'Mortality in the Democratic Republic of Congo: A Nationwide Survey,' *Lancet* 367:44–51.

Cohn, C. (2000) '"How Can She Claim Equal Rights When She Doesn't Have to Do as Many Pushups as I Do?": The Framing of Men's opposition to Women's Equality in the Military,' *Men and Masculinities* 3:131–151.

Cohn, C. (2004) 'Feminist Peacemaking: In Resolution 1325, the United Nations Requires the Inclusion of Women in All Peace Planning and Negotiation,' *Women's Review of Books* 21(5): 8–9.

Cohn, C. (2008) 'Mainstreaming Gender in UN Security Policy: A Path to Political Transformation?,' in S.M. Rai and G. Waylen (eds), *Global Governance: Feminist Perspectives*, London: Palgrave.

Cohn, C., Kinsella, H. and Gibbings, S. (2004) 'Women, Peace and Security: Resolution 1325,' *International Feminist Journal of Politics* 6(1): 130–140.

Cohn, C. and Ruddick, S. (2004) 'A Feminist Ethical Perspective on Weapons of Mass Destruction,' in H. Sohail and S. Lee (eds), *Ethics and Weapons of Mass Destruction: Religious and Secular Perspectives*, Cambridge: Cambridge University Press.

Collins, R. (2008) *Violence. A Micro-Sociological Theory*, Princeton, NJ: Princeton University Press.

Connell, R.W. (1987) *Gender and Power*, Cambridge: Polity Press.

Connell, R.W. (1995) *Masculinities*, Cambridge: Polity Press.

Connell, R.W. (1997) 'Men, Masculinities and Feminism,' *Social Alternatives* 16(3): 7–10.

Connell, R.W. (1998) 'Men in the World: Masculinities and Globalization,' *Men and Masculinities* 1(1): 3–23.

Connell, R.W. (2001) 'Masculinities, Violence, and Peacemaking,' *Peace News* 2443:14–16.

Connell, R.W. (2002) 'Masculinities, the Reduction of Violence and the Pursuit of Peace,' in C. Cockburn and D. Žarkov (eds), *The Postwar Moment: Militaries, Masculinities and International Peacekeeping—Bosnia and the Netherlands*, London: Lawrence and Wishart.

Connell, R.W. (2005) 'Globalization, Imperialism and Masculinities,' in M. Kimmel, J. Hearn and R.W. Connell (eds), *Handbook of Studies on Men and Masculinities*, Thousand Oaks, CA: Sage.

Connell, R.W. (2007) *Southern Theory: The Global Dynamics of Knowledge in Social Science*, Cambridge: Polity Press.

Constitution of the Republic of Turkey. (1980). Online. Available HTTP: <http://www.anayasa.gov.tr/images/loaded/pdf_dosyalari/THE_CONSTITUTION_OF_THE_REPUBLIC_OF_TURKEY.pdf> (accessed 10 January 2011).

Conway, D. (2008) 'Contesting the Masculine State,' in J.L. Parpart and M. Zalewski (eds), *Rethinking the Man Question. Sex, Gender and Violence in International Relations*, London: Zed Books.

Cooke, M. and Woollacott, A. (eds) (1993) *Gendering War Talk*, Princeton, NJ: Princeton University Press.

Coomaraswamy, R. (1997) 'Tiger Women and the Question of Women's Emancipation,' *Pravada* 4(9): 8–10.

Creighton, C. and Shaw, M. (eds) (1987) *The Sociology of War and Peace*, London: Macmillan.

Crépeau, F. (1995) *Droit d'asile. De l'hospitalité aux contrôles migratoires*, Brussels: Bruylant.

Crossette, B. (1996) 'When Peacekeepers Turn into Troublemakers,' *New York Times*, 7 January, 6.

Cushman, T. (2004) 'A Conversation on Religion and Violence with Veena Das,' *Hedgehog Review, Institute for Advanced Studies in Culture* 6(1).

Dandeker, C. (2000) 'On "the Need to Be Different": Recent Trends in Military Culture,' in H. Strachan (ed), *The British Army: Manpower and Society into the Twenty-First Century*, London: Frank Cass.

Dandeker, C. and Gow, J. (2004) 'Military Culture and Strategic Peacekeeping,' in J. Callaghan and M. Schönborn (eds), *Warriors in Peacekeeping: Points of Tension in Complex Cultural Encounters. A Comparative Study Based on Experiences in Bosnia*, New Brunswick, NJ: Transaction Publishers.

Danielsson, E. (2009) 'En enkönad fred är ingen fred—en studie av svenska riksdagsdebatter om FN-resolution 1325' [A Unisexual Peace Is No Peace—A Study of Debates on the UN Resolution 1325 in the Swedish Parliament], Essay, level III, Department of Political Science, Stockholm University.

Das, V. (2007) *Violence and the Descent into the Ordinary*, Berkeley: University of California Press.

Davis, A. (2009) 'A Vocabulary for Feminist Praxis: On War and Radical Critique,' in Riley R., C. T. Mohanty and M. B. Pratt (eds), *Feminism and War: Confronting US Imperialism*, London: Zed Books.

Davis, C. and Roulston, C. (eds) (2000) *Gender, Democracy an Inclusion in Northern Ireland*, Basingstoke: Palgrave.

Dawson, G. (1994) *Soldier Heroes: British Adventure, Empire and the Imagining of Masculinities*, London: Routledge.

D'Costa, B. (2006) 'Marginalized Identity: New Frontiers of Research for IR?,' in B. Ackerly, M. Stern and J. True (eds), *Feminist Methodologies for International Relations*, Cambridge: Cambridge University Press.

Dean, R.D. (2001) *Imperial Brotherhood: Gender and the Making of Cold War Foreign Policy*, Amherst: University of Massachusetts Press.

de Beauvoir, S. (1953) *The Second Sex*, London: Jonathan Cape.

Delestrac, D. (director) (2009) *Pax Americana and the Weaponization of Space*, Canada/France, Film, Color, HD, 85 min.

de Mel, N. (2001) *Women and the Nation's Narrative*, New Delhi: Kali for Women.

de Mel, N. (2007) *Militarising Sri Lanka: Popular Culture, Memory and Narrative in the Armed Conflict*, New Delhi: Sage.

Devlet Memurları Kanunu. (1965) Online. Available HTTP: <http://www.mevzuat.adalet.gov.tr/html/388.html> (accessed 12 October 2009).

de Vries, H. and Weber, S. (eds) (1997) *Violence, Identity and Self Determination*, Stanford, CA: Stanford University Press.

de Vylder, S. (2004) 'Costs of Male Violence,' in H. Ferguson, J. Hearn, Ø.G. Holter, L. Jalmert, M. Kimmel, J. Lang, R. Morrell and S. de Vylder (eds), *Ending Gender-Based Violence: A Call for Global Action to Involve Men*, Stockholm: SIDA.

Dittmer, C. and Apelt, M. (2008) 'About Intervening in Vulnerable Societies: Gender in Military Peacekeeping of the Bundeswehr,' in H. Carreiras and G. Kümmel (eds), *Women in the Military and Armed Conflict*, Wiesbaden: VS Verlag Für Sozialwissenschaften.

Dixon, N. (1976) *On the Psychology of Military Incompetence*, London: Jonathan Cape.

Dowler, L. (1998) 'And They Think I'm a Nice Old Lady' Women and War in Belfast, Northern Ireland,' *Gender, Place and Culture* 5(2): 159–176.

Downes, A.B. (2007) 'Restraint or Propellant? Democracy and Civilian Fatalities in Interstate Wars,' *Journal of Conflict Resolution* 51:872–904.

Duhaček, N. (2005) 'Panel Discussion Security Is an Absence of Fear, Violence, and Poverty: From Military Security towards a Feminist Concept of Security,' Conference on Women, Peace and Security, Belgrade, 31 October. Online. Available HTTP: <www.zeneucrnom.org> (accessed 22 October 2009).

Dunn, S. (1995) 'The Conflict as a Set of Problems,' in S. Dunn (ed), *Facets of the Conflict in Northern Ireland*, London: Macmillan/St. Martin's Press.

Eck, K. and Hultman, L. (2007) 'One-Sided Violence against Civilians in War: Insights from New Fatality Data,' *Journal of Peace Research* 44:233–246.
Eckhardt, W. (1992) *Civilizations, Empires and Wars: A Quantitative History of War*, Jefferson, NC: MacFarland and Company.
Edkins, J. (2002) 'After the Subject of International Security,' in A. Finlayson and J. Valentine (eds), *Politics and Post-Structuralism: An Introduction*, Edinburgh: Edinburgh University Press.
Eduards, M. (2007) *Kroppspolitik. Om Moder Svea och andra kvinnor* [Body Politics. On Mother Svea and Other Women], Stockholm: Atlas.
Eisenstein, H. (2009) *Feminism Seduced. How Global Elites Use Women's Labor and Ideas to Exploit the World*, Boulder, CO: Paradigm Publications.
Eisenstein, Z. (2007) *Sexual Decoys. Gender, Race and War in Imperial Democracy*, London: Zed Books.
El-Bushra, J. (2000) 'Transforming Conflict: Some Thoughts on a Gendered Understanding of Conflict Processes,' in S. Jacobs, R. Jacobson and J. Marchbank (eds), *States of Conflict: Gender, Violence and Resistance*, London: Zed Books.
Elshtain, J.B. (1995) *Women and War*, Chicago: University of Chicago Press.
Enloe, C. (1989) *Bananas, Beaches and Bases. Making Feminist Sense of International Politics*, Berkeley: University of California Press.
Enloe, C. (1993) *The Morning After: Sexual Politics at the End of the Cold War*, Berkeley: University of California Press.
Enloe, C. (1996) 'Margins, Silences and Bottom Rungs: How to Overcome the Underestimation of Power in the Study of International Relations,' in S. Smith, K. Booth and M. Zalewski (eds), *International Theory: Positivism and Beyond*, Cambridge: Cambridge University Press.
Enloe, C. (1998) *Does Khaki Become You?: The Militarization of Women's Lives*, London: Pandora.
Enloe, C. (2000) *Maneuvers—The International Politics of Militarizing Women's Lives*, Berkeley: University of California Press.
Enloe, C. (2004) 'Demilitarisation or more of the same?,' in C. Cockburn and D. Zarkov (eds), *The Postwar Moment*, London: Lawrence and Wishart.
Enloe, C. (2005) 'What if Patriarchy Is "the Big Picture"? An Afterword,' in D. Mazurana, A. Raven-Roberts and J. Parpart (eds), *Gender, Conflict and Peacekeeping*, Lanham, MD: Rowman and Littlefield.
Enloe, C. (2007) *Globalisation and Militarism. Feminists Make the Link*, London: Rowman and Littlefield.
Equality Ombudsman. (2006) *JämO, Kunskapsöversikt. Sexuella trakasserier och trakasserier på grund av kön i arbetslivet* [Sexual Harassment and Harassment because of Sex in Working Life—A Review]. Online. Available HTTP: <http://www.do.se/Documents/Material/konskapsoversikt_sextrak_rev_jan07.pdf> (accessed 5 May 2010).
Eyre, D.P. and Suchman, M.C. (1996) 'Status, Norms, and the Proliferation of Conventional Weapons: An Institutional Theory Approach,' in P.J. Katzenstein (ed), *The Culture of National Security: Norms and Identity in World Politics*, New York: Columbia University Press.
Fainaru, S. (2008) *Big Boy Rules: America's Mercenaries Fighting in Iraq*, Philadelphia: De Capo Press.
Faludi, S. (1991) *Backlash: The Undeclared War against American Women*, New York: Crown Publishers.
Fearon, K. and McWilliams, M. (2000) 'Swimming against the Mainstream: The Northern Ireland Women's Coalition,' in C. Davis and C. Roulston (eds), *Gender, Democracy and Inclusion in Northern Ireland*, Basingstoke: Palgrave.
Ferguson, H., Hearn, J., Holter, Ø.G., Jalmert, L., Kimmel, M., Lang, J., Morrell, R. and de Vylders, S. (2004) *Ending Gender-Based Violence: A Call for Global Action to Involve Men*, Stockholm: SIDA.

Ferguson, K. (2003) 'Silence: A Politics,' *Contemporary Political Theory* 2(1): 49–65.
Fidler, S. (2008) 'UK Becomes Largest Exporter of Arms,' *Financial Times*, 18 June. Online. Available HTTP: <http://www.ft.com/cms/s/0/8efb9db6-3cce-11dd-b958-0000779fd2ac.html?nclick_check=1> (accessed 18 June 2008).
Flén, E. (2010) 'Tuo sotilas on tyttö—Miksi naisia tarvitaan rauhanturvatehtäviin?' [Why Are Women Needed in Peace Operations?], in P. Jukarainen and S. Terävä (eds), *Tasa-arvoinen turvallisuus?* [Equal Security?], Helsinki: Minerva.
Florea Hudson, N. (2009) *Gender, Human Security and the United Nations: Security Language as a Political Framework for Women*, London: Routledge.
Fogarty, B.E. (2000) *War, Peace and the Social Order*, Boulder, CO: Westview Press.
Foucault, M. (1963/2003) *The Birth of the Clinic: An Archaeology of Medical Perception*, trans. A.M. Sheridan, New York: Routledge.
Freedman, J. (2007) *Gendering the International Asylum and Refugee Debate*, Basingstoke: Palgrave Macmillan.
Friedman E.J., Hochstetler, K. and Clark, A.M. (2005) *Sovereignty, Democracy, and Global Civil Society: State–Society Relations at UN World Conferences*, Albany: State University of New York Press.
Frontline Online. (2005) 'Behind the Mask.' Online. Available HTTP: <http://www.pbs/wgbh/pages/frontline/shows/IRA/conflict> (accessed 14 September 2005).
Galtung, J. (1969) 'Violence, Peace and Peace Research,' *Journal of Peace Research* 6(3): 167–191.
Garcia, S. (1999) 'Military Women in the NATO Armed Forces,' *Minerva* 17(2). Online. Available HTTP: <http://departments.oxy.edu/library/research/help/articles/index.htm> (accessed 3 June 2008).
Gareis, S.B. and Varwick, J. (2005) *The United Nations: An Introduction*, New York: Palgrave.
Gender Force. (2007) *Good and Bad Examples. Lessons Learned from Working with the Unites Nations Resolution 1325 in International Missions*. Online. Available HTTP: <http://www.genderforce.se/dokument/Good_and_bad_examples_English_A4.pdf> (accessed 1 June 2011).
Geraghty, T. (2009) *Soldiers of Fortune: A History of the Mercenary in Modern Warfare*, New York: Pegasus.
Giles, W. and Hyndman, J. (eds) (2004) *Sites of Violence: Gender and Conflict Zones*, Berkeley: University of California Press.
Godec, S.T. (2010) 'Between Rhetoric and Reality: Exploring the Impact of Military Humanitarian Intervention upon Sexual Violence—Post-Conflict Sex Trafficking in Kosovo,' *International Review of the Red Cross* 92(877): 235–258.
Goldstein, J.S. (2001) *War and Gender*, Cambridge: Cambridge University Press.
Goleman, D. (1997) *Tunneäly: Lahjakkuuden koko kuva* [Emotional Intelligence], trans. Jaakko Kankaanpää, Helsinki: Otava.
Gonsalves, T. (2003) 'Gender and Peacebuilding: A Sri Lankan Case Study,' IDRC Working Paper. Online. Available HTTP: <https://idlbnc.idrc.ca/dspace/bitstream/123456789/33539/1/Gonsalves_Tahira_paper.pdf> (accessed 20 February 2009).
Grant, R. and Newland, K. (eds) (1991) *Gender and International Relations*, Milton Keynes: Open University Press.
Gregory, D. (2004) *The Colonial Present*, Malden, MA: Blackwell.
Griffin, G. and Braidotti, R. (eds) (2002) *Thinking Differently: A Reader in European Women's Studies*, London: Zed Books.
Gurr, T.R. and Harff, B. (1994) *Ethnic Conflict in World Politics*, Boulder, CO: Westview Press.

Gustavsen, E. (2011) 'Siblings in Arms? Gender Perceptions in the US and Norwegian Armed Forces,' master's thesis, Oslo, University of Oslo, Department of Sociology and Human Geography.
Haakonsen, M.B. and Jansen T. (2010) *Trenger flere kvinner i kamp* [Need More Women in Combat]. Online. Available HTTP: <http://www.mil.no/start/article.jhtml?articleID=195194> (accessed 2 January 2011).
Haaland, T.L. (2008) *Small Forces with a Global Outreach. Role Perceptions in the Norwegian Armed Forces after the Cold War*, Oslo: Unipub forlag.
Hägglund, G. (2007) 'Natoonko?' [To NATO?], *Sotilas–aikakauslehti* 82:21–23.
Hall, E. (1995) *We Can't Even March Straight*, London: Vintage.
Hall, S. (2004) 'Army Recruits More Prone to Suicide than Civilians,' *Guardian*, 28 August. Online. Available HTTP: <http://www.guardian.co.uk/society/2004/aug/28/mentalhealth.politics> (accessed 28 August 2004).
Hammerstad, A. (2000) 'Whose Security? UNHCR, Refugee Protection and State Security after the Cold War,' *Security Dialogue* 31(4): 391–403.
Hanmer, J. (1990) 'Men, Power and the Exploitation of Women,' in J. Hearn and D. Morgan (eds), *Men, Masculinities and Social Theory*, London: Unwin Hyman/Routledge.
Hansen, L. (2000) 'The Little Mermaid's Silent Security Dilemma and the Absence of Gender in the Copenhagen School,' *Millennium: Journal of International Studies* 29(2): 285–306.
Haq, F. (2007) 'Militarism and Motherhood: Women of the Lashkar-e-Tayyaba,' *Signs* 32(4): 1023–1046.
Haraway, D. (1988) 'Situated Knowledges: The Science Question in Feminism as a Site of Discourse on the Privilege of Partial Perspective,' *Feminist Studies* 14(3): 575–99.
Harding, S. (1986) *The Science Question in Feminism*, Milton Keynes: Open University Press.
Harding, S. (1991) *Whose Science? Whose Knowledge? Thinking from Women's Lives*, Milton Keynes: Open University Press.
Harding, S. (2004a) *The Feminist Standpoint Theory Reader: Intellectual and Political Controversies*, New York: Routledge.
Harding, S. (2004b) 'Rethinking Standpoint Epistemology: What Is "Strong Objectivity"?,' in S. Harding (ed), *The Feminist Standpoint Theory Reader: Intellectual and Political Controversies*, New York: Routledge.
Harrell-Bond, B. (1999) 'Interview with Barbara Harrell-Bond,' in D. Indra (ed), *Engendering Forced Migration: Theory and Practice*, Oxford: Berghahn.
Harrell-Bond, B. (2002) 'Can Humanitarian Work with Refugees be Humane?,' *Human Rights Quarterly* 24:51–85.
Harris, J.J. and Segal, D.R. (1985) 'Observations from the Sinai: The Boredom Factor,' *Armed Forces and Society* 11(2): 235–248.
Hartmann, H. (1979) 'Capitalism, Patriarchy and Job Segregation by Sex,' in Z. Eisenstein (ed), *Capitalist Patriarchy and the Case for Socialist Feminism*, New York: Monthly Review Press.
Hartsock, N.C.M. (1983) *Money, Sex and Power: Toward a Feminist Historical Materialism*, Boston: Northeastern University Press.
Hartsock, N.C.M. (1998) *The Feminist Standpoint Revisited and Other Essays*, Boulder, CO: Westview Press.
Hawkesworth, M. (2009) 'Institutionalizing Insurgency,' *International Feminist Journal of Politics* 11(1): 10–20.
Hearn, J. (1987) *The Gender of Oppression*, New York: Wheatsheaf, Brighton/St. Martin's.
Hearn, J. (1997) 'The Implications of Critical Studies on Men,' *Nora* 3:48–60.

Hearn, J. (1998a) 'Theorizing Men and Men's Theorizing: Men's Discursive Practices in Theorizing Men,' *Theory and Society* 27(6): 781–816.
Hearn, J. (1998b) *The Violences of Men*, London: Sage.
Hearn, J. (2003a) 'Men: Power, Challenges of Power and the 'Big Picture' of Globalisation,' in I. Novikova and D. Kambourov (eds), *Men and Masculinities in the Global World: Integrating Postsocialist Perspectives*, Helsinki: Kikimora Publishers.
Hearn, J. (2003b) 'On Men, Women, Militarism and the Military,' in P. Higate (ed), *Military Masculinities: Identity and the State*, Westport, CT: Praeger.
Hearn, J. (2009) 'Patriarchies, Transpatriarchies and Intersectionalities,' in E. Oleksy (ed), *Intimate Citizenships: Gender, Sexualities, Politics*, London: Routledge.
Hearn, J. and McKie, L. (2008) 'Gendered Policy and Policy on Gender: The Case of "Domestic Violence,"' *Policy and Politics: An International Journal* 36(1): 75–91.
Hearn, J. and Morgan, D. (1990) 'The Critique of Men,' in J. Hearn and D. Morgan (eds), *Men, Masculinity and Social Theory*, London: Hyman Unwin.
Hearn, J. and Parkin, W. (2001) *Gender, Sexuality and Violence in Organizations: The Unspoken Forces of Organization Violations*, London: Sage.
Helvacıoğlu, B. (2006) 'The Smile of Death and the Solemncholy of Masculinity,' in L. Ouzgane (ed), *Islamic Masculinities*, London: Zed Books.
Higate, P. (2001) 'Theorizing Continuity: From Military to Civilian Life,' *Armed Forces and Society* 27(3): 443–460.
Higate, P. (ed) (2002) *Military Masculinities*, New York: Praeger.
Higate, P. (2004) *Gendered Relations and Peacekeeping in the Democratic Republic of Congo and Sierra Leone, Monograph No 91*, Pretoria: Institute for Security Studies.
Higate, P. (2007) 'Peacekeepers, Masculinities and Sexual Exploitation,' *Men and Masculinities* 10(1): 99–119.
Hill, F, Abotiz, M. and Poehlman-Doumbouya, S. (2003) 'Nongovernmental Organizations' Role in the Buildup and Implementation of Security Council Resolution 1325,' *Signs* 28(4): 1255–1269.
Hirsch, M. and Spitzer, L. (1993) 'Gendered Translations: Claude Lanzmann Shoah,' in M. Cooke and A. Woollacott (eds), *Gendering War Talk*, Princeton, NJ: Princeton University Press.
Hobsbawm, Eric (1994) *The Age of Extremes*, Harmondsworth: Penguin.
Hockey, J. (1986) *Squaddies: Portrait of a Subculture*, Exeter: Exeter University Press.
Hockey, J. (2003) 'No More Heroes: Masculinity in the Infantry,' in P. Higate (ed), *Military Masculinities. Identity and the State*, Westport, CT: Praeger.
Holmqvist, C. (2005) 'Private Security Companies: The Case for Regulation,' SIPRI Policy Paper No. 9, Stockholm, Sweden.
Holt, K. (2004) 'Will Congo's Women Ever Have Justice?' *The Independent*, 12 July. Online. Available HTTP: <http://departments.oxy.edu/library/research/help/articles/index.htm> (accessed 1 July 2007).
Holt, K. and Hughes, S. (2004) 'Sex and Death in the Heart of Africa,' *The Independent*, 25 May. Online. Available HTTP: <http://departments.oxy.edu/library/research/help/articles/index.htm> (accessed 1 July 2007).
Hopton, J. and Higate, P. (2005) 'War, Militarism and Masculinities,' in M. Kimmel, J. Hearn and R.W. Connell (eds), *Handbook of Studies on Men and Masculinities*, Thousand Oaks, CA: Sage.
Horowitz, D.L. (1985) *Ethnic Groups in Conflict*, Berkeley: University of California Press.
Howe, S. (2005) 'Mad Dogs and Ulstermen: The Crisis of Loyalism (Part 2).' Online. Available HTTP: <http://www.opendemocracy.net/democracy-protest/loyalism_2885.jsp.> (accessed 5 January 2009).

Hranjski, H. (1994) 'UN Dismisses Widespread Illegality among Troops in Former Yugoslavia,' *United Press International*, 27 January. Online. Available HTTP: <http://departments.oxy.edu/library/research/help/ articles/index.htm> (accessed 8 August 2007).
Huggins, M.K. and Haritos-Fatouros, M. (1998) 'Bureaucratizing Masculinities among Brazilian Torturers and Murderers,' in L.H. Bowker (ed), *Masculinities and Violence*, Thousand Oaks, CA: Sage.
Hughes, D. (1999) 'Feminista!' *An Online Journal of Feminist Construction* 3(1). Online. Available HTTP: <http://www.feminista.com/archieves/v3n1/hughes.html> (accessed 23 December 2005).
Huhtinen, A.M. (2004) 'Soldiership without Existence—The Changing Socio-Psychological Culture and Environment of Military Decision-Makers,' in J. Toiskallio (ed), *Identity, Ethics and Soldiership, ACIE Publications, No 1. National Defence College, Department of Education*, Helsinki: ACIE Publications.
Huhtinen, A.M. (2007) 'Strategically Leading for Identity in War on Terror,' *Tiede ja ase* 65:184–197.
Human Rights Council. (2009) 'Human Rights in Palestine and Other Occupied Arab Territories.' Report of the United Nations fact finding mission on the Gaza conflict.
Human Security Centre. (2005) *Human Security Report 2005: War and Peace in the 21st Century*, Oxford: Oxford University Press. Online. Available HTTP: <http://www.humansecurityreport.info/> (accessed 1 June 2011).
Hunt, K. (2006) '"Embedded Feminism" and the War on Terror,' in K. Hunt and K. Rygiel (eds), *(En)Gendering the War on Terror*, Aldershot: Ashgate.
Hutchings, K. (2007) 'Feminist Ethics and Political Violence,' *International Politics* 44:90–106.
Hutchings, K. (2008) 'Making Sense of Masculinity and War,' *Men and Masculinities* 10(4): 389–404.
Hutchings, K., Zalewski, M., Tickner, A., Sylvester, C., Light, M., Jabri, V. and Halliday, F. (2008) 'Roundtable Discussion: Reflections on the Past, Prospects for the Future in Gender and International Relations,' *Millennium—Journal of International Studies* 37(1): 153–179.
Hutchinson, J. (2005) *Nations as Zones of Conflict*, London: Sage.
Hyndman, J. (1998) 'Managing Difference: Gender and Culture in Humanitarian Emergencies,' *Gender Place and Culture* 5(3): 241–260.
Hyndman, J. (2000) *Managing Displacement: Refugees and the Politics of Humanitarianism*, Minneapolis: University of Minnesota Press.
Insats & Försvar. (2007) March. Monthly newsletter issued by the Swedish Armed Forces Headquarters.
Insats & Försvar. (2008) February. Monthly newsletter issued by the Swedish Armed Forces Headquarters.
İnsel, A. and Bayramoğlu, A. (eds) (2004) *Bir Zümre, Bir Parti: Türkiye'de Ordu*, Istanbul: Birikim.
Iversen, A., Dyson, C., Smith, N., Greenberg, N., Walvin, R., Unwin, C., Hull, L., Hotope, M., Dandeker, C., Ross, J. and Wessley, S. (2005) '"Goodbye and Good Luck": The Mental Health Needs and Treatment Experiences of British Ex-Service Personnel,' *British Journal of Psychiatry* 186:480–486.
Jabri, V. (2010) *War and the Transformation of Global Politics*, Basingstoke: Palgrave Macmillan.
Jackson, R.H. (1990) *Quasi-States: Sovereignty, International Relations, and the Third World*, New York: Cambridge University Press.
Jaggar, A. (1983) *Feminist Politics and Human Nature*, Totowa, NJ: Rowman and Allenheld.
Jaggar, A. (2005) 'Saving Amina': Global Justice for Women and Intercultural Dialogue,' *Ethics and International Affairs* 19(3): 55–75.

'Jails Hold 8,500 Ex-Servicemen.' (2008) 30 August. Online. Available HTTP: <http://news.bbc.co.uk/2/hi/uk_news/wales/7589953.stm> (accessed 30 August 2008).
Jeffords, S. (1989) *The Remasculinization of America: Gender and the Vietnam War*, Bloomington: Indiana University Press.
Joachim, J. (1999) 'Shaping the Human Rights Agenda: The Case of Violence against Women,' in M. Meyer and E. Prügl (eds), *Gender Politics in Global Governance*, Lanham, MD: Rowman and Littlefield.
Joachim, J. (2003) 'Framing Issues and Seizing Opportunities: The UN, NGOs, and Women's Rights,' *International Studies Quarterly* 47:247–274.
Johnson, R. (1986) 'Institutions and the Promotion of Violence,' in A. Campbell and J.J. Gibbs (eds), *Violent Transactions*, Oxford: Blackwell.
Jolly, R. (1996) *Changing Step: From Military to Civilian Life*, London: Brassey's.
Jones, A. (ed) (2004) *Gendercide and Genocide*, Nashville, TN: Vanderbilt University Press.
Jones, A. (2006) *Genocide: A Comprehensive Introduction*, London: Routledge.
Jukarainen, P. (2010) 'Vapaus, velvollisuus ja tasa-arvo'[Freedom, Duty and Equality], in S. Myllyniemi (ed), *Puolustuskannalla, Nuorisobarometri 2010* [In Defense, Youth Barometer 2010], Helsinki: Nuora & Nuorisotutkimusseura.
Jukarainen, P. and Terävä, S. (2010) *Tasa-arvoinen turvallisuus? Sukupuolten yhdenvertaisuus suomalaisessa maanpuolustuksessa ja kriisinhallinnassa* [Equal Security? Gender Equality in Finnish Defense and Crisis Management], Helsinki: Minerva.
Kääriäinen, S. (2006) 'Vakaa kansainvälinen järjestys on kaikkien etu'. Vieraskynä. [International Stablity Benefits All], *Helsingin Sanomat*, 11 August.
Kabat-Zinn, J. (2005) *Coming to Our Senses: Healing Ourselves and the World through Mindfulness*, New York: Hyperion.
Kaldor, M. (2004) *A Human Security Doctrine for Europe: Barcelona Report.* Online. Available HTTP: <http://www.abolishwar.org.uk/human_security_for_europe.pdf> (accessed 27 June 2008).
Kaldor, M. (2006) *New and Old Wars: Organised Violence in a Global Era*, Cambridge: Polity Press.
Kallio-Tamminen, T. (2008) *Kvanttilainen todellisuus: Fysiikka ja filosofia maailmankuvan muovaajina*, Helsinki: Gaudeamus Helsinki University Press.
Kandiyoti, D. (1994) 'The Paradoxes of Masculinity: Some Thoughts on Segregated Societies,' in A. Cornwall and N. Lindisfarne (eds), *Dislocating Masculinities: Comparative Ethnographies*, London: Routledge.
Karamé, K.H. (2001) 'Military Women in Peace Operations: Experiences of the Norwegian Battalion in UNIFIL 1978–98,' *International Peacekeeping* 8(2): 85–96.
Karns, M.P. and Mingst, K.A. (2004) *International Organizations: The Politics and Processes of Global Governance*, Boulder, CO: Lynne Rienner Publishers.
Kartikeyan, D.R. and Raju, R. (2004) *The Rajiv Gandhi Assassination: The Investigation*, Colombo: Vijitha Yapa Publications.
Kaskeala, J. (2006) 'Kriisinhallinnasta tukea Suomen puolustukseen. Vieraskynä.' [Support for the Defense from Crisis Management], *Helsingin Sanomat*, 22 July.
Keck, M. and Sikkink, K. (1998) *Activists beyond Borders. Advocacy Networks in International Politics*, Ithaca, NY: Cornell University Press.
Kelly, L. (2000) 'Wars against Women: Sexual Violence, Sexual Politics and the Militarised State,' in S. Jacobs, R. Jacobson and J. Marchbank (eds), *States of Conflict. Gender, Violence and Resistance*, London: Zed Books.
Kelman, H. (1973) 'Violence without Moral Restraint: Reflections on the Dehumanization of Victims and Victimisers,' *Journal of Social Issues* 29:25–61.

Kesic, V. (2000) 'From Reverence to Rape—An Anthropology of Ethnic and Genderized Violence,' in M.R. Waller and J. Rycenga (eds), *Frontline Feminisms. Women, War, and Resistance*, New York: Garland Publications.
Khan, S. (2008) 'Afghan Women: The Limits of Colonial Rescue,' in R.L. Riley, C.T. Mohanty and M.B. Pratt (eds), *Feminism and War: Confronting US Imperialism*, London: Zed Books.
Kiljunen, P. (2006), 'Kenraalimajuri Paavo Kiljunen: Sotilaallisen kriisinhallinnan haasteet' [Major General Paavo Kiljunen: Challenges of Military Crisis Management], Speech at the Paasikivi-Seura in Helsinki, 5 September. Online. Available HTTP: <http://www.paasikivi-seura.fi/58 > (accessed 19 May 2010).
Kilpiä, J. (2006) 'Kriisinhallinta muuttuu yhä haasteellisemmaksi. Vieraskynä' [Crisis Management Turns Out to Be Ever More Challenging], *Helsingin Sanomat*, 29 July.
Kimmel, M. (1996) *Manhood in American: A Cultural History*, New York: Free Press.
Kimmel, M., Hearn, J. and Connell, R.W. (eds) (2005) *Handbook of Studies on Men & Masculinities*, London: SAGE.
Kinsey, C. (2007) *Corporate Soldiers and International Security: The Rise of Private Military Companies*, London: Routledge.
Kirke, C. (2010) 'Orders Is Orders . . . Aren't They? Rule Bending and Rule Breaking in the British Army,' *Ethnography* 11(3): 359–380.
Klemola, T. (2004) *Taidon Filosofia: Filosofian taito*, Tampere, Finland: Tampere University Press.
Knauss, P.R. (1987) *The Persistence of Patriarchy: Class, Gender, and Ideology in Twentieth Century Algeria*, New York: Praeger.
Kneebone, S. (2005) 'Women within the Refugee Construct: "Exclusionary Inclusion" in Policy and Practice—The Australian Experience,' *International Journal of Refugee Law* 17(1): 7–42.
Knox, C. (2002) '"See No Evil, Hear No Evil": Insidious Paramilitary Violence in Northern Ireland,' *British Journal of Criminology* 42(1): 164–185.
Koyama, S. and Myrttinen, H. (2007) 'Unintended Consequences of Peace Operations on Timor Leste from a Gender Perspective,' in C. Aoi, C. De Coning and R. Thakur (eds), *Unintended Consequences of Peacekeeping Operations*, Tokyo: United Nations University Press.
Krahmann, E. (2003) 'Conceptualizing Security Governance,' *Cooperation and Conflict* 38(1): 5–26.
Kronsell, A. (2005) 'Gendered Practices in Institutions of Hegemonic Masculinity—Reflections from Feminist Standpoint Theory,' *International Feminist Journal of Politics* 7(2): 280–298.
Kronsell, A. (2006) 'Methods for Studying Silences: Gender Analysis in Institutions of Hegemonic Masculinity,' in B. Ackerly, M. Stern and J. True (eds), *Feminist Methodologies for International Relations*, Cambridge: Cambridge University Press.
Kronsell, A. (2010) 'Gender and Governance,' in Robert Denemark (ed), *The International Studies Compendium Project*, Oxford: Wiley-Blackwell.
Kronsell, A. and Svedberg, E. (2001) 'The Duty to Protect: Gender in the Swedish Practice of Conscription,' *Cooperation and Conflict* 36(3): 153–176.
Laitinen, K. (2006) 'Suomalaisen asevelvollisuuden tarina' [The Narrative of Finnish Conscription], in S. Rummakko (ed), *Tahdon asia* [Matter of Will], Helsinki: Like.
Lappalainen, T. (2007) 'Uusille vesille' [To New Waters], *Suomen Kuvalehti* 29:18–23.
La Ruta Pacifica de las Mujeres. (2003) *La Ruta Pacifica de Las Mujeres: No Parimos Hijos ni Hijas para la Guerra*, Medellin, Colombia: La Ruta Pacifica de las Mujeres.

Lambda-Istanbul (2006) *Ne Yanlışız Ne de Yalnızız: Bir Alan Çalışması, Eşcinsel ve Biseksüellerin Sorunları*, Istanbul: Berdan Matbaacılık.

Leander, A. (2009) 'Security: A Contested Commodity,' Working Paper organized for the Centre for Security Economics and Technology, the University of St. Gallen and the Geneva Centre for the Democratic Control over Armed Forces, Geneva, 2–3 November.

Leitenberg, M. (2006) 'Deaths in Wars and Conflicts in the 20th Century,' Cornell University Peace Studies Program, Occasional Paper #29. Online. Available HTTP: <http://www.cissm.umd.edu/papers/files/deathswarsconflictsjune 52006.pdf> (accessed 1 June 2011).

Lerner, G. (1986) *The Creation of Patriarchy*, Oxford: Oxford University Press.

Lindholm. (2008) 'Eksyksissä' [Lost], *Suomen Kuvalehti* 12–13:48–53.

Lister, D. (2005) 'Fiancée Leads Crusade against IRA Killers,' *The Times*, 14 February.

Locher, B. (2007) *Trafficking in Women in the European Union. Norms, Advocacy Networks and Policy Change*, Wiesbaden: Vs Verlag.

Locher, B. and Prügl, E. (2001) 'Feminism and Constructivism: Worlds Apart or Sharing the Middle Ground?,' *International Studies Quarterly* 45(1): 111–129.

Loescher, G. (2001) *The UNHCR and World Politics: A Perilous Path*, Oxford: Oxford University Press.

Lorentzen, A. and Turpin, J. (eds) (1998) *The Women and War Reader*, New York: New York University Press.

Lykke, N. (2010) *Feminist Studies. A Guide to Intersectional Theory, Methodology and Writing*, New York: Routledge.

Lynch, C. (2001) 'UN Halted Probe of Officers' Alleged Role in Sex Trafficking: Lack of Support from Above, in Field Impeded Investigators,' *Washington Post*, 27 December, A17.

Lysaker, K. and Håbjørg, G.E. (2002) *Aidsproblematikk—et forsvarsanliggende* [AIDS—A Matter of Defense], Oslo: Report Made to the Chief of the Army Staff.

Lyytikäinen, M. (2007) 'Gender Training for Peacekeepers: Preliminary Overview of United Nations Peace Support Operations,' Gender, Peace and Security Working Paper 4, New York, INSTRAW.

MacKenzie, M. (2009) 'Forgotten Warriors: The Reintegration of Girl Soldiers in Sierra Leone,' *Security Studies* 18(2): 241–261.

MacKenzie, M. (2010) 'Ruling Exceptions: Female Soldiers and Everyday Experience of Civil Conflict,' in Christine Sylvester (ed), *Experiencing War*, London: Routledge.

MacKinnon, C.A. (1987) *Feminism Unmodified. Discourses on Life and Law*, Cambridge, MA: Harvard University Press.

Macklin, A. (1995) 'Refugee Women and the Imperative of Categories,' *Human Rights Quarterly* 17(2): 213–277.

Maclellan, N. (2006) 'From Fiji to Fallujah: The War in Iraq and the Privatisation of Pacific Security,' *Pacific Journalism Review* 12(2): 47–65.

Mæland, B. (2004) *Skadeskutt idealisme. Norsk offisersmoral i Kosovo* [Morality of Norwegian Officers in Kosovo], Bergen: Eide forlag.

Mahmood, S. (2001) 'Feminist Theory, Embodiment, and the Docile Agent: Some Reflections on the Egyptian Islamic Revival,' *Cultural Anthropology* 6(2): 202–236.

Malkki, L. (1995) *Purity and Exile: Violence, Memory and National Cosmology among Hutu Refugees in Tanzania*, Chicago: University of Chicago Press.

Malkki, L. (1996) 'Speechless Emissaries: Refugees, Humanitarianism and Dehistoricization,' *Cultural Anthropology* 11(3): 377–404.

Mandel, R. (2002) *Armies without States: the Privatization of Security*, Boulder, CO: Lynne Rienner Publishers.

Manderson, L., Kelaher, M., Markovic, M., and McManus, K. (1998) 'A Woman without a Man Is a Woman at Risk: Women at Risk in Australian Humanitarian Programs,' *Journal of Refugee Studies* 11(3): 267–283.
March, J.G. and Olsen, J.P. (1989) *Rediscovering Institutions: The Organizational Basis of Politics*, New York: Free Press.
Marlies, G. and Kaldor, M. (2005) *Human Security Doctrine for Europe*, London: Routledge.
Marshall, T.F. (1996) 'The Evolution of Restorative Justice in Britain,' *European Journal on Criminal Policy and Research* 4(4): 21–43.
Martin, S. (2005) *Must Boys Be Boys? Ending Sexual Exploitation and Abuse in UN Peacekeeping Missions*, Washington, DC: Refugees International.
Masters, C. (2009) 'Femina Sacra: The "War on/of Terror," Women and the Feminine,' *Security Dialogue* 40(1): 29–49.
McCarry, M. (2007) 'Masculinity Studies and Male Violence: Critique or Collusion?,' *Women's Studies International Forum* 30(5): 404–415.
McCold, P. (2006) 'The History of Restorative Justice: Mediation, Circles, and Conferencing,' in D. Sullivan and L. Tifft (eds), *The Handbook of Restorative Justice*, New York: Routledge.
McEvoy, K. and Mika, H. (2002) 'Restorative Justice and the Critique of Informalism in Northern Ireland,' *British Journal of Criminology* 42(3): 534–562.
McDowell, S. (2008) 'Commemorating Dead "Men": Gendering the Past and Present in Post-Conflict Northern Ireland,' *Gender, Place and Culture* 15(4): 335–354.
McGrory, D. (2002) 'Woman Sacked for Revealing UN Links with Sex Trade,' *The Times*, 7 August. Online. Available HTTP: <http://departments.oxy.edu/library/research/help/articles/index.htm> (accessed 3 August 2007).
McWilliams, M. (1995) 'Struggling for Peace and Justice: Reflections on Women's Activism in Northern Ireland,' *Journal of Women's History* 6(4): 13–39.
Mechling, J. (2009) 'Is Hazing Play,' in C. Dell Clark (ed), *Transactions at Play*, New York: University of America Press.
Mendelson, S.E. (2005) *Barracks and Brothels: Peacekeepers and Human Trafficking in the Balkans*, Washington, DC: Center for Strategic and International Studies Report.
Mercier, P.J. and Mercier, J.D. (eds) (2000) *Battle Cries on the Home Front: Violence in the Military*, Springfield, IL: Charles C. Thomas.
Messerschmidt, J.W. (2010) *Hegemonic Masculinities and Camouflaged Politics: On the Bush Dynasty and Its War against Iraq*, Herndon, VA: Paradigm.
Metcalf, A. (1985) 'Introduction,' in A. Metcalf and M. Humphries (eds), *The Sexuality of Men*, London: Pluto.
Meyer, C. (2005) *DC Confidential*, London: Weidenfeld and Nicolson.
Micewski, E.R. (2004) 'Responsibilities of the Future Soldier and Military Leader—How Is Military Ethics Today?,' in J. Toiskallio (ed), *Identity, Ethics and Soldiership, ACIE Publications*, No 1. National Defence College, Department of Education, Helsinki: ACIE Publications.
Mies, M. and Shiva, V. (2004) 'The Subsistence Perspective,' in S. Harding (ed), *The Feminist Standpoint Theory Reader: Intellectual and Political Controversies*, New York: Routledge.
Miller, L.L. and Moskos, C. (1995) 'Humanitarians or Warriors? Race, Gender, and Combat Status in Operation Restore Hope,' *Armed Forces and Society* 21(4): 615–637.
Morgan, D. (1992) *Discovering Men*, London: Routledge.
Morgan, D. (1994) 'Theater of War: Combat, the Military and Masculinities,' in H. Brod and M. Kaufman (eds), *Theorizing Masculinities*, Thousand Oaks, CA: Sage.

234 Bibliography

Morgan, R. (1989) *The Demon Lover: On the Sexuality of Terrorism*, New York: W.W. Norton.
Morgan, V. (1995) 'Women and Conflict in Northern Ireland,' in A. O'Day (ed), *Terrorism's Laboratory: The Case of Northern Ireland*, Aldershot: Dartmouth.
Moser, C.O.N. and Clark, F.C. (eds) (2001) *Victims, Perpetrators or Actors? Gender, Armed Conflict and Political Violence*, London: Zed Books.
Moskos, C.C. and Burk, J. (1994) 'The Postmodern Military,' in J. Burk (ed), *The Military in New Times. Adapting Armed Forces to a Turbulent World*, Boulder, CO: Westview Press.
Mosse, G. (1996) *The Image of Man: The Creation of Modern Masculinity*, Oxford: Oxford University Press.
Murphy, C.N. (1996) 'Seeing Women, Recognizing Gender, Recasting International Relations,' *International Organization* 50(3): 513–538.
Murphy, R. (2006) 'An Assessment of UN Efforts to Address Sexual Misconduct by Peacekeeping Personnel,' *International Peacekeeping* 13(4): 531–546.
Nagel, J. (1998) 'Masculinity and Nationalism: Gender, Sexuality and the Making of Nations,' *Ethnic and Racial Studies* 21(2): 242–269.
Naim, CM (2008) 'The Mothers of the Lashkar,' Outlook India, Available HTTP: <http://www.outlookindia.com/fullprint.asp?choice=1&fodname=20081215&fname=naim&sid=1 > (accessed 8 February 2009).
NAP. (2009) *Regeringens handlingsplan för perioden 2009–2012 för att genomföra säkerhetsrådets resolution 1325 (2000) om kvinnor, fred och säkerhet* [Swedish Government's Action Plan to Implement SCR 1325 on Women, Peace and Security]. Online. Available HTTP: <htpp//:www.operation1325.se/images/stories/Dokument/nationell_handlingsplan_1325.pdf> (accessed 8 March 2009).
Narayan, U. and Harding, S. (eds) (2000) *Decentering the Center: Philosophy for a Multicultural, Postcolonial, and Feminist World*, Bloomington: Indiana University Press.
Narayan Swamy, M.R. (1994) *Tigers of Lanka: From Boys to Guerrillas*, Colombo: Vijitha Yapa Publications.
Nash, B. and Hillen, J. (2001) 'Debate: Can Soldiers Be Peacekeepers and Warriors?,' *NATO Review* 49(2). Online. Available HTTP: <http://www.nato.int/docu/review/2001/0102-04.htm> (accessed 10 August 2008).
Nduka-Agwu, A. (2009) '"Doing Gender" after the War: Dealing with Gender Mainstreaming and Sexual Exploitation and Abuse in UN Peace Support Operations in Liberia and Sierra Leone,' *Civil Wars* 11(2): 179–199.
Network for Ethics and Codes of Conduct. (2004) *Nätverket för Etiska Regler och Uppförandekoder: Rekommenderad uppförandekod för svensk personal i internationella uppdrag* [Recommended Code of Conduct for Swedish Personnel On International Missions]. Online. Available HTTP: <http://www.srv.se/upload/Internationellt/Hjalpinsatser/Personal/rekommenderad_uppförandekod.pdf> (accessed 3 September 2009).
Norges Forsvar. (2007a) April.
Norges Forsvar. (2007b) September.
Norman, H. (1904) *All the Russias. Travel and Studies in Contemporary Russia, Finland, Siberia the Caucasus and Central Asia*, New York: Charles Scribner's Sons. Online. Available HTTP: <http://www.archive.org/stream/allrussias00norm#page/n0/mode/2up.> (accessed 21 June 2010).
North Atlantic Treaty Organization. (2004a) 'NATO Policy on Combating Trafficking in Human Beings,' Istanbul Summit, 29 June. Online. Available HTTP: <http://www.nato.int/docu/comm/2004/06-istanbul/docu-traffic.htm> (accessed 20 August 2008).

North Atlantic Treaty Organization. (2004b) 'US, Norwegian Envoys to NATO Brief on Anti-Trafficking Policy,' 8 July. Online. Available HTTP: <http://www.nato.int/docu/speech/2004/s040708a.htm> (accessed 20 August 2008).
North Atlantic Treaty Organization. (2007a) 'Assistant Secretary General Defense Policy and Planning Biography.' Online. Available HTTP: <http://www.nato.int/cv/is/asg-dpp/sedivy-e.html> (accessed 5 August 2008).
North Atlantic Treaty Organization. (2007b) 'Committee on Women in NATO Forces Handbook,' Online. Available HTTP: <http://www.nato.int/issues/women_nato/handbook_2007.pdf> (accessed 20 August 2008).
North Atlantic Treaty Organization. (2009) 'Final Decision on MC 0249/2: The NATO Committee on Gender Perspectives,' 20 May. Online. Available HTTP: <http://www.nato.int/nato_static/assets/pdf/pdf_2009_ 06/20090611_Signed_ MC_0249_2_FINAL_ENG_NU.pdf> (accessed 11 December 2010).
Norwegian Armed Forces. (2011) *Menneskene* [The Men and Women]. Online. Available HTTP: <http://www.mil.no/fakta/start/menneskene/#0> (accessed 2 January 2011).
Norwegian Armed Forces Headquarters Defense Command. (1992) *Letter to the Norwegian Ministry of Defense Dated 18 March 1992*, Oslo: Archives of Headquarters Defense Command.
Norwegian Battalion in SFOR II. (1997) 'Contingent Report,' Norwegian Headquarters Defense Command.
Norwegian Battalion in SFOR III. (1998) 'Contingent Report,' Norwegian Headquarters Defense Command.
Norwegian Contingent Commander KFOR. (1999) *Letter to Headquarters Defense Command Dated 26 October 1999*, Oslo: Archives Headquarters Defense Command.
Norwegian Contingent Commander UNIFIL. (1992) *Letter to Headquarters Defense Command Dated 13 August 1992*, Oslo: Archives of Headquarters Defense Command.
Norwegian Contingent Commander UNIMOG. (1990) *Letter to Headquarters Defense Command Dated 19 April 1990*, Oslo: Archives of Headquarters Defense Command.
Norwegian Ministry of Defense. (2007) 'Økt rekruttering av kvinner' [Increased Recruitment of Women], White Paper 36, Norwegian Ministry of Defense.
Nuwer, H. (ed) (2004) *The Hazing Reader*, Bloomington: Indiana University Press.
Oakley, A. (1972) *Sex, Gender and Society*, London: Temple Smith.
O'Brien, M.M. (2009) *America's Failure in Iraq*, Bloomington: AuthorHouse.
O'Brien, S. (1993) 'Morale and the Inner Life in the Armed Forces,' *Therapeutic Communities* 14(4): 285–295.
Office to Monitor and Combat Trafficking in Persons. (2007) 'Trafficking in Persons Report, 2007,' Office of Electronic Information, Bureau of Public Affairs. Online. Available HTTP: <http://www.state.gov/g/tip/rls/tiprpt/2007/> (accessed 1 June 2008).
Oliver, K. (2007) *Women as Weapons of War. Iraq, Sex, and the Media*, New York: Columbia University Press.
Olsson, L. and Tryggestad, T.L. (eds) (2001) *Women and International Peacekeeping*, London: Frank Cass.
O'Malley, P. (1990) *Biting at the Grave*, Boston: Beacon Press.
Oosterveld, V.L. (1996) 'The Canadian Guidelines on Gender-Related Persecution: An Evaluation,' *International Journal of Refugee Law*, 8(4): 569–596.
Oxfam. (2005) *Foreign Territory: The Internationalisation of EU Asylum Policy*, Oxford: Oxfam.

Pääesikunta. (2009) 'YK:n turvallisuusneuvoston PL 1325 "naiset, rauha ja turvallisuus" kansallisen toimintaohjelman toimeenpano puolustusvoimissa—lisäselvityspyyntö. Raportti 29.5.2009' [Implementation of the Finland's National Action Plan for UN Security Council Resolution 1325 Women., Peace and Security Further Clarification], Report, 29 May.

Pankhurst, D. (2007a) 'Introduction: Gendered War and Peace,' in D. Pankhurst (ed), *Gendered Peace: Women's Struggles for Post-war Justice and Reconciliation*, London: Routledge.

Pankhurst, D. (2007b) 'Post-War Backlash Violence against Women: What Can 'Masculinity' Explain?,' in D. Pankhurst (ed), *Gendered Peace: Women's Struggles for Post-War Justice and Reconciliation*, London: Routledge.

Parashar, S. (2009) 'Feminist IR and Women Militants: Case Studies from South Asia,' *Cambridge Review of International Affairs* 22(2): 235–256.

Parashar, S. (2011) 'Gender *Jihad* and Jingoism: Women as Perpetrators, Planners and Patrons of Militancy in Kashmir,' *Studies in Conflict and Terrorism* 34:4.

Parpart, J.L. (2009) 'Choosing Silence: Rethinking Voice, Agency and Women's Empowerment,' paper presented at the annual meeting of the International Studies Association, Theory vs. Policy? Connecting Scholars and Practitioners, New Orleans, LA, 17 February.

Parpart, J. and Zalewski, M. (eds) (2008) *Rethinking the Man Question: Sex, Gender and Violence in International Relations*, London: Zed Books.

Pateman, C. (1988) *The Sexual Contract*, Cambridge: Polity Press.

Penttinen, E. (2004) 'Whose Voice's Matter: Feminist Stretch the Boundaries Of International Relations Discipline,' in S. Durlabhji (ed), *Power in Focus, Perspectives from Multiple Disciplines*, Lima, OH: Wyndham Hall Press.

Penttinen, E. (2006) 'Power and Hegemony in Saving "Other" Women,' in M. Haugaard and H. Lentner (eds), *Hegemony and Power*, Lanham, MD: Lexington Books.

Penttinen, E. (2009) 'Feminist Imaginings or Feminist Problem-Making? Creating the World through Observation,' paper presented at the Touching War Programme, Lancaster University, 20 March.

Pershing, J.L. (2003) 'Why Women Don't Report Sexual Harassment: A Case Study of an Elite Military Institution,' *Gender Issues* 21(4): 3–30.

Peterson, S.V. (1999) 'Political Identities: Nationalism as Heterosexism,' *International Feminist Journal of Politics* 1(1): 34–65.

Peterson, S.V. (2010) 'Gendered Identities, Ideologies, and Practices in the Context of War and Militarism,' in L. Sjoberg and S. Via (eds), *Gender, War, and Militarism: Feminist Perspectives*, Santa Barbara, CA: Praeger.

Peterson, V.S. (ed) (1992a) *Gendered States: Feminist (Re)Visions of International Relations Theory*. Boulder, CO: Lynne Rienner Publishers.

Peterson, V.S. (1992b) 'Security and Sovereign States: What Is at Stake in Taking Feminism Seriously?,' in V.S. Peterson (ed), *Gendered States: Feminist (Re)Visions of International Relations Theory*, Boulder, CO: Lynne Rienner Publishers.

Petersson, S. (2008) 'Frivillighet och Plikt—an analys av manliga normer och särskilda kompetenser i delbetänkandet *Totalförsvarsplikten i framtiden*' [Volunteer or Conscript. An Analysis of Male Norms and Specific Competences], Essay, level III, Department of Political Science, Stockholm University.

Pettman, J.J. (1996/2002) *Worlding Women. A Feminist International Politics*, London: Routledge.

Pittaway, E. and Bartolomei, L. (2003) 'An Examination of the Role of Identity and Citizenship in the Experiences of Women in Kakuma Refugee Camp in Northern Kenya,' *Development* 46(3): 87–93.

Pittaway, E. and Bartolomei, L. (2006) *The Case for an UNHCR Conclusion on 'Refugee Women at Risk,'* Sydney: Centre for Refugee Research.

Pitzke, M. (2007) '"Whores of War" Under Fire,' *Spiegel Online International*. Online. Available HTTP: <http://www.spiegel.de/international/world/0,1518, 506554,00.html> (accessed 18 April 2010).
Plummer, K. (1983) *Documents of Life*, London: George Allen Unwin.
Porter, E. (1998) 'Women and Politics in Northern Ireland,' *Politics* 18(1): 25–32.
Porter, E. (2000) 'Participatory Democracy and the Challenge of Dialogue across Difference,' in C. Davis and C. Roulston (eds), *Gender, Democracy and Inclusion in Northern Ireland*, Basingstoke: Palgrave.
Porter, E. (2007) *Peacebuilding: Women in International Perspective*, London: Routledge.
Puechguirbal, N. (2007) 'Våldshandlingar bland FN:s fredsbevarande styrkor,' in C. Ockrent and S. Treiner (eds), *Kvinnornas svarta bok: en antologi om kvinnors situation i världen idag* [The Black Book of Women's Conditions], Stockholm: Damm Förlag.
Puheloinen, A. (2006) 'Vaikka puolustusvoimat supistuu, tarvitsemme yleisen asevelvollisuuden' [Even If the Defense Forces Contracts We Need a General Conscription], Speech of a commander-in-chief in the opening ceremony of the 178th Defense Course, 18 September. Online. Available HTTP: <http://www. mil.fi/puolustusvoimainkomentaja/2408.dsp> (accessed 18 April 2010).
Puistola, J.-A. (2008) 'Sotilaat rauhan asialla' [Soldiers for the Peace], *Sotilas-aikakauslehti* 83:49–50.
Racioppi, L. and Sullivan See, K. (2001) '"This We Will Maintain": Gender, Ethno-Nationalism and the Politics of Unionism in Northern Ireland,' *Nations and Nationalism* 7(1): 93–112.
Rai, S. (2004) 'Gendering Global Governance,' *International Feminist Journal of Politics* 6(4): 579–601.
Rai, S.M. and Waylen, G. (eds) (2008) *Global Governance: Feminist Perspectives*, London: Palgrave.
Rajaram, P.K. (2002) 'Humanitarianism and Representations of the Refugee,' *Journal of Refugee Studies* 15(3): 247–264.
Rajasingham-Senanayake, D. (2001) 'Ambivalent Empowerment: The Tragedy of Tamil Women in Conflict,' in R. Manchanda (ed), *Women, War and Peace in South Asia: Beyond Victimhood to Agency*, New Delhi: Sage.
Rao, A. (2006) 'Gender Equality Architecture and UN Reforms.' Online. Available HTTP: <http://www.wedo.org/files/Gender%20Equality%20Architecture%20 and%20UN%20Reform0606.pdf> (accessed 15 July 2007).
Rao, A. and Kelleher, D. (2002) 'Unravelling Institutionalised Gender Inequality,' AWID Occasional Paper, No. 8.
Ratner, H. (2005) *Refugee Women and Stories of Sexual Violence: Agents in their Victimisation?* Unpublished manuscript, Copenhagen: Institute for Anthropology.
Rauhanturvaajaliitto. (2001) '19 vuotta rauhanturvaamista Libanonissa' [19 Years of Peacekeeping in Lebanon], *Sinibaretti 5*. Online. Available HTTP: <http:// www.rauhanturvaajaliitto.fi/lehti/5_01/lipsi.htm > (accessed 1 June 2011).
Razack, S. (2004) *Dark Threats and White Knights: The Somalia Affair, Peacekeeping and the New Imperialism*, Canada: University of Toronto Press.
Reardon, B.A. (1985/1996) *Sexism and the War System*, New York: Teacher's College Press.
Reardon, B.A. (1993) *Women and Peace: Feminist Visions of Global Security*, Albany: State University of New York Press.
Rehn, E. and Johnson Sirleaf, E. (2002) *Women, War and Peace: The Independent Experts' Assessment on the Impact of Armed Conflict on Women and Women's Role in Peace-Building*, New York: United Nations Development Fund for Women (UNIFEM).

Røkenes, T.H. (2004) '"Sønner av Norge" En studie av den norske bataljonen i Kosovo, perioden 2002–2003' ['Sons of Norway' A Study of the Norwegian Battalion in Kosovo 2002–2003], master's thesis, Bergen, the University of Bergen, Department of Administration and Organization Theory.

Rose, H. (1983) 'Hand, Brain and Heart: Towards a Feminist Epistemology for the Natural Sciences,' *Signs: Journal of Women in Culture and Society* 9(1): 73–96.

Roth, R. (2005) 'Interview with Jane Holl Lute, Joey Lowe, and Nachman Shai on "Diplomatic License,"' *CNN International*, 18 February. Online. Available HTTP: <http://departments.oxy.edu/library/research/ help/articles/index.htm> (accessed 11 January 2008).

Roy, S. (2007) 'The Everyday Life of the Revolution: Gender, Violence and Memory,' *South Asia Research* 27(2): 187–204.

Roy, S. (2009) 'The Ethical Ambivalence of Resistant Violence: Notes from Postcolonial South Asia,' *Feminist Review* 91:135–153.

Rubin, G. (1975) 'The Traffic in Women,' in R. Reiter (ed), *Towards an Anthropology of Women*, New York: Monthly Review Press.

Ruddick, S. (1989) *Maternal Thinking: Towards a Politics of Peace*, London: Women's Press.

Ruddick, S. (2004) 'Maternal Thinking as a Feminist Standpoint,' in S. Harding (ed), *The Feminist Standpoint Theory Reader: Intellectual and Political Controversies*, New York: Routledge.

Rummel, R.J. (1994) *Death by Government*, New Brunswick, NJ: Transaction.

Sabuni, N. and Tolgfors, S. (2007) 'Fler kvinnor i försvaret' [More Women in the Defense], *Sydsvenskan*, 5 November. Online. Available HTTP: <http://www.sweden.gov.se/sb/d/9318/a/91453> (accessed 5 November 2007).

Salonius-Pasternak, C. and Visuri, P. (2006) *Suomi rauhanturvaajana 1991–2006* [Finland in Peacekeeping 1991–2006], Helsinki: Puolustusministeriö.

Sandoval, C. (2004) 'US Third World Feminism: The Theory and Method of Differential Oppositional Consciousness,' in S. Harding (ed), *The Feminist Standpoint Theory Reader: Intellectual and Political Controversies*, New York: Routledge.

Savaş Karşıtları. (2009) 'Türkiye'de vicdani retlerini açıklayanlar.' Online. Available HTTP: <http://www.savaskarsitlari.org/arsiv.asp?ArsivTipID=2&ArsivAnaID=27221&ArsivSayfaNo=1> (accessed 1 November 2009).

Scahill, J. (2007a) *Blackwater*, New York: Nation Books.

Scahill, J. (2007b) *The Mercenary Revolution: Flush with Profits from the Iraq War, Military Contractors See a World of Business Opportunities*. Online. Available HTTP: <http://www.independent.org/2007/08/10/the-mercenary-revolution-flush-with-profits-from-the-iraq-war-military-contractors-see-a-world-of-business-opportunities/> (accessed 26 August 2008).

Schalk, P. (1992) 'Birds of Independence. On the Participation of Tamil Women in Armed Struggle,' *Lanka* 7:44–142.

Scharff, C. (2008) 'Perspectives on Feminist (Dis-)Identification in the British and German Contexts: A Performative Approach.' Online. Available HTTP: <www.lse.ac.uk/collections/newFemininities/Perspectives%20on%20feminist%20dis-identification,%20feminist%20review%20format.pdf> (accessed 9 May 2009).

Schofield, S. (1994) 'Militarism, the UK Economy and Conversion Policies in the North,' in G. Tansey, K. Tansey and P. Rogers (eds), *A World Divided: Militarism and Development after the Cold War*, London: Earthscan Publications.

Schultz, S. and Yeung, C. (2005) 'Private Military Security Companies and Gender,' Report prepared for Geneva Centre for the Democratic Control of Armed Forces (DCAF: component of Gender and SSR toolkit, tool #10).

Seidler, V. (1997) *Man Enough—Embodying Masculinities*, London: Sage.
Selek, P. (2009) *Sürüne Sürüne Erkek Olmak*, Istanbul: İletişim.
Selignam, M.E. and Csikszentmihalyi, M. (2000) 'Positive Psychology an Introduction,' *American Psychologist* 55(1): 5–14. Online. Available HTTP: <http://www.ppc.sas.upenn.edu/ppintroarticle.pdf> (accessed 17 October 2009).
Shapiro, M.J. (1997) *Violent Cartographies: Mapping Cultures of War*, Minneapolis: University of Minnesota Press.
Shaw, M. (2002) 'Risk-transfer Militarism, Small Massacres and the Historic Legitimacy of War', in *International Relations*, 16(3): 343–359.
Shepherd, B. (2008) *The Circuit*, London: Pan Books.
Shepherd, L. (2008) *Gender, Violence, and Security: Discourse as Practice*, London: Zed Books.
Shepherd, L. (ed) (2010) *Gender Matters in Global Politics: A Feminist Introduction to International Relations*, London: Routledge.
Shirlow, P., Graham, B., McEvoy, K., Ó hAdhmaill, F. and Purvis, D. (2005) *Politically Motivated Former Prisoner Groups: Community Activism and Conflict Transformation*, Belfast: The Authors.
Shirlow, P. and McEvoy, K. (2008) *Beyond the Wire: Former Prisoners and Conflict Transformation in Northern Ireland*, London: Pluto Press.
Sinclair-Webb, E. (2000) 'Our Bülent Is a Commando: Military Service and Manhood in Turkey,' in M. Ghoussoub and E. Sinclair-Webb (eds), *Imagined Masculinities: Male Identity and Culture in the Modern Middle East*, London: Saqi.
Singer, P.W. (2005) *Corporate Warriors: The Rise of the Privatized Military Industry*, Ithaca, NY: Cornell University Press.
Sion, L. (2006) '"Too Sweet and Innocent for War"? Dutch Peacekeepers and the Use of Violence,' *Armed Forces and Society* 32:454–474.
Sjoberg, L. (2006a) *Gender, Justice and the Wars in Iraq. Feminist Reformulation of Just War Theory*, Lanham, MD: Lexington Books.
Sjoberg, L. (2006b) 'Gendered Realities of the Immunity Principle: Why Gender Analysis Needs Feminism,' *International Studies Quarterly* 50:889–910.
Sjoberg, L. (ed) (2009a) *Gender and International Security: Feminist Perspectives*, London: Routledge.
Sjoberg, L. (2009b) 'Introduction to Security Studies: Feminist Contributions,' *Security Studies* 18(2): 183–213.
Sjoberg, L. and Gentry, C. (2007) *Mothers, Monsters, Whores: Women's Violence in Global Politics*, London: Zed Books.
Sjoberg, L. and Via, S. (eds) (2010) *Gender, War, and Militarism: Feminist Perspectives*, Santa Barbara, CA: Praeger.
Skjelsbaek, I. and Smith, D. (eds) (2001) *Gender, Peace & Conflict*, London; Thousand Oaks, CA: Sage.
Smith, D. (1987) *The Everyday World as Problematic: A Feminist Sociology*, Boston: Northeastern University Press.
Smith, D. (2004) 'Women's Perspective as a Radical Critique of Sociology,' in S. Harding (ed), *The Feminist Standpoint Theory Reader: Intellectual and Political Controversies*, New York: Routledge.
Smith, J. (1993) *Misogynies*, London: Faber and Faber.
Smith, R. (2006) *The Utility of Force: The Art of War in the Modern World*, Harmondsworth: Penguin.
Snyder, C. (1999) *Citizen-Soldiers and Manly Warriors: Military Service and Gender in the Civic Republican Tradition*, Lanham, MD: Rowman and Littlefield.
Sorenson, D.S. and Wood, P.C. (eds) (2005) *The Politics of Peacekeeping in the Post-Cold War Era*, New York: Frank Cass.
SOU. (2008) 98, Totalförsvarsplikten i framtiden. Online. Available HTTP: <http://www.sweden.gov.se/sb/d/10636/a/114421> (accessed 12 December 2009).

Spivak, G.C. (1988) 'Can the Subaltern Speak?,' in C. Nelson and L. Grossberg (eds), *Marxism and the Interpretation of Culture*, Urbana-Champaign: University of Illinois Press.
Spivak, G.C. (1993) 'Can the Subaltern Speak?,' in P. Williams and L. Chrisman (eds), *Colonial Discourse and Postcolonial Theory*, London: Harvester Wheatsheaf. 66–111.
Statement of Government Policy. (2007) The Parliamentary Debate on Foreign Affairs, 14 February. Online. Available HTTP: <http://www.sweden.gov.se/sb/d/5298/a/39592> (accessed 28 December 2009).
Statement of Government Policy. (2009) The Parliamentary Debate on Foreign Affairs, 18 February. Online. Available HTTP: <http://www.sweden.gov.se/sb/d/5298/a/120758> (accessed 28 December 2009).
Steans, J. (2006) *Gender and International Relations. Issues, Debates and Future Directions*, Cambridge: Polity Press.
Steans, J. and Ahmadi, V. (2005) 'Negotiating the Politics of Gender and Rights: Some Reflections on the Status of Women's Human Rights at "Beijing Plus Ten,"' *Global Society* 19(3): 227–245.
Stecklow, S. and Lauria, J. (2010) 'UN Mum on Probes of Sex-Abuse Allegations,' *Wall Street Journal*, 21 March. Online. Available HTTP: <http://departments.oxy.edu/library/research/dbs/ frame.asp?UID=PROQUEST> (accessed 22 November 2010).
Stiehm, J.H. (1982) 'The Protected, the Protector, the Defender,' *Women's Studies International Forum* 5:367–376.
Stiglitz, J. and Bilmes, L. (2008) *The Three Trillion Dollar War; The True Cost of the Iraq Conflict*, New York: W.W. Norton.
Stockholm International Peace Research Institute. (2002) *Yearbook: Armaments, Disarmament and International Security*, Oxford: Oxford University Press.
Stockholm International Peace Research Institute. (2003) *Yearbook: Armaments, Disarmament and International Security*, Oxford: Oxford University Press.
Stockholm International Peace Research Institute. (2008) *Yearbook: Armaments, Disarmaments and National Security*. Online. Available HTTP: <http://www.sipri.org/yearbook/2008> (accessed 1 June 2011).
Strømmen, W. and Leraand, D. (2005) *I kamp for fred. Norge i UNIFIL 1978–1998* [Fighting for Peace. Norway in UNIFIL], Oslo: Gazette bok as.
Swedish Armed Forces. (2003) Internal mission report [Försvarsmakten], *FMUG rapport—C GRO uppdrag* 2003:02.
Swedish Armed Forces. (2006–2008) 'Plan of Action for Gender Equality 2006–2008 and 2009–2011' [Försvarsmakten, Jämställdhetsplan 2006–2008 and 2009–2011].
Swedish Armed Forces. (2007a) 'Ethical Guidelines and Codes of Conduct for Swedish Staff on International Missions' [Försvarsmakten, Etiska regler och uppförandekod för svensk personal inför och under internationella uppdrag]. Skrivelse 16 150:64 273.
Swedish Armed Forces. (2007b) [Försvarsmakten], Råd & Tips. Online. Available HTTP: <http://www.rekryc.mil.se/article.php?id=11755> (accessed 17 September 2007).
Swedish Armed Forces. (2009) Gal [Försvarsmakten, Tjej]. Online. Available HTTP: <http://www.mil.se/sv/Arbete-och-utbildning/Varnplikt/Tjej/> (accessed 7 March 2009).
Swedish Armed Forces. (2009–2011) 'Plan of Action for Gender Equality 2006–2008 and 2009–2011' [Försvarsmakten, Jämställdhetsplan 2006–2008 and 2009–2011].
Swedish Civil Contingencies Agency. (2009) 'Code of Conduct' [MSB/Myndigheten för samhällsskydd och beredskap, Uppförandekod]. Online. Available

HTTP: <http://www.msb.se/Upload/Insats_och_beredskap/Delta_insats/Uppförandekodex%20MSB.pdf?epslanguage=sv> (accessed 15 February 2010).
Swidler, A. (1986) 'Culture in Action: Symbols and Strategies,' *American Sociological Review* 51(2): 273–286.
Sylvester, C. (1994) *Feminist Theory and International Relations in a Postmodern Era*, Cambridge: Cambridge University Press.
Sylvester, C. (2005), 'The Art of War/The War Question in (Feminist) IR,' *Millennium* 33(3): 855–878.
Sylvester, C. (2009) 'Review of Laura J. Shepherd's *Gender, Violence and Security: Discourse as Practice*,' *Minerva Journal of Women and War* 3(1):94–96.
Sylvester, C. (ed) (2010a) *Experiencing War*, London: Routledge.
Sylvester, C. (2010b) 'Tensions in Feminist Security Studies,' *Security Dialogue* 41(6): 607–614.
Sylvester, C. (2010c) 'War, Sense and Security,' in L. Sjoberg (ed), *Gender and International Security: Feminist Perspectives*, London: Routledge.
Sylvester, C. and Parashar, S. (2009) 'The Contemporary Mahabharata and the Many Draupadis: Bringing Gender to Critical Terrorism Studies,' in R. Jackson, M. Breen Smyth and J. Gunning (eds), *Critical Terrorism Studies: A New Research Agenda*, London: Routledge.
Syrén, H. (2006). April statement. Online. Available HTTP: <http://www.newsdesk.se/pressroom/forsvarsmakten/event/view/2363> (accessed 1 November 2007).
Tallberg, T. (2009) *The Gendered Social Organisation of Defence: Two Ethnographic Case Studies in the Finnish Defence Forces*, Helsinki: Hanken School of Economics. Online. Available HTTP: <http://www.hanken.fi/staff/tallber/blog/files/Lopullinen_julkaisuversio.pdf> (accessed 1 June 2011).
Tatchell, P. (1995) *We Don't Want to March Straight: Masculinity, Queers and the Military*, London: Cassell.
Telegol. (2009) *Haberturk*. Online. Available HTTP: <http://videonuz.ensonhaber.com/izle/escinsel-hakem-halil-ibrahim-dincdag-ilk-kez-canli-yayinda> (accessed 7 December 2010).
Theweleit, K. (1987) *Male Fantasies*, vol. 1, Cambridge: Polity Press.
Thompson, A. and Ferguson, D. (1997) 'Military Abuses to Be Aired—Peacekeeping Troops in Bosnia Accused of Sexual Assault,' *Toronto Star*, 17 January, A4.
Thrift, N. (2000) 'It's the Little Things,' in K. Dodds and D. Atkinson (eds), *Geopolitical Traditions: A Century of Geopolitical Thought*, London: Routledge.
Tickner, J.A. (1992) *Gender in International Relations*, New York: Columbia University Press.
Tickner, J.A. (2001) *Gendering World Politics. Issues and Approaches in the Post-Cold War Era*, New York: Colombia University Press.
Tickner, J.A. (2006a) 'Feminism Meets International Relations: Some Methodological Issues,' in B. Ackerly, M. Stern and J. True (eds), *Feminist Methodologies for International Relations*, Cambridge: Cambridge University Press.
Tickner, J.A. (2006b) 'On The Frontlines or Sidelines of Knowledge and Power?,' *International Studies Review* 8(3): 386–388.
Tilly, C. (1990) *Coercion, Capital, and European States, AD 990–1990*, Cambridge, MA: Basil Blackwell.
Titunik, R. (2007) 'The Myth of the Macho Military,' *Polity* 40:137–163.
Toiskallio, J. (2004) 'Action Competence Approach to the Transforming Soldiership,' in J. Toiskallio (ed), *Identity, Ethics and Soldiership, ACIE Publications, No 1. National Defense College, Department of Education*, Helsinki: ACIE Publications.
Tolson, A. (1977) *The Limits of Masculinity*, London: Tavistock.
Tomforde, M. (2005) 'Motivation and Self-Image among German Peacekeepers,' *International Peacekeeping* 12(4): 576–585.

Totland, O.M. (2009) 'Det operative fellesskapet. En sosialantropologisk studie av kropp, kjønn og identitet blant norske soldater i Telemark Bataljon' [A Study of Body, Sex and Identity among Norweigan Soldiers in Telemark Battalion], master's thesis, Oslo, University of Oslo, Department of Social Anthropology.

True-Frost, C. (2007) 'The Security Council and Norm Consumption,' *International Law and Politics* 40:115–218.

Tuominen, R. (2008) 'Rauhanturvaajien rajoitettu arki'[The Limited Everyday Life of the Peacekeepers], *Ruotuväki* 46:6.

Türk Silahlı Kuvvetleri Sağlık Yeteneği Yönetmeliği. (1986). Online. Available HTTP: <http://www.mevzuat.adalet.gov.tr/html/20176.html> (accessed 16 November 2009).

Türkiye Futbol Federasyonu Merkez Hakem Kurulu. (2009) 'Hakemliğe giriş ünvan ve klasmanlara ayrılma ile vize yenileme kural, prensip ve yöntemleri.' Online. Available HTTP: <http://www.tff.org/Resources/TFF/Documents/2009DK/TFF/talimatlar/Hakemlige-Giris-Ic-Talimati-_Nisan-2009_.pdf> (accessed 10 January 2011).

United Nations. (1979) 'Convention on Elimination of All Forms of Discrimination against Women,' 18 December. Online. Available HTTP: <http://www.un.org/womenwatch/daw/cedaw/text/econvention.htm> (accessed 15 March 2010).

United Nations. (1996) 'Report of the Fourth World Conference on Women,' A/CONF.177/20. Online. Available HTTP: <http://www.un.org/womenwatch/daw/beijing/pdf/Beijing%20full%20report%20E.pdf> (accessed 15 September 2005).

United Nations. (1997) 'Agreed Conclusions of the Economic and Social Council,' 18 July.

United Nations. (2000a) 'Protocol to Prevent, Suppress and Punish Trafficking in Persons, Especially Women and Children,' 15 November. Online. Available HTTP: <http://www.uncjin.org/Documents/Conventions/dcatoc/final_documents_2/convention_%20traff_eng.pdf> (accessed 12 June 2005).

United Nations. (2000b) 'United Nations Convention against Transnational Organized Crime,' 10 November. Online. Available HTTP: <http://www.un-documents.net/uncatoc.htm> (accessed 12 June 2005).

United Nations. (2002) 'Report of the Inter-Agency Standing Committee Task Force on Protection from Sexual Exploitation and Abuse in Humanitarian Crises,' 13 June. Online. Available HTTP: <http://www.reliefweb.int/ library/documents/2003/iasc-report-2002.pdf> (accessed 1 August 2008).

United Nations. (2003a) 'Public Information Guidelines for Allegations of Misconduct Committed by Personnel of United Nations Peacekeeping and other Field Missions,' Online. Available HTTP: <http://www.un.org/en/pseataskforce/docs/public_information_guidelines_for_allegations_of_misconduct_.pdf>(accessed 15 March 2008).

United Nations. (2003b) 'Secretary-General's Bulletin: Special Measures for Protection from Sexual Exploitation and Sexual Abuse,' ST/SGB/2003/12, 9 October. Online. Available HTTP: <http://www.womenwarpeace.org/ webfm_send/1549> (accessed 15 March 2008).

United Nations. (2004) 'Gender Resource Package for Peacekeeping Operations,' Department of Peacekeeping Operations, Peacekeeping Best Practices Unit. Online. Available HTTP: <http://pbpu.unlb.org/pbps/library/ GRP%20Full%20Version.pdf> (accessed 15 March 2008).

United Nations. (2005) 'A Comprehensive Strategy to Eliminate Future Sexual Exploitation and Abuse in United Nations Peacekeeping Operations,' A/59/710, 24 March. Online. Available HTTP: <http://www.stimson.org/fopo/pdf/Prince_ZeidRpt.pdf> (accessed 15 March 2008).

Bibliography 243

United Nations. (2006) 'Report of the Secretary-General: Special Measures for Protection from Sexual Exploitation and Sexual Abuse,' A/60/861, 24 May. Online. Available HTTP: <http://daccess-ddsny.un.org/ doc/UNDOC/GEN/ N06/360/40/PDF/N0636040.pdf> (accessed 11 November 2007).

United Nations. (2007a) 'Report of the Secretary-General on Women and Peace and Security,' S/2007/567, 12 September. Online. Available HTTP: <http:// daccess-dds-ny.un.org/doc/UNDOC/GEN/N07/503/69/PDF/ N0750369.pdf?> (accessed 3 February 2008).

United Nations. (2007b) 'UN in Liberia Report Shows Decline in Sex Abuse Allegations; Envoy Says Some Progress,' *UN Daily News*, 9 March. Online. Available HTTP: <http://www.un.org/apps/news/story.asp?NewsID =21817&Cr= liberia&Cr1=> (accessed 11 November 2007).

United Nations. (2010) 'Report of the Office of Internal Oversight Services, Part Two: Peacekeeping Operations,' A/64/326, Part II, 23 February. Online. Available HTTP: <http://daccess-dds-ny.un.org/doc/ UNDOC/GEN/N10/249/64/ PDF/N1024964.pdf?> (accessed 21 November 2010).

United Nations High Commissioner for Refugees. (1991) *Guidelines on the Protection of Refugee Women*, Geneva: UNHCR.

United Nations High Commissioner for Refugees. (2001) *Respect Our Rights, Partnership for Equality: Report on the Dialogue with Refugee Women, Geneva, Switzerland, 20–22 June 2001*, Geneva: UNHCR.

United Nations High Commissioner for Refugees. (2002) 'Sexual Violence & Exploitation: The Experience of Refugee Children in Guinea, Liberia and Sierra Leone,' 26 February. Online. Available HTTP: <http://www.unhcr. org/3c7cf89a4.pdf> (accessed 11 November 2007).

United Nations High Commissioner for Refugees. (2006) *Measuring Protection by Numbers*, Geneva: UNHCR.

United Nations High Commissioner for Refugees. (2007) *The State of the World's Refugees*, Geneva: UNHCR.

Urquhart, D. (2000) *Women in Ulster Politics, 1890–1940: A History Not Yet Told*, Portland, OR: Irish Academic Press.

Üsküll, Z. (1989) *Siyaset ve Asker: Cumhuriyet Döneminde Sıkıyönetim Uygulamaları*, Istanbul: Afa Yayınları.

Valenius, J. (2007) 'A Few Kind Women: Gender Essentialism and Nordic Peacekeeping Operations,' *International Peacekeeping* 14(4): 510–523.

van Staden, L.N., Fear, N., Iversen, A., French, C., Dandeker, C. and S. Wessely (2007) 'Young Military Veterans Show Similar Help Seeking Behaviour,' *British Medical Journal* 334:382.

Varoğlu, A.K. and Bıçaksız, A. (2005) 'Volunteering for Risk: The Culture of the Turkish Armed Force,' *Armed Forces and Society* 31(4): 583–598.

Väyrynen, R. (2001) 'Funding Dilemmas in Refugee Assistance: Political Interests and Institutional Reforms in UNHCR,' *International Migration Review* 35(1): 143–167.

Väyrynen, T. (2004) 'Gender and UN Peace Operations: The Confines of Modernity,' *International Peacekeeping* 1(1): 125–142.

Vesa, U. (2007) 'Continuity and Change in the Finnish Debate on Peacekeeping,' *International Peacekeeping* 14:524–537.

Vuković, J. (2007) 'Security, The Activities of Women in Black, and UN Security Council Resolution 1325,' in S. Zajović, M. Perković and M. Urošević (eds),*Women for Peace*, Belgrade: Women in Black.

Wadley, J.D. (2010) 'Gendering the State. Performativity and Protection in International Security,' in L. Sjoberg (ed), *Gender and International Security. Feminist Perspectives*, London: Routledge.

Walby, S. (1990) *Theorizing Patriarchy*, Oxford: Basil Blackwell.

Weber, M. (1948) *From Max Weber: Essays in Sociology*, London: Routledge and Kegan Paul.
Weeks, K. (1998) *Constituting Feminist Subjects*, Ithaca, NY: Cornell University Press.
West, L. (1999) 'The United Nations Women's Conferences and Feminist Politics,' in M. Meyer and E. Prügl (eds), *Gender Politics in Global Governance*, Lanham, MD: Rowman and Littlefield Publishers.
White, M. (2001) *Historical Atlas of 20th Century*. Online. Available HTTP: <http://users.erols.com/mwhite28/20centry.htm> (accessed 1 June 2011).
Whitehead, S.M. and Barrett, F.J. (2001) *The Masculinities Reader*, Cambridge: Polity Press.
Whitworth, S. (2004) *Men, Militarism, and UN Peacekeeping. A Gendered Analysis*, Boulder, CO: Lynne Rienner Publishers.
Whitworth, S. (2008) 'Militarized Masculinity and Post-Traumatic Stress Disorder,' in J.L. Parpart and M. Zalewski (eds), *Rethinking the Man Question. Sex, Gender and Violence in International Relations*, London: Zed Books.
WHO. (2002) *World Report on Violence and Health, Statistical Appendix*, Geneva: WHO.
Williams, J. (2008) 'Space, Scale and Just War: Meeting the Challenge of Humanitarian Intervention and Trans-National Terrorism,' *Review of International Studies* 34:581–600.
Williams, K. (2005) *Love My Rifle More Than You: Young and Female in the US Army*, London: Weidenfeld and Nicolson.
Winslow, A. (1995) *Women, Politics, and the United Nations*, Westport, CT: Greenwood Press.
Winslow, D. (1998) 'Misplaced Loyalties: The Role of Military Culture in the Breakdown of Discipline in Peace Operations,' *Canadian Review of Sociology and Anthropology* 35(3): 345–367.
Woodward, R. and Winter T. (2007) *Sexing the Soldier. The Politics of Gender and the Contemporary British Army*, London: Routledge.
Women in Black. (1994a) '"Femmes en Noir" Contre La Guerre' [Women in Black Against the War] (leaflet, June 1992), in *Compilation of Information on Crimes of War against Women in Ex-Yugoslavia*, Montpellier: Women Living Under Muslin Law.
Women in Black. (1994b) 'Is There a Specifically Female Pacifism?' (workshop report, 1993), in S. Zajović, M. Perković and M. Urošević (eds), *Women for Peace*, Belgrade: Women in Black.
Women in Black. (1994c) 'Proclamation on the Second Anniversary of Women in Black' (leaflet, 1993), in S. Zajović, M. Perković and M. Urošević (eds), *Women for Peace*, Belgrade: Women in Black.
Women in Black. (1994d) 'Women as the Driving Force of Peace' (workshop report, 1993), in S. Zajović, M. Perković and M. Urošević (eds), *Women for Peace*, Belgrade: Women in Black.
Women in Black. (2005a) *Gender, Nation, Identity*, Belgrade: Women in Black.
Women in Black. (2005b) 'History.' Online. Available HTTP: <http://www.womeninblack.org/history.html> (accessed 3 December 2007).
Women in Black. (2006) 'We Are Still on the Streets: Our 15 Years.' Online. Available HTTP: <http://www.zeneucrnom.org/index.php?option=com_content&task=view&id=235&Itemid=4&lang=en> (accessed 14 October 2009).
Women in Black. (2007) 'Draft Resolution,' in S. Zajović, M. Perković and M. Urošević (eds), *Women For Peace*, Belgrade: Women in Black.
Women's Commission for Refugee Women and Children. (2002) *UNHCR Policy on Refugee Women and Guidelines on Their Protection: An Assessment of Ten Years of Implementation*, New York: Women's Commission for Refugee Women and Children.

Woolf, V. (1993) *A Room of One's Own*, London: Bloomsbury Classics.
Young, I.M. (2003) 'The Logic of Masculinist Protection: Reflections on the Current Security State,' *SIGNS* 29(1): 1–25.
Young-Pelton, R. (2006) *Licensed to Kill. Hired Guns in the War on Terror*, New York: Three Rivers Press.
Yuval-Davis, N. (1997) *Gender and Nation*, London: Sage.
Yuval-Davis, N. and Anthias, F. (eds) (1989) *Women, Nation, State*, London: Macmillan.
Zajović, S. (ed) (1994) *Women for Peace 1994*, Belgrade: Women in Black.
Zajović, S. (2007a) *Always Disobedient*, Belgrade: Women in Black.
Zajović, S. (2007b) 'Not in Our Name!,' in S. Zajović, M. Perković and M. Urošević (eds), *Women for Peace*, Belgrade: Women in Black.
Zajović, S. (2007c) 'Peace and Security from a Feminist-Pacifist Perspective,' in S. Zajović, M. Perković and M. Urošević (eds), *Women for Peace*, Belgrade: Women in Black.
Zajović, S., Perković, M. and Urošević, M. (eds) (2007) *Women for Peace 2007*, Belgrade: Women in Black.
Zalewski, M. and Parpart, J. (eds) (1998) *The 'Man' Question in International Relations*, Oxford: Westview.
Zarkov, D. (2002) 'Srebrenica Trauma: Masculinity, Military and National Self-Image in Dutch Daily Newspapers,' in C. Cockburn and D. Zarkov (eds), *The Postwar Moment: Militaries, Masculinities and International Peacekeeping*, London: Lawrence and Wishart.
Zarkov, D. (2007) *The Body of War: Media, Ethnicity and Gender in the Break-up of Yugoslavia*, Durham, NC: Duke University Press.
Zehr, H. (1990) *Changing Lenses*, Scottsdale, PA: Herald Press.
Zubaida, S. (1996) 'Turkish Islam and National Identity,' *Middle East Report* 199 (April–June): 10–15.
Zürcher, E. J. (2003) *Turkey: A Modern History*, 2nd edn, New York: I.B. Tauris.

Index

A
activism, 3–6, 11, 24–26, 122–124, 138, 178, 200, 203
activists, 6, 10–11, 19, 21–28, 33, 122, 213
Al Qaeda, 167, 190
Ali, Ayan Hirsi, 178
Allred, Keith, 112
Andrabi, Asiya, 171
Annan, Kofi, 111
antiwar activists, 6, 19, 21–28, 33
Aristotle, 94
Ashe, Fidelma, 2, 14, 197, 210
asylum seekers, 121–125, 131–133. *See also* refugee protection
Aurén, Chaplain, 100

B
Baron, Ilan Zvi, 94
Barrett, Frank, 70
Bastick, Megan, 37
bath towels, 51–56, 61
Bergoffen, Debra, 58
Bildt, Carl, 51, 57
bin Laden, Osama, 167
Biricik, Alp, 2, 3, 9, 76
boat people, 123–124
Burk, James, 91
Burns, Nicholas, 113
Bush, George W., 29, 167
Bush, Laura, 29
Butler, Judith, 22, 166, 175

C
Cadet's Oath, 95
Charlesworth, Hillary, 56
civilian crisis management, 97, 153–154. *See also* crisis management
class exploitation, 23

Clinton, Hillary, 191
Cockburn, Cynthia, 2, 5–6, 19, 209, 212
colonization, 23, 41
Colston, John, 113
combat training, 169, 173
conflict transformation: gender politics and, 14, 197–205, 210–211; masculinities and, 197–205, 210–211; in Northern Ireland, 197–205
conscientious objectors, 33, 87, 89n7
conscription: in Finland, 90–94; practice of, 3; resisting, 9; in Turkey, 77–81, 87–88
continuum effect, 27–30
covert operations, 189–190
Creighton, Colin, 26
crisis management: civilian crisis management, 97, 153–154; gender equality in, 154–157; international crisis management, 153–165; women in, 153–165

D
Dabic, Nada, 142–143
Das, Veena, 176
Dean, Robert, 30
deaths in wars, 37, 42
demilitarization, 197–205
Department of Peacekeeping Operations (DPKO), 110, 111
Dinçdað, Halil Ýbrahim, 76–77, 86
discrimination, 8, 59–60, 94, 114–115, 130, 176
division of labour, 20–21, 25, 102
domestic violence, 37, 40, 43, 45, 146
Downs, Alexander B., 98
Duhacek, Nadja, 142

Index

E
Eckhardt, William, 31
Eduards, Maud, 8, 51, 52, 60, 209, 210
effeminate army, 71
effeminate man, 31, 82–86
Eisenstein, Hester, 62
Eisenstein, Zillah, 56
Enloe, Cynthia, 2, 22, 32, 185

F
female activists, 6, 10–11, 19, 21–28, 33, 122, 213
female police officers, 153–158, 160–164, 165n6
female subordination, 5, 23–25, 46, 211. *See also* subordination
feminism: activism and, 4–6, 11, 19, 21–28, 33, 122, 200, 213; militarism and, 209–213; pacifism and, 14–15, 22, 136–141; as positive tool, 3–4; transnational feminism, 12, 22–23, 213; violence and, 3, 14, 212; war and, 14–15, 212
feminist organizations: SCR 1325 and, 3, 10–11, 135–149, 210–211; security and, 135–149; transnationalism and, 22–23; views on war, 27–28
Feminist Security Studies, 2, 63, 161, 209
feminist standpoint theory, 6, 19–34
Finland: conscription in, 90–103; protectors of, 97–101; sacrifices for, 99–100
Finnish Armed Forces (FAF), 9, 92
Flén, Elli, 97
Fogarty, Brian, 28, 29
Freedman, Jane, 11, 121, 212–213
Freud, Sigmund, 193

G
Gandhi, Rajiv, 173
gender: conceptualizing, 5–7, 17–48; making, 1–15, 49–103; militarism and, 5–8, 78–79, 140; military practices and, 2–3, 61; peace building and, 209; refugee protection and, 121–134; security and, 108–109, 140; violence and, 2–7, 54–57, 116, 122, 127, 131; war and, 19–48, 63–75, 209–212. *See also* men; women
gender equality: in crisis management, 154–157; in Norwegian Armed Forces, 8–9, 63–75; policies of, 59–62, 129, 131; power and, 205, 213; refugees and, 129, 131; in Swedish Armed Forces, 51–56
gender identities, 26, 32–33, 119, 197–200, 205
gender inequality, 52–56, 115, 126–130, 204–205, 213
gender mainstreaming: constraints on, 125–126; feminist activism and, 11; feminization threat and, 114–119; NATO and, 107, 116–119; progress in, 126–129, 211; refugee protection and, 11, 121–122, 212–213; SCR 1325 and, 107, 117, 135–136; UN and, 107, 114–119; UNHCR and, 11–12
gender-neutral military, 38, 43–45, 55, 59–61
gender order, 1, 5–7, 24–27, 41–42
gender politics: conflict transformation and, 14, 197–205, 210–211; demilitarization and, 197–205; national identity and, 210; security and, 144–147
gender power, 1–2, 6, 14, 22, 26–30, 204–205, 210–212
gender relations: changing, 212; gender-power relations, 212; militarism and, 211; transformative change in, 23; in war, 19–34, 63–75, 209–212
gender roles, 82–83, 98, 119, 169, 176–177
gender security: concept of, 10–13; SCR 1325 and, 136, 147–148; WiB and, 11–13, 136–137
gender subjectivity, 2, 13–15, 151–213
gender subordination, 1, 161, 176. *See also* subordination
gender transformation, 32–33
gender trouble, 51–62
gendercide, 39, 47
global histories, 40–41
'globalizing masculinities,' 40–41
Goffman, Erving, 186
Gregory, Derek, 101
guerrilla warfare, 168–169, 172–173

H
Haaland, Torunn Laugen, 8–9, 63, 96, 102, 210

Hägglund, General, 94
Häkämies, Minister, 96–97
Hansen, Lene, 2
Haraway, Donna, 20
Harding, Sandra, 20, 21, 33
Hartsock, Nancy, 20, 21, 22
Harvey, David, 184
hazing practices, 192–193
Hearn, Jeff, 2, 6, 35, 209, 212
Hebert, Laura, 12, 107, 211
Heikka, Jani, 98
heroism, 9, 90–91, 102, 209
Higate, Paul, 2, 14, 73, 182, 209
Hockey, John, 71
homelessness, 173–174, 176, 178
homophobia, 64, 69, 72–73
homosexuality: hazing practices and, 192–194; military service and, 9, 39, 73; performance of 76–89
hope, politics of, 153–165
human trafficking, 107, 112
Hutchings, Kimberly, 5, 62

I
identity politics, 166–169
Immonen, Petri, 100
institutional practices: gendered practices in, 211–212; traveling concepts and, 10–13, 105–149, 211; war and, 3–4
international crisis management, 153–165. See also crisis management
international organizations, 4, 10–11, 117, 211–212
international peacekeeping, 8, 90–100, 107, 210–211
international relations (IR), 1–2, 38, 41–45, 166, 175–179
intersectionality, 30–31
invisible women, 9, 63, 210

J
Jabri, Vivienne, 58
Jeffords, Susan, 30
Jukarainen, Pirjo, 9, 90, 209
'Just War' theory, 90–91, 94–100, 102–103

K
Kääriäinen, Seppo, 94
Karuna, Colonel, 173–174

Kashmir, 14, 167–172, 176–179
Kaskeala, Juhani, 94
Kemalist ideology, 78, 88n4
Ki-moon, Ban, 115
Kiljunen, Paavo, 99
Kilpiä, Juha, 93
Kronsell, Annica, 1, 209

L
labour, division of, 20–21, 25, 102
Laitinen, Kari, 102
Lerner, Gerda, 31
Liberation Tigers of Tamil Elam (LTTE), 167–169, 172–178, 179n7, 180n12, 180n14
Lykke, Nina, 213

M
MacKenzie, Megan, 179
MacKinnon, Catharine A., 55–56
male domination, 24–25, 48, 62, 65–66, 102, 211
male police officers, 163, 165n6
male power, 24–25, 31
'man question,' 41–42, 194–195
Martin, Sarah, 67
Marx, Karl, 20, 21
masculine heroism, 9, 90–91, 102, 209
masculine protection, 90–91, 100–102
masculinities: conflict transformation and, 197–205, 210–211; expressions of, 69–73; globalizing, 40–41; militarism and, 6, 8–9, 35–48; militarization and, 52; military practices and, 3; military protection and, 90–91, 100–102; patriarchy and, 24–29, 33; politics and, 198; re-envisioning, 197–205; reproduction of, 76–89; in security companies, 14, 182, 188, 190; soldiers and, 68, 72–73; violence and, 3, 33, 36–48, 52, 209, 212–213; war and, 2–3, 30, 35–48, 63–75, 213. See also men
mavericks, 182, 188
McLeod, Laura, 2, 12, 135, 153, 211
Mechling, Jay, 193
memory books, 8, 64, 66–68, 71–73, 74n1
men: effeminate men, 31, 82–86; histories of, 40–41; militarism and, 6, 8–9, 35–48; in security companies, 14, 182, 188, 190;

subordination to, 209; war and, 2–3, 30, 35–48, 63–75, 213. *See also* masculinities
mercenaries, 182, 187, 189–190
Meyer, Christopher, 44
Mies, Maria, 21
migrations, forced, 123–124, 133
militant movements, 14, 166, 170, 179
militarism: conceptualizing, 17–48; definition of, 5; feminism and, 209–213; gender and, 5–8, 78–79, 140; gender-neutral military, 38, 43–45, 55, 59–61; men and, 6, 8–9, 35; nation building and, 209, 210; opposing, 19; transnational militarism, 47; in Turkey, 76–79, 87–88; violence and, 36–48; women and, 39–40, 62. *See also* militarization; military service
militarization: definition of, 5; gender relations in, 19, 23–24, 28–30, 32; masculinities and, 52; opposing, 19; war and, 19–23, 31–32. *See also* militarism
military companies, 4, 98–99
military deaths, 37, 42
military practices: gender and, 2–3, 61; masculinities and, 3; national identity and, 3, 7, 79, 87, 209–210; new wars and, 3, 209; peacekeeping and, 1–3, 8
military service: avoiding, 33, 87; effects of, 39–40; homosexuality in, 9, 39, 73; mandatory military service, 77, 87, 88n3, 90; women in, 39–40, 51–62, 65–73, 98–99. *See also* militarism
military spending, 36–39, 43–44
military violence, 2–3, 7, 40, 45–46. *See also* violence
Milosevic regime, 138, 143, 147
misogyny, 64, 69, 72–73
mission life, 160, 162, 164
Morgan, David, 185
Moskos, Charles C., 91

N

Nafisi, Azar, 178
nation: remaking, 3, 7–10, 49, 209; reproduction of, 87
nation building, 3, 7, 40, 90, 209–210
National Action Plan (NAP), 95, 97, 140, 153
national identity: in Finland, 9, 90, 101; militant movements and, 179; military practices and, 3, 7, 79, 87, 209–210
new wars: feminist IR and, 175–178; identity politics and, 167–169; masculine protection and, 100–102; military practices and, 3, 209
NGOs: refugee protection and, 132–133; SCR 1325 and, 3, 10–11, 135–137, 139–141, 143–148, 210–211
Nordic crisis management, 153–155; holistic approach and 155–157; women on mission and, 157–161; responsibility of, 161–164. *See also* crisis management
North Atlantic Treaty Organization (NATO): gender mainstreaming and, 116–119; as model for UN, 112–114; responses to sexual misconduct, 11, 107, 109–114, 116, 118–120, 211; role of, 108–109
Northern Ireland: gender identities in, 14, 197–200; demilitarization and, 200–203; masculinities and, 203–205, 210–211
Norwegian Armed Forces (NAF): deployments abroad, 66–69; friendly war-fighters, 63–75; gender issues in, 8–9, 63–75; masculinities in, 69–73; women in, 65–73

O

Oliver, Kelly, 62
organized violence, 3, 45–46, 119, 212. *See also* violence

P

pacifism: feminism and, 14–15, 22, 136–141; security and, 139–141
Parashar, Swati, 2, 14, 166, 209
Parpart, Jane, 176
patriarchal manipulations, 166
patriarchal relations, 6, 19, 23–30, 45
patriarchal societies, 169–170
patriarchal structures, 87–88, 101–102, 137–138, 146
patriarchy, 24–29, 33
peace: conscription and, 92–94; honorable protector and, 97–100; 'Just

War' principle and, 94–96; making, 90–91; masculine protection and, 99–102; women and, 62, 96–97, 213
peace building missions: gender and, 209; masculine heroism and, 9, 90–91, 102; military practices and, 1–3, 8; violence and, 2–3
peace, struggle for, 32–33
peacekeeping operations: armed forces in, 63–64; gender perspective in, 11, 74; international peacekeeping, 8, 90–100, 107, 210–211; men in, 90–93, 101–102; military practices and, 2–3, 8; sexual misconduct in, 12, 107, 109–114, 116, 118–120, 210; UN and, 108, 111, 115–116; violence and, 2–3; women in, 12–13, 92–93, 101–102, 161–162
Penttinen, Elina, 13, 153, 177–179, 209
personality tests, 80, 89n6
police officers: crisis management and, 153, 155; security and, 157; women on mission and, 157–161; responsibility of, 161–164, 165n6
political responsibility, 137–138, 147–148
political violence, 27, 138, 166, 175–177, 199–204
politics: gender politics, 14, 197–205, 210–211; of hope, 13, 153–165; men's dominance in, 198; women in, 198–199
Powell, Jonathan, 44
Prabhakaran, Vellupillai, 167, 169, 172–173
private militarized security companies (PMSC), 188–189, 191, 194–195
private military companies, 4, 98–99
private security companies (PSCs): gender silences and, 194; locating, 186–187; masculinities in, 14, 182; nationality and, 190–191; plausible deniability and, 189–190
protectors: masculine protector, 209, 210, 212; of refugees, 133; of 'victims,' 209
Puheloinen, Commander-in-Chief, 97
Puistola, Juha-Antero, 101

R
racism, 63–64, 69, 72–73
'Rambo tendencies,' 71
rape: female experiences, 25; focus on, 57, 59, 109; gang rape, 110; implication of, 25; male experiences, 25; mass rape, 15, 23; of minors, 110; reports of, 121; sexual misconduct and, 109–110, 113–115; violence and, 42–46, 123; women at risk and, 130
Reardon, Betty, 5, 26–27
refugee protection: gender identities and, 121–122; gender mainstreaming and, 11, 121–129, 212–213; representations of, 131–133; women at risk and, 129–131
Resolution 1325, 3, 135–149, 210–211. See also SCR 1325
Resolution 1820. See also SCR 1820
Rich, Adrienne, 22
Ruddick, Sara, 21, 147
Runeberg, Johan Ludwig, 94–95

S
Sabuni, Nyamko, 53
Saed, Hafiz, 171
Sandoval, Chela, 24
Santos, Aida, 24
Schofield, Steve, 28
SCR 1325: adoption of, 10, 107; equality plans and, 8; feminist activism and, 4–5; feminist organizations and, 3, 10–11, 135–149, 210–211; in Finland, 95, 97; gender mainstreaming and, 117, 135–136; gender security and, 136, 147–148; military practices and, 8; protection by, 57, 60; purpose of, 3, 135; sexual violence and, 23–24
SCR 1820, 11, 57, 107, 117, 135
security: business of, 182; concept of, 10–13; feminist organizations and, 135, 144–149; gender and, 108–109, 140; gender politics and, 144–147; gender security, 136, 147–148; holistic approach to, 155–157; pacifism and, 139–141; private security, 14, 182; reproduction of, 76–89; women and, 210

Security Council Resolution 1325. *See also* SCR 1325
Security Council Resolution 1820. *See also* SCR 1820
security policy issues, 51–53, 62
security threats, 12, 108, 118–119
Sedivy, Jiri, 113
Serbia, 12, 27, 33, 41; feminist-pacifist and, 137–143, 145; militarized structures in, 143; draft resolution and, 145–148
sex/gender system, 24–25
sex objects, 54, 61
sex trafficking, 107, 110, 112
sexism, 63–67, 73, 210
sexual abuse, 107, 110
sexual assault, 42, 59, 115
sexual divisions, 23–25
sexual exploitation, 67, 73, 107, 110–111, 116, 162
sexual harassment, 52–55, 58–59, 61, 63, 110, 113, 162
sexual misconduct, 11–12, 107–120, 210–211
sexual violence, 23–24, 27, 43, 57, 60, 107–109, 121–123, 127–129
'sharp missions,' 71
Shaw, Martin, 26
Shepherd, Laura J., 58, 136
Shiva, Vandana, 21
silence of women, 170–179
Sion, Liora, 108
Sjoberg, Laura, 1, 100
Smith, Dorothy, 21
Smith, Rupert, 28
social constructionists, 23
soldiering, 25–26, 35–48, 66, 92, 102, 113
soldiers, traits of, 67–74
'space of one's own,' 141–144
Special Forces, 189–191
Spivak, Gayatri, 61
Sri Lanka, 14, 153, 160, 167–168, 172–173, 176, 179
states: international relations and, 41–45; 'man question' and, 41–42; para-states, 40–45; state sovereignty, 42, 139
subordination, 1, 5, 23–25, 46, 161, 176, 209, 211
suicide bombings, 169, 173–174, 191
supremacy; male 3, 5, 24; white 30
Svedberg, Erika, 1, 209
Swedish Armed Forces (SAF): gender equality in, 51–56; gender issues in, 8; gender trouble in, 51–62; role in, 210–211
Swedish security policy, 51–62
Sylvester, Christine, 2, 14, 58, 142, 177–179

T

terrorist groups, 167, 190
Tickner, Ann, 2, 62
Tilly, Charles, 31, 117, 210
transnational antiwar activists, 27
transnational militarism, 47
transnationalism: feminism and, 12, 22–23, 213; principles of, 213; women activists and, 213
traveling concepts: feminist theory and, 211; gender security and, 147–148; institutional practices and, 10–13, 105, 121, 124–125, 147, 211
'Troubles,' 197–198
Turkey: conscription in, 77–81, 87–88; masculinities in, 3, 9; military institutions in, 78–82; protectors of nation, 78–79; security in, 76–89

U

United Nations High Commissioner for Refugees (UNHCR), 4, 11–12, 121–132
United Nations (UN): gender mainstreaming and, 114–119; peacekeeping policies of, 108, 111, 115–116; responses to sexual misconduct, 11, 107, 109–114, 116, 118–120, 211; role of, 108–109
universalism, 129, 213

V

Väyrynen, Tarja, 96
victimhood, 97, 167–168, 174–178
violence: acts of, 209, 212; aggression and, 69, 71; analyses of, 45–47; conceptualizing, 17–48; domestic violence, 37, 40, 43, 45, 146; femininity and, 3, 14, 212; gender and, 2–7, 54–57, 116, 122, 127, 131; gender subjectivity and, 2, 151–213; masculini-

ties and, 3, 33, 36–48, 52, 209, 212–213; military violence, 2–3, 7, 40, 45–46; organized violence, 3, 45–46, 119, 212; peacekeeping and, 2–3; political violence, 27, 138, 166, 175–177, 199–204; sexual violence, 23–24, 27, 42–46, 57, 60, 107–109, 121–123, 127–129; war and, 26, 36–48, 213

W

war: causes of, 19–34; continuum effect of, 27–30; deaths in, 37, 42; feminism and, 14–15, 212; feminist standpoint on, 6, 19–34; friendly war-fighters, 63; gender relations in, 19, 23–25, 28–30, 32, 63, 209–212; identity politics and, 167–169; institutional practices and, 3–4; invisible women and, 63; 'Just War' theory, 90–91, 94–100, 102–103; making, 1–15; masculinities and, 2–3, 30, 35–48, 63–75, 213; militarization and, 19–23, 31–32; peace and, 1, 90–103; perceptions of, 26–28; protection for 'victims' of, 121–134; sexual divisions of, 23–25; systemic view of, 26–27; violence and, 26, 36–48, 213
War on Terror, 7, 10, 185
'war question,' 2, 7–10, 13–15, 166, 179n1, 184–186, 194, 211–212
war stories, 170–179
war system, 26–27
Weeks, Kathi, 21–22

Whitworth, Sandra, 9, 64, 69, 72
Williams, John, 100
Williams, Kayla, 25
'womanly' skills, 1, 13
women: crisis management and, 153–165; invisible women, 9, 63, 210; in militant movements, 14, 166, 170, 179; in military, 39–40, 51–62, 65–73, 98–99; peace and, 62, 213; peacekeeping operations and, 12–13, 92–93, 101–102, 161–162; in politics, 198–199; protection of, 133; roles of, 2, 52, 57–58, 116, 138–140, 146, 155, 166–172, 197–199; as security problem, 210; as sex objects, 54, 61; silence of, 170–179; subordination of, 209. *See also* gender
women activists, 6, 10–11, 19, 21–28, 33, 122, 213
Women at Risk Program, 129–131
women cadres, 169, 173, 176, 180n12
Women in Black (WiB): gender security and, 11–13, 136–137; network of, 19, 22, 137, 149n2; transnational feminists, 22
women's rights, 23, 56–58, 117, 124, 143, 154–155

Y

Young, Iris Marion, 60
Yuval-Davis, Nira, 22, 210

Z

Zajovic, Stasa, 137, 142, 144–147
Zeid Al-Hussein, Zeid Ra'ad, 111
zero-tolerance policy, 110–112, 116